RELATIONAL EGAL

Over the last twenty years, many political philosophers have rejected the idea that justice is fundamentally about distribution. Rather, justice is about social relations, and the so-called distributive paradigm should be replaced by a new relational paradigm. Kasper Lippert-Rasmussen seeks to describe, refine and assess these thoughts and to propose a comprehensive form of egalitarianism which includes central elements from both relational and distributive paradigms. He shows why many of the challenges which luck egalitarianism faces reappear, once we try to specify relational egalitarianism more fully. His discussion advances our understanding of the nature of the relational ideal and introduces new conceptual tools for understanding it and for exploring the important question of why it is desirable in the first place to relate as equals. Even severe critics of the distributive understanding of justice will find that this book casts important new light on the ideal to which they subscribe.

KASPER LIPPERT-RASMUSSEN is Professor of Political Theory, University of Aarhus, and Professor II in Philosophy, University of Tromsø. His books include *Born Free and Equal?* (2013) and *Luck Egalitarianism* (2015).

RELATIONAL EGALITARIANISM

Living As Equals

KASPER LIPPERT-RASMUSSEN

Aarhus Universitet, Denmark

CAMBRIDGE
UNIVERSITY PRESS

CAMBRIDGE
UNIVERSITY PRESS

University Printing House, Cambridge CB2 8BS, United Kingdom

One Liberty Plaza, 20th Floor, New York, NY 10006, USA

477 Williamstown Road, Port Melbourne, VIC 3207, Australia

314-321, 3rd Floor, Plot 3, Splendor Forum, Jasola District Centre, New Delhi - 110025, India

79 Anson Road, #06-04/06, Singapore 079906

Cambridge University Press is part of the University of Cambridge.

It furthers the University's mission by disseminating knowledge in the pursuit of education, learning and research at the highest international levels of excellence.

www.cambridge.org
Information on this title: www.cambridge.org/9781316613672
DOI: 10.1017/9781316675847

First published 2018
First paperback edition 2020

A catalogue record for this publication is available from the British Library

ISBN 978-1-107-15890-0 Hardback
ISBN 978-1-316-61367-2 Paperback

For Cæcilie, Hannah, Kira, Mona, Samuel and William

Contents

Preface   *page* xi
Acknowledgements   xiii

1   Introduction   1
     1.1 The Distributive Ideal of Justice   1
     1.2 The Relational Ideal of Justice   4
     1.3 Relational Egalitarianism: A Thumbnail Sketch of Its Recent History   11
     1.4 An Overview of the Book   16
     1.5 Summary   20

PART I NATURE

2   Relational Egalitarianism   23
     2.1 Introduction   23
     2.2 Luck Egalitarianism versus Relational Egalitarianism   24
     2.3 Anderson's Critique of Luck Egalitarianism   28
     2.4 Democratic Equality   36
     2.5 Scheffler's Critique of Luck Egalitarianism   41
     2.6 The Egalitarian Deliberative Constraint   51
     2.7 A Comparison   57
     2.8 Conclusion   59

3   Relating to One Another As Equals   61
     3.1 Introduction   61
     3.2 Equals with Regard to What?   63
     3.3 Relating, Regarding and Treating   70
     3.4 Treating As   73
     3.5 Equals   80
     3.6 Regarding As Equals   85
     3.7 The Ideal of Relational Equality and Ideal Ways of Relating As Equals   87
     3.8 Conclusion   92

4 Equality and Being in a Position to Hold Others Accountable:
    A Case Study   94
    4.1 Introduction   94
    4.2 What Is Hypocritical Blame?   97
    4.3 Wallace's Egalitarian Account of the Distinctive Wrongness of Hypocrisy 102
    4.4 Why Not Hypocrisy?   105
    4.5 Hypocrisy and Relational Equality   110
    4.6 Conclusion   116

PART II SITE, SCOPE AND JUSTIFICATION

5 Egalitarian Relations: Time, Site and Scope   121
    5.1 Introduction   121
    5.2 Intergenerational Justice   123
    5.3 Age   130
    5.4 Site   136
    5.5 Scope   146
    5.6 Conclusion   153

6 Justification of and by the Ideal   154
    6.1 Introduction   154
    6.2 Instrumentally Valuable   155
    6.3 Non-Instrumentally Valuable for Persons   159
    6.4 Impersonally Valuable   166
    6.5 Not (Primarily) Valuable, but Required   170
    6.6 Aims of Real-Life Egalitarians and the Value of Equality   174
    6.7 Conclusion   177

PART III RELATIONAL AND DISTRIBUTIVE EQUALITY

7 Pluralist Egalitarianism   181
    7.1 Introduction   181
    7.2 Consistency   182
    7.3 An Underlying Disagreement about Justification?   185
    7.4 Reduction   192
    7.5 Dispositional Egalitarianism   201
    7.6 Pluralist Egalitarianism   205
    7.7 Conclusion   210

8 Often the Twain Meet   211
    8.1 Introduction   211
    8.2 Anderson on Equality of Opportunity and/or Capability   212
    8.3 Offensive Tastes   217
    8.4 Snobbery   222

8.5 Dworkinian Bureaucracy   227
8.6 Cohen on Justificatory Community   230
8.7 Communal Camping   233
8.8 Conclusion   235

9 Conclusion   236

References   239
Index   247

Preface

The main title of this book might seem slightly odd. Is not any idea about equality relational? After all, by definition equality is a relation that obtains between individuals when they have equal amounts of, say, resources. In a sense this is true. However, 'relational equality' refers to a particular kind of relations, namely egalitarian social relations; and this important addendum largely vindicates the title, since in much of the literature on justice, it is assumed that one can specify what justice, or at least distributive justice, requires without saying anything – or at any rate not that much – about *social* relations.

Over the last twenty years or so, many political philosophers have rejected this view, suggesting that, fundamentally, justice is all about social relations and that the so-called distributive paradigm, which was once dominant in political philosophy, should be replaced by a new relational paradigm. This book seeks to describe, refine and assess these thoughts. *Pace* the paradigm replacement view just described, I propose an ecumenical form of egalitarianism, which includes central elements from both relational and distributive paradigms. In the course of doing so, I show why the family of different relational views on justice is much larger than the present body of literature might lead one to think, and that many of the differences between different relational views mirror differences between different distributive views. Specifically, I will show why many of the challenges faced by luck egalitarianism reappear, *mutatis mutandis*, once we try to specify relational egalitarianism more fully. This suggests that the two strands of thinking about justice and equality are not that different at all and, in particular, that the differences – and I am not denying that there are important differences – are not so large that an ecumenical project of the sort this book engages in makes no sense. Last, but definitely not least, I also seek to advance our understanding of the relational ideal, for example by offering a broader view of the way in which it is embodied in our practice of giving and receiving blame and by introducing new conceptual tools for understanding this view (and its many variations) and for exploring the important question of why it is desirable in the first place to relate as equals. Hence, I hope that even readers of a relational egalitarian persuasion who reject any ecumenical ambitions of the sort I pursue in the book will find that, nevertheless, it casts important new light on the ideal to which they subscribe.

I should like to acknowledge a deep academic debt to my former D.Phil. supervisor in connection with this book. When I worked with – or, perhaps more correctly, in academic respects at least, under – G. A. Cohen (an especially noteworthy fact, given the topic of this book), I did not see as clearly as I should have what a brilliant mind he was. At the time I did not work on equality, but on deontology (which is not to say that the two topics are unrelated). My interest in equality came later and I have always found Jerry's work on equality tremendously insightful and inspiring. With all due modesty, I would like to think of this book as one that brings together two broad lines of thought in Jerry's work about justice (and more generally in egalitarian political philosophy) which, to my knowledge, he never explicitly connected in any worked-out way: the idea of luck egalitarianism and distributive equality, on the one hand, and the idea of relating as equals, on the other. As we shall see, Jerry was very sympathetic to both ideas, despite the impression one might reasonably develop if one reads some of the contemporary relational egalitarian critiques of luck egalitarianism in general and critiques of Jerry's work in particular. Hence, I like to think of this book not only as one that reconciles two ways of thinking about egalitarian justice which, presently, are often thought of as incompatible, but also, and partly for more personal reasons, as a book that brings to fruition two lines of thought that were present in Jerry's work and which, due to his untimely death, he never put together – at least not at length and systematically.

Acknowledgements

In part, this manuscript builds on work that I have presented on a number of occasions over the last five years. Hence, I would like to thank the following persons for useful feedback: Andreas Albertsen, Richard Arneson, Gustaf Arrhenius, Cristina Astier, David Axelsen, Katharina Berndt Rasmussen, Juliana Bidadanure, Simon Birnbaum, Åsa Carlson, Erik Carlsson, Ian Carter, Paula Casal, Naima Chahboun, Andreas Christiansen, Matthew Clayton, Hugh Collins, Roger Crisp, Jens Damgaard Thaysen, Göran Duus-Otterström, Eva Erman, David Estlund, Nir Eyal, Jessica Flanagan, Carina Fourie, Anca Gheaus, Pablo Gilabert, Antje Gimmler, Sara Goering, Axel Gosseries, Les Green, Siba Harb, Deborah Hellman, Blake Hereth, Iwao Hirose, Nils Holtug, Brad Hooker, Kristian Højer Toft, Pietro Intropi, Magnus Jedenheim-Edling, Kristian Jensen, Jens Johansson, Klemens Kappel, Tarunabh Khaitan, Nadim Khoury, Frej Klem Thomsen, Carl Knight, Kjartan Koch Michalsen, Annabelle Lever, Sune Lægaard, Martin Marchman Andersen, Andrew Mason, Tim Meijers, Zoltan Miklosi, Sophia Moreau, Per Mouritsen, Viki Møller Lyngby Pedersen, Chris Nathan, Charlotte Newey, Geraldine Ng, Lasse Nielsen, Serena Olsaretti, Mike Otsuka, Tom Parr, Fabienne Peter, Adina Preda, Massimo Renzo, Juha Räikkä, Raffaele Rodogno, Eric C. Rowse, Shlomi Segall, Johanna Seibt, Thomas Sinclair, Adam Slavny, David Sobel, Rasmus Sommer Hansen, Katie Steel, Asbjørn Steglich-Petersen, Zofia Stemplowska, Philip Stratton-Lake, Julie Suk, Adam Swift, Jørn Sønderholm, Victor Tadros, Robert Talisse, Folke Tersman, Patrick Tomlin, Kartik Upadhyaya, Laura Vallentini, Peter Vallentyne, Tore Vincent Olsen, Annamari Vitikainen, Kristin Voigt, Alex Voorhoeve, Steve Wall and Andrew Williams. I thank Søren Flinch Midtgaard in particular for providing helpful comments on the entire manuscript and Kate Thulin for proofreading.

I should also like to thank the Norwegian Research Council for its financial support in connection with my work on this book, which in part was conducted in relation with the *Globalizing Minority Rights* (GMR) project (NFR 259017).

Finally, I thank the relevant publishers (Wiley, and Taylor & Francis, respectively) for permission to reprint material (Lippert-Rasmussen, 2013b; 2015b), details of which can be found in the References section of the present book.

CHAPTER I

Introduction

1.1 The Distributive Ideal of Justice

Suppose, realistically, that some people are starving, while others live a life of opulence. Absent special facts about how this situation arose – perhaps however it arose – it appears to involve an injustice, and that this injustice consists of a deficient distribution of goods. Examples such as these suggest:

> *The distributive ideal of justice*: A situation is just only if the distribution of goods it involves has a particular set of desirable features.

The distributive ideal of justice only states a necessary condition for a distribution being just. One reason this is so is that most acknowledge that there are other aspects of justice than the distributive aspect (Rawls, 1999: 8; Cohen, 2008: 6; cp. Dworkin, 2000: 12).[1] For instance, there is retributive justice, and in some cases deviations from the distribution favoured by distributive justice might be more just, all things considered, given the concern for, say, punishing criminals.

Friends of the distributive ideal of justice disagree over which goods the distributive ideal pertains to, and about which features a distribution must have in order for it to be desirable justice-wise. In light of the opening example, it is natural to say that the distributive ideal pertains to the distribution of resources, since, presumably, the injustice of that situation consists of the fact that the distribution of resources is undesirable in a certain way. However, the inclination to take this view might simply reflect that we assume that people's level of well-being is strongly correlated with their level of resources and, accordingly, that we assume that starving people have a very low level of well-being, while those who live in opulence have a very high one. However, once we pry apart resources and well-being, we see that what we really care about non-instrumentally is the distribution

---

[1] Rawls focuses on distributive justice under strict compliance. Retributive justice concerns situations characterized by partial compliance.

of well-being. We can refer to the issue of which goods the distributive ideal of justice pertains to as the *distribuendum of distributive justice* issue.

Whatever is the correct distribuendum of the distributive ideal, friends of that ideal also disagree about the shape a distribution must have for it to be desirable from the point of view of distributive justice. Sufficientarians believe that a situation is distributively just only if the distribution of goods is such that everyone has enough (Axelsen & Nielsen, 2015; Casal, 2007; Crisp, 2003; Fourie & Rid, 2017: 1–120; Frankfurt, 1988: 134; Huseby, 2010; Shields, 2012).[2] Setting aside a number of complications, friends of the Rawlsian difference principle believe that a situation is just only if the distribution is such that the worst off are as well off as possible (Rawls, 1999: 266).[3] Prioritarians believe that a situation is just only if the distribution is such that the weighted moral value of people's well-being is maximized (Holtug, 2010; Parfit, 1998: 12). And, finally, egalitarians believe that a distribution is just only if everyone has the same amount of goods. Arguably, all four views described imply that the situation of poverty and opulence is unjust. We can refer to the issue of what pattern the distributive ideal of justice endorses as the *pattern of distributive justice* issue (Nozick, 1974: 153–5).[4]

For nearly the last fifty years of political philosophy, the issues of the distribuendum and pattern of distributive justice have had a central place in discussions of justice (Arneson, 1989; Cohen, 2011: 3–43; Dworkin, 2000: 11–119; Parfit, 1998; Sen, 1979; Temkin, 1993). In the next section, I explain why some think that this is unfortunate. But before I do so, I will introduce one more complication in relation to the distributive ideal, using the ideal of distributive equality as a stepping stone for making a point about distributive ideals in general. This complication concerns the role of responsibility.

As I formulated the distributive egalitarian ideal of justice two paragraphs above, it amounts to:

> *Distributive outcome egalitarianism*: A situation is just only if everyone has the same amount of goods.

---

[2] Frankfurt's sufficientarianism concerns the distribution of 'economic assets' (Frankfurt, 1988: 134), but the structure of his sufficientarianism can be applied to other goods.

[3] Among the complications ignored here are: that Rawls' principles of justice apply to the basic structure of society; that the difference principle applies to groups; and that the principles of equal liberty and fair equality of opportunity are lexically prior to the difference principle.

[4] In Nozick's (1974: 155) terminology, all four of the principles mentioned here are 'end-state principles'. Nozick rejects all end-state principles of justice and canvasses a libertarian, historical entitlement theory instead.

Distributive outcome egalitarianism, however, seems to be refuted by the objection from irresponsibility (Cohen, 2011: 120–2).[5] In one of its forms, this objection asks us to assume that we start with an initial state of perfect equality such that everyone has the same of whatever is the distribuendum of egalitarian justice. Suppose that one person – call him Terry – voluntarily engages in imprudent behaviour and as a result ends up worse off than another person – call her Selma. Selma acts prudently and as a result ends up better off than she was initially. Now there is an unequal distribution in Selma's favour, which outcome egalitarianism condemns as unjust. However, says the objection from irresponsibility, there is nothing unjust about this inequality, since Terry is responsible for being worse off. Indeed, it would be unjust if someone redistributed Selma and Terry's holdings in order to restore outcome equality. Friends of the egalitarian distributive ideal who find this objection compelling often retain their egalitarian commitments in the face of this objection by endorsing:

> *Luck egalitarianism*: It is just only if everyone's distributive shares reflect nothing other than their comparative exercise of responsibility.[6]

Just a word on terminology: by 'luck' is meant something for which the relevant individual is not responsible.[7] Accordingly, luck egalitarianism contrasts with distributive outcome egalitarianism, because the latter view ascribes no significance to the distinction between what is a matter of luck so construed and what is not.

Many think that it was a great leap forward when Dworkin in 1981 defended a version of luck egalitarianism which appeared immune to the objection from irresponsibility (Cohen, 2011: 32). According to Dworkin, the state has a duty to show equal concern and respect for its citizens and, as he saw it, the state fails to do so if it forces some people to subsidize others

---

[5] I write 'seems' for the following reason. Suppose the relevant good to be distributed equally is opportunities of some kind and you define opportunity in such a way that if, at some point in time, people have equally good opportunities and, at some point later in time, they no longer do, then the latter inequality is such that the worse-off person is responsible for being worse off (opportunity-wise) (cp. Arneson, 2000: 339). Suppose also that you specify opportunity outcome egalitarianism in such a way that if at some point in time two persons have equally good opportunities, then their having unequal opportunities at some later point in time need not be unjust. Given these two suppositions the objection of irresponsibility does not refute – indeed, does not even challenge – the opportunity-focused version of outcome egalitarianism. For present purposes, I can ignore this complication.

[6] Suppose there is more than one way in which people's distributive shares can reflect nothing but their comparative exercises of responsibility, e.g. because such a reflection depends on people's reasonable expectations and these can vary. If so, luck egalitarianism is a seriously incomplete theory of distributive justice (cp. Anderson, 2008b).

[7] There are other ways to conceptualize luck (Lippert-Rasmussen, 2014; 2015a: 59–62; Hurley, 2003: 106–12).

who voluntarily engage in risky behaviour and suffer from bad option luck.[8] Hence, sensitivity to the choices of citizens is internal to the duty of the state to express equal concern and respect for its citizens. While these were not the exact terms in which Dworkin described what for him was a crucial distinction, many saw him as promoting a crucial and luck-egalitarian distinction between disadvantages which reflected people's choices and disadvantages which did not (Kymlicka, 2002: 75–9).

The distinction between outcome- and luck-focused theories has only attracted serious attention in relation to egalitarian distributive ideals. However, a similar distinction applies to the other distributive ideals that I mentioned above (Lippert-Rasmussen, 2015a: 25–33). For instance, while almost all defenders of a sufficientarian distributive ideal have subscribed to an outcome-focused version of this ideal, there is no reason why one might not prefer a luckist version of the sufficientarian distributive ideal. Indeed, insofar as one finds the objection from irresponsibility against outcome egalitarianism persuasive, it is unclear why one should not similarly think that the most plausible version of the sufficientarian distributive ideal is luckist.

1.2   The Relational Ideal of Justice

It is time to shift focus away from the distributive ideal to the main topic of this book, the relational ideal of justice or, more specifically, relational egalitarianism. Consider:

> *The odd slave society*: In a forgotten Greek polis, the population was divided into two equally large groups, slaves and masters. The masters were firm egalitarian believers in the distributive ideal of justice, where the scope of their ideal extended not just to the citizens of the polis, but also to slaves owned by members of the polis. Accordingly, the slave-owning citizens of this extraordinary polis organized their society in such a way that everyone falling within the scope of their egalitarian distributive ideal was equally well off overall in terms of the relevant distribuendum of distributive justice.[9] However, none of this affected the nature of social relations between masters and slaves. Slaves had to obey the orders of their masters; they had to

---

[8] Dworkin (2000: 1) omits 'respect' from the 'show equal concern and respect' part.

[9] Suppose the distribution of legally protected rights and liberties form the distribuendum of justice, or more plausibly, part of it. In that case, the odd slave society is not a scenario of the sort I stipulate it to be. I have considerable sympathy with this objection, which, for the moment, I ignore – but see Chapter 7.4. Often counterexamples to distributive ideals of justice that involve a description of an unjustly unequal situation purportedly nevertheless realizing distributive equality presuppose a particular and disputable idea about what constitutes the relevant distribuendum.

approach them in a servile manner; they had no rights under the law; their testimony was systematically discounted relative to that provided by free people; and they were held in contempt and considered incapable, by their masters as well as by themselves, of exercising self-control. (cp. Scheffler, 2003a: 37)

If the odd slave society was not an ideally just society, as I conjecture most readers think it was not, the distributive ideal does not exhaust the ideal of justice.[10] In a sense, we knew that already, since, as I noted when I introduced the distributive ideal, the ideal only states a necessary condition of a situation being just. However, the reason I gave for not including a sufficient condition was that there is such a thing as retributive justice in addition to distributive justice, and what is at stake here is not retributive justice. The present reason we might have for finding the egalitarian slave society unjust seems to operate on the same field, as it were, as the distributive ideal.[11]

What makes the odd slave society unjust? At this point one might appeal to:

> *The relational ideal of justice*: A situation is just only if social relations have certain specific, desirable features.[12]

The relational and the distributive ideals of justice ascribe different loci of justice – social relations and distributions.[13] Logically speaking, one could think that justice has both loci – call such a view the pluralistic view of justice (see Chapter 7.2; Gheaus, 2016).[14] Presently, this is not the dominant position in political philosophy, but, arguably, Rawls' theory of

---

[10] 'The relationship between master and slave is often used as the standard example for an inegalitarian (and therefore unjust) relationship' (Schuppert, 2015: 112).

[11] Some would agree in that they think both situations that I have decribed involve social injustice. However, they might add that social justice has two dimensions – political and distributive justice – and that the odd slave society might involve social injustice only because it involves political injustice (cp. Tan, 2014: 6–7). Relational egalitarians think it involves more than that.

[12] On some views, relational equality is a social ideal distinct from justice – for an informative discussion, see Schemmel (2015: 146–66). In this book, I am primarily interested in relational equality as an ideal of justice, in part because this is how the ideal is commonly presented, in part because only on this assumption is it a potential competitor with distributive ideals of justice.

[13] By the 'locus of justice' I mean that to which principles of justice apply, e.g. distributions, actions, social institutions or social relations. The question about the site of justice is normally distinguished from the issue of the scope of justice, which is normally taken to mean how far principles of justice extend to whatever they apply. For instance, cosmopolitan and statist egalitarians are normally taken to disagree about the scope of justice – cosmopolitans think justice mandates global equality, whereas statists think it mandates equality within states – even if they agree about the site of justice – e.g. because they believe that justice applies to basic institutions (Tan, 2014: 1–2; cp. Chapter 5).

[14] 'Pluralistic' here signals that pluralists are open to there being even more than just the two loci of justice presently in focus. I return to this in Chapter 7.6.

justice involves both loci.[15] Most positions defended presently are probably monistic, locus-wise, in that they claim either that, fundamentally, the relevant part of justice is simply a matter of the distribution of goods, or simply a matter of social relations.

In defending a monistic relational ideal of justice, one might suggest that when we think of situations which are seemingly unjust because of the relevant distribution of goods, we assume these go hand in hand with objectionable social relations, e.g. exploitation, and that once we pry them apart, we realize that, fundamentally, what we really care about is that the social relations have a suitable (egalitarian) character. We are indifferent to distributions per se, once we isolate them and assess them on their own (cp. O'Neill, 2008; Scanlon, 2000: 202–18; see Brown, 2014).

When I introduced the distributive ideal I noted that its friends differed among themselves on two issues: which good(s) should be distributed and which distributive pattern is just. Two analogous differences arise in relation to specifying the relational ideal, although the fact that the distributive and the relational ideals are parallel in this respect tends to be ignored.

First, friends of the relational ideal must say something about what is the relevant distribuendum of the relational ideal – that is, which dimension(s) are relevant for assessment of social relations. Or, to introduce a term similar to distribuendum: *relationendum*. Just as we might say that, from the point of view of distributive equality, it is crucial to give an account of the sort of goods distributive equality pertains to, it is crucial from the point of view of relational justice to specify the dimension(s) in which people should relate as equals (Chapter 3). Unfortunately, relational egalitarians have not given this topic the attention it deserves. Perhaps they have not – mistakenly, in my view – even seen it as a topic that is quite similar to, say, the 'equality of what' issue that has occupied luck egalitarians a great deal.

Here are two such issues about the relevant relationendum. As noted, friends of distributive equality disagree about whether the relevant good to be distributed is outcomes or opportunities, e.g. should people have equal amounts of well-being or should they instead have equally good opportunities for well-being? A similar issue divides friends of relational justice, i.e. does justice require that people relate to one another in certain valuable

[15] Rawls' difference principle is one way to flesh out the distributive ideal. Rawls' first principle of justice – 'Each person is to have an equal right to the most extensive total system of equal basic liberties compatible with a similar system of liberty for all' (Rawls, 1999: 266) – is one way of fleshing out (one aspect of) the relational ideal.

ways or rather that they have (equally/sufficiently good etc.) opportunities for relating to one another in certain valuable ways? It might be true that, with some qualifications to be explained later, people who have actually defended relational justice have tended to endorse an outcome-focused version of relational egalitarianism:

> *Outcome relational egalitarianism*: A situation is just only if everyone relates to one another as equals.[16]

However, this is not a commitment which is inherent in the ideal of relational egalitarianism per se, let alone in the ideal of relational justice per se. Nothing prevents friends of relational egalitarianism from subscribing to:

> *Luck relational egalitarianism*: A situation is just only if no one relates to others as (superiors/) inferiors through no responsibility of their own.[17]

One important lesson to learn from this is that the often-drawn distinction between luck egalitarianism on the one hand and relational egalitarianism on the other hand is seriously misleading, because it confuses two distinctions: first, the distinction between distributive and relational ideals of justice and, second, the distinction between outcome-focused and luckist versions of justice.[18] Hence, the common distinction ignores outcome versions of the distributive ideal and luckist versions of the relational ideal of justice.

Another question in relation to the relationendum of justice is whether the dimension on which people should relate as equals is expressive content

---

[16] Becase outcome relational egalitarianism is the only form of relational justice that I have seen anyone explicitly defend, in what follows I often refer to that position simply as 'relational egalitarianism'.

[17] This view is ambiguous in relation to the content of its responsibility component, as are similar statements of the responsibility component in luck egalitarianism (Lippert-Rasmussen, 2011). Further, some might say that 'relating to others as (superiors/) inferiors' as a result of the involved parties' exercise of responsibility is compatible with relating as equals in the relevant and attractive sense. However, for the present purpose, which is not to defend luck relational egalitarianism, we can ignore these matters. My purpose here is simply to show that, in principle at least, a concern for the nature of social relations might be fleshed out differently in relation to the concern for responsibility. Some might think that holding one another responsible for our choices is crucial to our treating one another as equals, e.g. Dworkin thinks that taxing people to support voluntary gamblers who had bad option luck involves a failure to treat non-gambling citizens as equals. The point here is that people who endorse a social-relations-focused view of justice might differ among themselves as to whether they adopt a luckist or a non-luckist version of this view. The impression held by some that it is otherwise reflects the fact that relational egalitarian theorists have developed their views in opposition mainly to luck egalitarianism – not any inherent feature of the relational egalitarian ideal of justice.

[18] Two paragraphs below I introduce some non-egalitarian forms of the relational ideal of justice. The distinction between outcome-focused and luckist theories applies to these forms as well.

(Nath, 2015: 189; Pogge, 2006; Pogge, 2008: 47–8; Schemmel, 2012a: 127–8, 143) or whether it is something else, e.g. social power or how citizens regard each other independently of how their views of one another are expressed in their actions etc.[19] Friends of relational justice often give examples of injustices that lend themselves to the view that what really is unjust about the relevant objectionable social relations is their objectionable expressive content. For instance, in most contexts a situation where men but not women have the right to vote would seem to express a certain objectionable, sexist view of men and women, and at least some prominent relational egalitarians have offered an expressivist account of wrongness in general (Anderson & Pildes, 2000).[20]

However, expressive content is not the only dimension on which friends of relational justice might assess social relations (or, for that matter, a dimension in terms of which friends of relational justice necessarily will assess social relations) (Voigt, forthcoming). Friends of the relational ideal might instead think that what is crucial is the way in which people regard one another, whether or not they express these views. Admittedly, how people subjectively regard others and what view of others they express in their actions are variously connected, but, analytically, they are different and when they come apart, friends of relational justice might differ significantly in their views as to what justice requires (Chapter 3). Moreover, there could be social relations that are objectionable independently of what they express or how people who are involved in them regard one another. For instance, Richard Norman thinks that domination and

---

[19] Schemmel takes the site of expressive justice to be institutions, but he also notes that 'radical egalitarians' believe that justice requires that individuals, and not just institutions, express the right sort of attitudes 'in their private lives' (Schemmel, 2012a: 137). The disagreement between these radical expressive egalitarians and those who think that only attitudes expressed by institutions matter mirror the disagreement among friends of the distributive ideal about whether the difference principle pertains to the basic structure of society or whether it also pertains to people's actions in the course of their daily lives (cp. Chapter 5.4; Cohen, 2008: 116–50).

[20] Some of Dworkin's formulations suggest that he subscribes to an expressivist account of justice, since he believes that justice requires that the state show 'equal concern' for its citizens (Dworkin, 2000: 1). Nevertheless, Dworkin is normally seen as a friend of the distributive ideal, because he thinks that certain distributions manifest that the state fails to express 'equal concern and respect' (cp. Schemmel, 2012a: 146 n33; Chapter 8.5). Note that in one sense at least we might think that the equal distribution in the odd slave society expresses hierarchical social relations: to wit, it is the result of these hierarchical social relations and conforms to the intentions of the unjustly ruling minority. Hence, if we say that a distribution might be unjust because it expresses unjust social relations, we will have to say that the *equal* distribution in the odd slave society is unjust (cp. Anderson, 2008b: 261). If we say that '[d]istributions are objectionable from an egalitarian point of view to the extent that they are the . . . effect of inegalitarian social relations' (Anderson, 2008b: 263), the equal distribution in the odd slave society is as objectionable from an egalitarian point of view as an extremely unequal distribution in a normal slave society. This I take to be a *reductio*.

exploitation violate the relational ideal of justice (Norman, 1998: 44). However, the reason he thinks so is not grounded in some view about the expressive content of relations of domination or exploitation or on any assumptions about how, say, dominators regard dominatees, but simply in the view that if someone dominates and exploits another then they relate to one another in an objectionable, inegalitarian way.

Second, friends of the relational ideal must specify which shape social relations should take for them to be just. Interestingly, something similar to the range of views that are available to friends of the distributive ideal is available to friends of the relational view. For instance, one can subscribe to relational sufficientarianism. According to this view, a situation is just only if everyone relates to one another as – if I may coin a phrase parallel to 'equals' – sufficients, where a sufficient is one whose standing is sufficiently high. If we consider this view in its luckist form – it comes in a non-responsibility-sensitive form as well, which I suspect will be more attractive than its luckist cousin to many friends of the relational ideal of justice – we get:

> *Luck relational sufficientarianism*: It is just only if no one relates to others as non-sufficients through no responsibility of their own.

The most plausible versions of such a position condemn as unjust those social relations that are most objectionable from the point of view of relational egalitarians, e.g. the relations between slaves and masters in my odd slave society. However, relational sufficientarianism might be compatible with the unequal relations between a worshipping religious follower and a sufficiently respectful guru; a world-famous, but non-harrassing, well behaved, professor and a first-year student; or a boss with suitably circumscribed powers and an employee with alternative employment opportunities.[21]

Another possibility would be to model the relational ideal on the difference principle and say that justice requires that those who are worst off in terms of social relations should be as well off as possible in terms of social relations.[22] One might think that, on the one hand, if everyone would benefit from the introduction of certain kinds of non-egalitarian social relations and, in particular, if those who would be worst off relative

---

[21] The ideal that we relate to one another as sufficients, aesthetically speaking, is implicit in Anderson's (1999: 335) idea that justice does not require that we adopt aesthetic norms such that we are all equally beautiful, only norms which are such that we are all deemed 'an acceptable presence in civil society' (cp. Chapter 3.2).

[22] Not all forms of relational egalitarianism can be articulated in this way, cp. Chapter 6.4.

to others under such a non-egalitarian scheme would be better off than under any other scheme, no one would have any complaint against people not relating as equals in the relevant ways and, thus, no injustice would arise from such inegalitarian social relations.[23]

Some might find the leximin version of the relational ideal implausible by virtue of the fact that it gives lexical priority to those who are worst off in terms of social relations and, thus, rejects social relations that would render them slightly worse off at the gain of making many more people better off.[24] In view of this concern, one can subscribe to relational prioritarianism. On this view, social relations should be such that the weighted valued of moral status (or social standing) is maximized. Some might say that the only way to do so is to have equality of moral status or social standing. However, in itself relational prioritarianism is silent on which distributive pattern maximizes the relevant weighted value of moral status, and at least some theorists have suggested that unequal social relations might actually benefit us all. The conservative thinker Edmund Burke believed that, in a certain way, social relations are not a zero-sum matter – hierarchy, instead of thoroughly egalitarian social relations, gives those who end up at the lower end of the hierarchy the chance of virtuous modesty and deference which might be better for them, social relations-wise, than some bland form of equality, which homogenizes and vulgarizes everything: 'the order of civil life establishes ['the true moral equality of mankind', i.e. natural hierarchy] as much for the benefit of those whom it must leave in a humble state, as those whom it is able to exalt to a condition more splendid' (Burke, 1987 [1790]: 124; cp. 170).[25]

---

[23] This implies that Anderson's (2010a) attempt to tie the idea of relational egalitarianism to the idea of individual complaints understood in the indicated way fails (Chapter 7.3). If she is right about the former, justice does not – at a fundamental level – require that people relate as equals. Justice might require – at a fundamental level – that we relate to one another in such a way that those who are worst off, social relations-wise, are as well off as possible, and if the only way to make the worst off as well off as possible is by people relating as equals, then – at a non-fundamental level – this is what justice requires. But this would not turn friends of the complaint model into relational *egalitarians*, any more than the fact – assuming it to be one – that the worst off fare as well as possible only under an equal distribution turns friends of Rawls' difference principle into friends of distributive equality at the level of fundamental principles of justice.

[24] The leximin version of the relational ideal instructs us to maximize the social standing of those with the least social standing first. Having done that, we should then maximize the social standing of those who are second-most worst off social standing-wise, and so on and so forth (cp. Hirose, 2015: 25).

[25] Not all relational egalitarians think that egalitarian social relations are required by justice because of how they are good for people (Chapters 6.4 and 6.5). However, no one denies that social relations can benefit or harm people.

A fourth possibility, and the one which has received by far the most attention, is relational egalitarianism, which I have already introduced in its outcome-focused as well as its luckist versions and whose recent history I will briefly sketch in the next section. The present section's two main points are, first, that just as there are outcome-focused and luckist versions of the distributive ideal, so there are of the relational ideal. Second, in a way that is analogous to how the distributive ideal of justice comes in different versions depending on the preferred distributive pattern, so does the relational ideal. Specifically, we can be friends of the *relational* ideal of justice, but not be relational *egalitarians*.

1.3 Relational Egalitarianism: A Thumbnail Sketch of Its Recent History

In the previous two sections, I introduced the distributive and relational ideals of justice. In particular, I introduced the luck egalitarian version of the former and the egalitarian, outcome-focused version of the latter. The last twenty-five years of political philosophy have seen much work that, in one way or another, points to various limitations of, or flaws in, the ideal of distributive justice – in particular, in its luck egalitarian variants – and defends, as a supplement, or as a replacement, some version of the relational ideal – in particular, relational egalitarianism.

An early proponent of relational egalitarianism is Iris Marion Young.[26] In *Justice and the Politics of Difference*, she criticizes the distributive paradigm within theories of justice, 'which tends to focus on the possession of material goods and social positions' (Young, 1990: 8).[27] While she concedes that some friends of this paradigm extend a concern for distribution 'to

---

[26] It is rare that anything in (political) philosophy is truly new. If we go back further in time, we can point to other 'early' relational egalitarians. Anderson (2010a) thinks of Rawls as articulating important aspects of relational egalitarianism, and in developing their accounts of social relations informed by equal respect, Miller (1998) and Wolff (1998) both point to R. H. Tawney as their source of inspiration. Going back further, one might see Hegel's master-slave dialectic and the theme of recognition which it embodies – a theme which has recently been explored by critical theory thinkers like Axel Honneth (2007) and Nancy Fraser (Fraser & Honneth, 2003) – as well as Rousseau's (1973 [1754]) critique of his contemporaries' obsession with proving themselves superior to others as anticipating central aspects of contemporary relational egalitarianism (cp. O'Neill, 2008: 129; Anderson, 2008b: 263). Schemmel (2012a: 125) and Young (1990: 15) refer to Marx's critique of the Gotha programme's preoccupation with issues about distribution and its similarities to recent critiques of the distributive paradigm. No doubt there are other canonical thinkers lurking in the historical background of relational egalitarianism.

[27] Criticisms that purport to show that if one endorses a certain theory, then one is likely to have a certain deficient focus or misconstrue certain matters, almost invariably, and even when sound, are criticisms of those who embrace the focus and not criticisms of the theory in question. Almost

cover such goods as self-respect, opportunity, power and honour', such
extensions result in distorted understandings of these goods 'as identifiable
things or bundles distributed in a static pattern among identifiable, separate individuals' (Young, 1990: 8).[28] Distribution is important in Young's
view, but *pace* Rawls among others, the concern for distribution should be
limited to a concern for the distribution of material goods and 'oppression
and domination . . . should be the primary terms for conceptualizing
injustice' (Young, 1990: 8–9; cp. Navin, 2011).[29] A view informed by
such an understanding of justice would, Young contends, involve
a 'process-oriented and relational conceptualization' of justice. Along
these lines, she introduces the notion of 'five faces of oppression' – exploitation, marginalization, powerlessness, cultural imperialism and violence –
as that which should primarily occupy those who theorize justice.

Other early and influential works defending relational egalitarianism
include pieces by Jonathan Wolff and David Miller. Wolff's work is
interesting for a number of reasons, one being that, unlike many other
relational egalitarians, he thinks of the ideal of relational equality as one
that supplements, rather than replaces, the ideal of distributive justice (cp.
Wolff, 2010: 347). In a 1998 article in *Philosophy & Public Affairs*, he
expresses his discontent with the then-dominant luck egalitarian position
within theories of equality. Among other things, 'the goal of equality', as he
understands it along with socialist egalitarians, 'is not so much to achieve
an egalitarian distribution of material goods, but to create a society in
which each individual can think of themselves as valued as an equal'
(Wolff, 2010: 337).[30] From that perspective, liberal egalitarian theories

---

invariably, theories do not issue injunctions regarding focus (though they might render certain
focuses more natural than others) and are rarely incompatible with a correction of the relevant
misconstruals. Accordingly, I do not think Young's critique is best construed as a critique of the
distributive theories as such as opposed to a (in some respects well-taken) critique of *theorists* working
within the 'distributive paradigm' (cp. Chapter 2.3). Admittedly, the primary target of Young's
critique is the distributive paradigm. While the distributive paradigm includes distributive theories
of justice, it also includes much more, e.g. *inter alia*, 'characteristic questions' and 'specific theories
and their typical scope and mode of application' (Young, 1990: 16). I have no intention of defending
the distributive *paradigm* (in this sense) in this book.

[28] It is unclear what Young means by 'identifiable things or bundles'. People who are concerned about
an unequal distribution of power do not misconstrue power as an 'identifiable thing or bundle' or 'a
kind of stuff' that we can take from some people and give to others, who will then have less or more
of the 'thing, bundle or stuff' as a result of the relevant intervention, in the same way that we can
redistribute land or money (cp. Young, 1990: 25, 30–3; Norman, 1998: 46). Young does not offer any
examples of theorists who make such a blatant error.

[29] Young (1990: 33) thinks that the 'scope of justice is wider than distributive justice'. Hence, she thinks
that the latter falls within the scope of the former, though it far from exhausts it.

[30] In hindsight Wolff notes that one of his dissatisfactions with luck egalitarianism is that it is not
informed by a 'vision of the good society' (Wolff, 2010: 337; cp. Young, 1990: 35–6). Note, however,

such as Dworkin's ideal of equality of resources seem 'rather soulless' (Wolff, 2010: 337). More concretely, under a wide range of circumstances, the egalitarian concern for fairness as reflected in the distinction between deserving and undeserving poor clashes with the realization of another important set of values that Wolff takes to be defining of socialist equality, namely respect, where this includes mutual respect among citizens as well as everyone enjoying self-respect. This is so because in order to determine whether someone – say, an unemployed person – should receive welfare benefits from the luck egalitarian state, it would need to know whether this person is responsible for being worse off, and this requires respect-undermining 'shameful revelations' on the part of that person.[31] Collecting such information involves the risk of harming 'the very people that [luck egalitarianism] is designed to help' (Wolff, 2010: 335). Accordingly, at least in the circumstances of the actual world, we should refrain from realizing distributive justice as much as we can in the interest of 'other egalitarian concerns' (Wolff, 1998: 122).

In a contribution to an edited volume on the ideal of equality, Miller, like Wolff, distinguishes between 'two different kinds of valuable equality, one connected with justice, and the other standing independently of it. Equality of the first kind is distributive . . . The second kind is not . . . It does not specify directly any distribution of rights or resources. Instead it identifies a social ideal, the ideal of a society in which people regard and treat one another as equals, in other words a society that is not marked by status divisions such that one can place different people in hierarchically ranked categories, in different classes for instance. We can call this second kind of equality *equality of status*, or simply *social equality* (Miller, 1998: 23; cp. Miller, 2015: viii).[32]

Miller is critical of the first kind of equality, distributive equality, but favours social equality. He thinks that justice requires that each gets his or

---

that a criticism to the effect that luck egalitarianism does not capture everything that one thinks that a theory of equality should capture is different from a criticism to the effect that luck egalitarianism is a false account of justice (cp. Lippert-Rasmussen, 2018; Chapter 3.7).

[31] It is not crucial to Wolff's challenge that respect is unequal, i.e. unemployed people have to show that they are unable to work, but better-off, employed people do not. Suppose everyone is required to make shameful revelations about themselves to everyone else. This would not be a regrettable state of affairs fairness-wise, but it would be regrettable from the point of view of the egalitarian value of respect (Wolff, 1998: 117). Wolff thinks that Anderson's relational ideal of democratic equality is no less vulnerable to the shameful-revelations objection than is luck egalitarianism (Wolff, 2010: 348).

[32] This formulation is compatible with a society with many local hierarchies provided that it is not the same individuals who come out on top (or at the bottom) in sufficiently many of them, because if the individuals who come out on top in too many local hierarchies are the same, individuals could plausibly be placed in a global hierarchy (cp. Chapter 5.5; Anderson, 2008b: 266–7).

her due and that what one is due depends on the nature of the specific good in question and on the context. Sometimes, e.g. in 'manna-from-heaven cases, cases where a group of people find themselves in possession of a divisible good for whose existence none of them is in any way responsible and on which none has any special claim of need, say', giving each his or her due involves equal distributions (Miller, 1998: 25). Such cases, however, are 'limiting cases', and in most cases justice does not require an equal distribution.[33]

Three important points emerge from Miller's characterization of the ideal of social equality. First, equality of status is not something people are entitled to. The ideal does not reflect individual claims, but reflects an impersonal concern that 'our society should not be like that', i.e. a society of unequals (Miller, 1998: 24; cp. Miller, 2015: viii).[34] 'Our' is important in this quote, because Miller thinks that for, say, non-moderns, things might have been different and for them a hierarchical society might have been compatible with solidarity, dignity and respect (Miller, 1998: 33).

Second, equality of status is not incompatible with any ranking of people across the board: 'Where there is social equality, people feel that each member of the community enjoys an equal standing with all the rest that overrides their unequal ratings along particular dimensions' (Miller, 1998: 31). Hence, I might defer to the advice of an expert, say, compatibly with the ideal of relating as equals.[35]

Third, while social equality is compatible with certain kinds of, or certain degrees of, distributive inequality, the former constrains the latter. For instance, 'large-scale, cumulative inequalities of advantage' can 'make it difficult for people to live together on terms of equality' (Miller, 1998: 34).

While I definitely do not want to belittle the early contributions to the relational egalitarian literature just mentioned, it is probably fair to say that what really brought relational egalitarianism into the spotlight of political philosophy was an article in *Ethics* by Elizabeth Anderson, to which I will return in much more detail in the next chapter. In that article, Anderson

---

[33] Miller (1998: 26–31) also mentions two additional cases where justice requires distributive equality, one involving complete uncertainty about people's respective claims and one involving equal entitlements based on group membership. Note also that Miller does not reject the distributive ideal as such, e.g. he accepts a sufficientarian account of distributive justice (Miller, 1998: 26n9).

[34] Presumably, Miller does not think that equality of status does not have personal value in addition to impersonal value, since he thinks that '[a]ssociating as equals provides us with a kind of recognition that is essential to the modern self' (Miller, 1998: 30).

[35] Miller's notion of social equality is informed by Walzer's (1983) idea of complex equality (cp. Anderson, 2008b: 264).

pursues two main aims. The first and negative one is to rebut luck egalitarianism. The second and positive aim is to sketch the contours of her particular version of the relational ideal of justice, to wit, democratic equality. One central aspect of democratic equality is that it holds that, setting aside certain important but less well advertised qualifications, justice requires that everyone at all times has the capability to interact as equals qua citizens, e.g. in the political sphere, and qua members of civil society, e.g. in the private sphere. As part of her project of carving out a space for democratic equality, she takes care to emphasize that, at most, democratic equality is indirectly concerned with distribution of goods and, as a matter of fact, democratic equality can obtain even if the distribution of goods, be that welfare, money or resources in general, is fairly unequal. However, as a matter of contingent fact, democratic equality implies limits to the degree of permissible distributive inequality. But in itself – i.e. independently of how it affects, or is a reliable indicator of, or is expressive of, whether people relate as equals – distributive equality is of no concern to egalitarians. As we have already seen is the case with David Miller, this way of paying tribute to the attraction of the distributive ideal is also found in the work of other relational egalitarians (Scanlon, 2000: 54; Scheffler, 2015).[36] In her later work, Anderson has explored additional aspects of relational egalitarianism, e.g. its relation to a so-called second-person conception of moral justification and its implications for racial segregation, and it is probably fair to say that she is one of the two leading proponents of relational egalitarianism (see Chapter 7.3).

The other relational egalitarian that I have in mind in the previous sentence, and whose work will also be scrutinized more carefully in the next chapter, is Samuel Scheffler.[37] Like Anderson and Wolff, he criticizes luck egalitarianism for its obsession with responsibility. And, like Miller and Anderson, he canvasses an ideal of justice according to which people ought to relate as equals, where this involves that their relations are 'in certain crucial respects, at least, unstructured by differences of rank, power or status' (Scheffler, 2005: 18). In his most recent work, Scheffler explicates this ideal in greater detail, arguing that an important dispositional constraint on relating as equals is that the parties to this

---

[36] This tribute relies on an empirical assumption: to wit, that huge distributive inequalities are incompatible with relating as equals. However, the tribute turns into an assault should the empirical circumstances be different, i.e. if relating as equals requires huge distributive inequality.

[37] Other important theorists working on relational egalitarianism include Fourie (2012); Fourie et al. (2015); Hausman & Waldren (2011); Norman (1998); O'Neill (2008); Pogge (2006; 2008); Schemmel (2011; 2012a; 2012b).

relation place equal weight on their own interests and those of the other party (see Chapter 2.6).

1.4   An Overview of the Book

While relational equality has received a fair of amount attention recently, the theory is still at a relatively early stage in terms of its development. Indeed, one of the main aims of this book is to articulate the ideal of relational equality more fully. In the course of doing so, it will address its nature (Chapters 2, 3 and 4), its site and scope (Chapter 5), its justifiability (Chapter 6) and its relation to the distributive ideal, in particular luck egalitarianism (Chapters 7 and 8).

Chapter 2 focuses on Anderson's and Scheffler's work on relational egalitarianism and presents their views in much greater resolution than that offered in the previous section's thumbnail sketch. I present their criticisms of luck egalitarianism as well as their positive accounts of their favoured relational ideals. As far as their critiques of luck egalitarianism are concerned I argue that these are not decisive and, in relation to Anderson's critique, I distinguish between theorist- and theory-focused critiques of luck egalitarianism, arguing that her critique is of the former kind. When it comes to their respective relational ideals, I identify some important differences between them, e.g. that Anderson's ideal, unlike Scheffler's, focuses on expressive content.

Chapters 3 and 4 say something about the nature of relating as equals. Chapter 3 offers an analysis of what it is to relate as equals. Surprisingly little has been written on this topic (Miller 1998, 31; Fourie et al., 2015: 108; Schemmel, 2012a: 134; but see Wolff, 2015: 221). I conjecture that an important reason for this is that, to a large extent, relational egalitarianism has been articulated as an alternative to luck egalitarianism; accordingly, much energy has been channelled into criticizing that view and, in the course of doing so, pointing out what relational egalitarianism is *not* (Tomlin, 2015; cp. Schemmel, 2012a: 124). Accordingly, many have provided examples of relations that, intuitively, are incompatible with the relational egalitarian ideal (cp. Fourie et al., 2015: 3; Young, 1990). Yet such examples do not add up to a positive account of what relational egalitarianism is or requires. Relating as equals, I argue, has two components: treating others as equals and regarding others as equals. These can come apart, such as when I treat someone as an equal despite the fact that I do not regard him as one but fear the consequences of not relating to him as one. I will also address the relationendum issue, which I briefly introduced in

Section 1.2, arguing that there are a number of different dimensions in which people can relate as (un)equals.

Chapter 4 explores one way – the way in which we give and receive blame – in which we relate as equals. One central assumption underlying this practice is that, roughly, you are not in a position to blame others for a fault which you also have, and you need not accept blame from others who are at fault in the same way that they blame you for being. If, despite being at greater fault yourself, you engage in blaming, others can dismiss your blame as hypocritical. There are obvious alternative inegalitarian, but to our minds quite alien, ways of giving and receiving blame; e.g. it might be the case that we deferentially accept blame from superior people, e.g. nobility, who are at greater fault than we ourselves are ('Who am I to criticize his Lordship?' etc.). Ironically, this is an aspect of relating as equals that relational egalitarians have not addressed, unlike the more politically charged failures to relate as equals that racism, sexism etc. involve, but which has had the attention of one of the most prominent defenders of luck egalitarianism, G. A. Cohen (2013: 115–42).

Chapter 5 scrutinizes what friends of relational equality can and should say about the site and scope of their ideal. The analogous question for luck egalitarians has received considerable attention and there are, I contend, considerable, but not full, similarities in terms of the available luck egalitarian positions and the answers relational egalitarians can give.[38] First, I raise a dilemma for relational egalitarians with respect to intergenerational justice. Either there is such a thing as intergenerational justice, or there is not. The latter horn of the dilemma is implausible. If so, relational egalitarians must give us some account of intergenerational justice. But it is very difficult to see how they can do that. Either they concede, plausibly, that we – members of the present generation – have no social relations to members of future generations, who will be born only once we are dead, in which case any claim of justice they have upon us must be grounded in something other than our social relations. Or they argue that we do indeed have social relations with members of future generations. However, in so doing they make the notion of social relations too thin, as it were, in a way

---

[38] Roughly, luck egalitarians divide into those who think that there is no egalitarian justice across generations and those who think there is (Segall, 2016); those who think that distributive equality concerns people's lives as a whole (Nagel, 1991) and those who think that it (also) concerns segments of people's lives (McKerlie, 1996; Temkin, 1993); those who think that the site of luck egalitarian justice is restricted to social institutions (Tan, 2014) and those who think that the site of luck egalitarian justice also includes individual actions (Cohen, 2008); and those who think that the scope of luck egalitarianism is restricted to include co-citizens (Nagel, 1991) and those who defend cosmopolitan versions of luck egalitarianism (Caney, 2005).

that is incompatible with other of their commitments (cp. Pogge, 2008: 172–8). Next, I address relations between different age groups. There are significant periods of our lives, e.g. childhood, where we cannot relate to others as equals in the way two competent adults can. For instance, relational egalitarians see paternalism between competent adults as incompatible with relational equality. However, some degree of paternalism (whereby I mean acting against someone's will in matters that they have a defeasibly primary say over and for their own benefit) is a desirable element of the relationship between parents and children, so the requirement that, at any given moment, everyone relates to one another as equals seems implausible. One way to address this problem is to adopt a whole-lives version of relational egalitarianism, which allows that people do not at all times in their lives relate to others as equals provided that, when considering their lives as a whole, they do. I defend the view that relational egalitarians must adopt a lifetime perspective in addition to a time-relative perspective. Third, in relation to the site issue, most relational egalitarians believe that relational equality pertains not only to institutions, e.g. the state, but also to people's actions in the course of their everyday lives (cp. Schemmel, 2012a: 135–7). I argue that this view is the most plausible one, partly in light of my view of what the value of relating as equals consists of. Finally, Chapter 5 addresses the question of whether the scope of relational equality is statist or cosmopolitan. I submit that individuals who are not fellow citizens can relate to one another as (un)equals and that, in the end, relational egalitarians should also be concerned with the (in)egalitarian character of relations between non-co-citizens. This amounts to a cosmopolitan version of the ideal of treating one another as equals (Nath, 2015).

Chapter 6 builds on the three previous chapters in order to focus on wherein the value of relating as equals consists. One possibility is that it is good for us – whether instrumentally, non-instrumentally or both – to relate as equals. This might be so, but if this is the only way egalitarian relations are valuable, the concerns of relational egalitarians can be accommodated fully by distributive egalitarians. Indeed, the relevant view seems to call for a principle for how the relevant personal good should be distributed across persons. Another possibility is that relating as equals is impersonally valuable, i.e. valuable whether or not it is valuable for anyone. I do not deny that this might be the case. However, I show why there are considerable problems in providing a more detailed and plausible account of that value, e.g. do we make the world a better place by bringing more people into existence, whom we then relate to as equals, and, better in one respect, by eliminating people to whom we do not relate as equals?

The third option I consider is that, whatever value relating as equals has, relating as equals simply reflects a deontic requirement grounded in our equal moral status as persons. This view, I argue, fits better with standard relational egalitarian views than the impersonal value view.

Chapter 7 distinguishes between three forms of egalitarianism: distributive luck egalitarianism, relational egalitarianism and dispositional egalitarianism – the latter of which is a view which, in effect, Scheffler articulates in his attempt to work out some of the details of the relational ideal of equality. I argue that these views are consistent and distinct, i.e. strictly speaking, though not substantively speaking, relational egalitarianism is not reducible to a form of distributive egalitarianism with an unusual equalisandum, e.g. social standing. Also, *pace* Anderson, I argue that these three egalitarian views mentioned are not incompatible because rooted in some deep disagreement about the nature of moral justification. Indeed, I propose an ecumenical view of egalitarian justice, according to which they are grounded in fairness, understood as the claim that to the extent individuals are differently situated – whether in terms of how well off they are or in terms of how they are treated relative to others – this is unfair unless the relevant difference is motivated by their differential exercise of responsibility. If my arguments in Chapter 7 are sound, luck and relational egalitarianism are much less different from one another than most theorists tend to assume.

Chapter 8 builds on this view and explores two issues. First, I show how a concern for the distribution of opportunities, which is not simply grounded in its being instrumental for making or enabling people to relate as equals, sometimes appears inherent in Anderson's position. Second, I argue – and at greater length – that we find relational egalitarian concerns expressed in the work of prominent luck egalitarians, most notably G. A. Cohen. For instance, Cohen's critique of Rawlsian justifications of inequality rests on a certain ideal of people forming a justificatory community, which in itself can be seen as a way of fleshing out part of what it is to relate to each other as equals (cp. Chapter 7.3). Like Chapter 7, albeit in a theorist- as opposed to a theory-focused way, Chapter 8 shows that the distance between luck and relational egalitarianism is much less marked than the impression one might develop from reading relational egalitarian criticisms of luck egalitarianism.

Like relational egalitarians, I believe that people relating as equals has a particular kind of egalitarian value beyond how their so relating to one another affects distributions, at least on the standard conceptions of what distributions involve. Like pluralist relational egalitarians, I do not believe that this rules out that luck egalitarianism captures part of what the ideal of egalitarian justice is about. As already mentioned, I believe that the two forms of egalitarianism might both be rooted in a concern for fairness. That such an ecumenical version of egalitarian justice is possible, even plausible, is one of the main claims of this book. It is in the spirit of this ecumenical view that I will elaborate a number of respects in which the distance between luck and relational egalitarians is smaller than they apparently imagine.

I fear not all readers will be friends of ecumenical egalitarian justice once they stop reading this book. Accordingly, it is worth pointing to this book's other main aim, namely to show that there are many ways of being a relational egalitarian, some of which involve being no less concerned with responsibility than luck egalitarians. Larry Temkin (1993) famously noted that the ideal of distributive equality is complex. Here I argue, though in much less detail than Temkin does in his book, that something similar is true of relational egalitarianism. In particular, I show that some of the issues of contention that arise in connection with various ways of fleshing out the luck egalitarian ideal, e.g. in relation to the distribuendum, site and scope of luck egalitarian justice, appear in analogous forms in relation to different versions of relational egalitarianism. Finally, I suggest a luckist, partially complete-lives version of relational egalitarianism which is quite different from the forms of relational egalitarianism presently on offer, and explore which answers relational egalitarians can give to the 'What is the point of relational equality?' question.

1.5 Summary

In this chapter I have contrasted distributive and relational ideals of justice. The ideal of relational justice comes in different versions, and relational egalitarianism, on which I will focus in the remainder of this book, is just one version thereof. Moreover, while this is widely ignored, there are outcome as well as luckist versions of the relational ideal. I have also briefly mentioned some of the main contributions to the recent literature on relational egalitarianism as well as set out the three main aims of this book: first, to defend a pluralist version of egalitarian justice which incorporates a luckist version of relational equality; second, to argue that relational egalitarianism is considerably more complex than has been noted so far and, in the course of noting this, to clarify its nature and develop the theory further, e.g. by offering a detailed analysis of the concept of relating as equals and a critical reflection on what makes relating as equals desirable; and, third, to show that relational egalitarianism is complex in ways quite analogous to the ways in which luck egalitarianism is complex.

PART I

Nature

CHAPTER 2

Relational Egalitarianism

2.1 Introduction

In Chapter 1, I sketched out how the objection from irresponsibility has led many who are sympathetic to an egalitarian distributive ideal to reject outcome egalitarianism in favour of some form of luck egalitarianism. Building on the insight encapsulated in that objection, for almost two decades after Dworkin's influential 1981 articles, many egalitarian-inclined philosophers invested a great deal of energy in refining Dworkin's cut between brute luck disadvantages, for which people are not responsible, and option luck disadvantages, for which they are responsible and, thus, do not merit compensation (e.g. Lippert-Rasmussen, 2001). Similarly, much ink was spilled over what is the right metric of distributive shares, e.g. welfare, resources (as Dworkin thought), both or something altogether different. Most egalitarian philosophers assumed that something along the lines of luck egalitarianism was the correct theory of egalitarian justice and, thus, that they could legitimately commit themselves to luck-egalitarian puzzle solving, as Kuhnians might put it, and ignore the foundational task of justifying the ideal of equality itself. With some justification, Scheffler (2003a: 14) compares the situation to one in which utilitarians channel all their argumentative energies into settling which of different versions of utilitarianism is the best, but neglect to defend utilitarianism against competing moral theories despite its many counterintuitive implications.

This luck-egalitarian hegemony in political philosophy ended with the publication of Elizabeth Anderson's 'What is the point of equality?' in 1999. Negatively, the article offered a barrage of (often highly polemical) criticisms of the views of most of the main luck egalitarian theorists at the time. Positively, it sketched a relational alternative to luck egalitarianism, namely democratic equality. Relational egalitarianism, as we discuss it today, has been shaped first and foremost by this article as well as by Anderson's ensuing work and a series of important pieces by Samuel

Scheffler (2003a; 2003b; 2005; 2015), who has taken up and developed many of the themes that are found in Anderson's work. This chapter focuses on the views of Anderson and Scheffler.

Section 2.2 elaborates the distinction between luck and relational egalitarianism on the basis of Anderson and Scheffler's work. Section 2.3 surveys Anderson's critique of luck egalitarianism. I argue that many of her criticisms apply to distributive views other than luck egalitarianism and that they are mostly independent of relational egalitarianism, i.e. one might accept or reject them independently of whether one subscribes to relational egalitarianism. Section 2.4 describes Anderson's positive version of relational egalitarianism, namely democratic equality. Section 2.5 presents Scheffler's critique of luck egalitarianism, while Section 2.6 lays out his account of relational egalitarianism. I argue that Scheffler's criticisms of luck egalitarianism are no more compelling than Anderson's. Section 2.7 compares Anderson and Scheffler's relational ideals in light of the five previous sections, highlighting some significant differences between them.

My main claims in this chapter are: (1) neither Anderson's nor Scheffler's objections to distributive equality refute the distributive ideal of equality, (2) nor do their objections provide compelling motivation for embracing their relational ideals instead of, say, modified versions of the distributive ideal that accommodate the relevant objections, (3) and yet they succeed in describing something that is a concern from the point of view of egalitarian justice.

2.2 Luck Egalitarianism versus Relational Egalitarianism

In her 1999 article, Anderson contrasts her own relational view of justice – democratic equality – with luck egalitarianism, or 'equality of fortune', as she calls it below:

> democratic equality is . . . a relational theory of equality: it views equality as a social relationship. Equality of fortune is a distributive theory of equality: it conceives of equality as a pattern of distribution. Thus, equality of fortune regards two people as equal as long as they enjoy equal amounts of some distributable good – income, resources, opportunities for welfare and so forth. Social relations are largely seen as instrumental to generating such patterns of distribution. By contrast, democratic equality regards two people as equal when each accepts the obligation to justify their actions by principles acceptable to the other, and in which they take mutual consultation, reciprocation and recognition for granted.[1] Certain patterns in the

---

[1] In many cases – apparently compatible with relating as equals – we do not in any straightforward sense accept an obligation to justify ourselves to one another, to consult one another, etc. Suppose

distribution of goods may be instrumental to securing such relationships, follow from them, or even be constitutive of them. But democratic egalitarians are fundamentally concerned with the relationships within which goods are distributed, not only with the distribution of goods themselves.[2] (Anderson, 1999: 313–14; cp. Anderson, 2008a: 143)

The ideal of distributive equality can be satisfied even if the ideal of democratic equality is not. There can be distributive equality between Robinson Crusoe-like characters with no social relations, e.g. they all live lives that are equally good (and lonely). Conversely, it is possible for people to have different levels of income etc. not rooted in any differential exercise of responsibility and still accept 'the obligation to justify their actions by principles acceptable to the other', taking 'mutual consultation, reciprocation and recognition for granted' – something that appears to ensure the satisfaction of Anderson's ideal of democratic equality as stated above.

Samuel Scheffler draws a contrast which is similar to Anderson's:

> According to [distributive equality, the most influential version of which is luck egalitarianism], equality is an essentially distributive value. We can directly assess distributions as being more or less egalitarian, and justice requires that we strive to achieve fully egalitarian distributions, except insofar as other values forbid it. This is the view taken by Jerry Cohen when he says, 'I take for granted that there is something that justice requires people to have equal amounts of, not no matter what, but to whatever extent is allowed by values that compete with distributive equality' . . . According to the . . . relational view, equality is an ideal governing certain kinds of interpersonal relationships. It plays a central role in political philosophy because justice requires the establishment of a society of equals, a society whose members relate to one another on a footing of equality. For those who accept this view, one important task is to consider what kinds of institutions and practices a society must put in place if it is to count as a society of equals. The relevant institutions and practices will include those that govern the distribution of goods within society, and so the ideal of equality, understood as an ideal that governs the relations among the members of society, will have important distributive implications. But, according to this view, equality is a more general, relational ideal, and its

---

I prevent you from stealing my vital organs. While most believe that there are valid principles that permit my preventing you from doing so, most neither think that I am under any obligation to justify myself to you – I do not wrong you by simply thwarting your plans, by offering you no justification for doing so or thinking that I owe you none, or by failing to consult you about the location of my kidneys – nor that I fail to treat you as an equal on that account. Scheffler recognizes this and emphasizes the importance of determining which 'resource allocation[s] decision falls within the scope of a relationship' (Scheffler, 2015: 32).

[2] Here I take for granted that we know what a social relation is (see Chapter 7.4).

bearing on questions of distribution is indirect. (Scheffler, 2015: 21–2; cp. Scheffler, 2003a: 21–2, 31)

Drawing on these two characterizations, and on what Anderson and Scheffler write elsewhere, we might contrast the following two official dramatis personae of their work (see Chapters 1.1 and 1.2):

> *Luck egalitarianism*: It is just only if everyone's distributive shares reflect nothing other than their comparative exercise of responsibility.
> *Outcome relational egalitarianism*: A situation is just only if everyone relates to one another as equals.[3]

Anderson and Scheffler's characterizations of the view they oppose as well as the view they canvass are quite similar, though I shall qualify this observation considerably as we move along (Section 2.7; Chapter 5.3). It is also worth noting that, at least in part, their rejection of luck egalitarianism stems from their rejection of the broader distributive ideal of justice (Chapter 1) as well as (a fortiori):

> *The strong distributive ideal of justice*: A situation is just if, and only if, the distribution of goods it involves has a particular set of desirable features.

Hence, they reject all the other distributive ideals that I introduced in Chapter 1.2 that take justice to be concerned exclusively and non-instrumentally with the distribution of goods. More specifically, they reject distributive views that, unlike luck egalitarianism, ascribe no significance to people's choices or exercise of responsibility, e.g. outcome egalitarianism, and their objections apply, *mutatis mutandis*, to such views that, unlike luck egalitarianism, do not take equality to be the distributive pattern mandated by justice. For instance, according to resource sufficientarians, justice is satisfied when, in a distribution involving two people, both of them have enough resources, whatever their social relations are. More generally, it is a striking feature of much of Anderson and Scheffler's critique of luck egalitarianism that, in large part, it is a critique of luck egalitarianism by virtue of its focus on distribution and, accordingly, that the real target of these parts of their criticism is much broader than just luck egalitarianism.

Anderson and Scheffler might find some distributive ideals less implausible than luck egalitarianism. For instance, they might think outcome sufficientarianism is a more plausible view than luck egalitarianism, but

---

[3] Chapter 7.4 returns to whether the distinction drawn here can be upheld or whether the concern for social relations can be reduced to a concern for the distribution of a certain social good. Chapter 7.2 reflects on the fact that the two views do not state sufficient conditions for justice.

since it shares with the latter the assumption that justice is a matter of distribution, ultimately, as relational egalitarians, they reject it too.[4] Similarly, in their embrace of outcome relational egalitarianism, they implicitly reject other versions of the relational ideal, e.g. they reject luckist versions and they reject the view that everyone should relate as sufficients.

Before proceeding to their objections to luck egalitarianism, I need to address one particular complication in relation to the quote from Anderson. Her formulations are qualified in that she writes that luck egalitarians take a 'largely' instrumental view of social relations, which suggests that in part they take a non-instrumental view. Similarly, she describes relational egalitarians in such a way that certain distributions of goods may be 'constitutive of social relations' and that relational egalitarians are fundamentally concerned '*not only* [my italics] with the distribution of goods', suggesting that they do indeed have such a concern, although it is not their only one.

I ignore these qualifications for the time being (see Chapter 8.2). I do so for two reasons. First, in effect the qualifications suggest the possibility of some sort of hybrid position between luck egalitarians and relational egalitarians, which holds that justice is non-instrumentally concerned with distributions as well as social relations. While I will eventually defend such a hybrid position (Chapter 7.6), for the time being introducing it muddies the waters.

Second, exegetically speaking my neglect of Anderson's reservations is permissible, because she does not explain what motivates them, and some of her views undermine a hybrid position of any sort. For instance, Anderson (2010a) argues that luck egalitarianism and relational egalitarianism are rooted in different views about moral justification – second- and third-person views respectively (Chapter 7.3). A hybrid view of the sort Anderson's guarded formulations suggest embodies both views of justification – views which Anderson takes to be incompatible.[5] With this brief

---

[4] A similar point applies to Rawls' difference principle, at least when it is seen as a fundamental principle of justice not simply grounded in the requirements of equal respect. Scheffler suggests, however, that the difference principle is grounded in a relational ideal, i.e. a 'fair system of cooperation among free and equal people, each of whom is taken to have the capacity for a sense of justice and pursue a rational plan of life which is constitutive of his or her good' (Scheffler, 2003a: 25). This possibility brings into play a distinction between first-order and foundationally distributive (/relational) views, which I return to later (Chapter 8.2) but ignore for now.

[5] In Anderson (2008b: 242, 263), she drops the relevant qualification: '[e]quality refers fundamentally to the social relations in which we stand, and only derivatively to distributive outcomes . . . Distributions are objectionable from an egalitarian point of view to the extent that they are the cause (by act or omission) or effect of egalitarian social relations, as embodied in inegalitarian social interactions, processes or rules'.

sketch of Anderson and Scheffler's taxonomical map of the theoretical landscape behind us, I proceed to fill out some of the details.

2.3 Anderson's Critique of Luck Egalitarianism

In 1999 Anderson asked whether if 'much recent academic work defending equality [i.e. the work of luck egalitarians] had been secretly penned by conservatives' the results could have been 'any more embarrassing for egalitarians?' (Anderson, 2015: 287).[6] Her uncompromisingly critical stand suggests that, on her view, it really would have been no worse had Steve Bannon and his ilk conspired to publish fake academic articles posing as egalitarians with the secret aim of compromising the real thing. Why does she hold this remarkable view?

She objects to luck egalitarianism on a number of different grounds, and in what follows I limit myself to what appear to be her three most important objections (cp. Lippert-Rasmussen, 2015a: 194–201): the site, the harshness and the pity objections. Her most basic objection to luck egalitarianism is the site objection:

> recent egalitarian writing has lost sight of the distinctively political aims of egalitarianism. The proper negative aim of egalitarian justice is not to eliminate the impact of brute luck from human affairs, but to end oppression, which by definition is socially imposed. Its proper positive aim is not to ensure that everyone gets what they morally deserve, but to create a community in which people stand in relations of equality to others. (Anderson, 1999: 288–9)

This objection is her most basic one in the sense that it sums up, in a principled way, what she finds misguided about luck egalitarianism, i.e. its focus on distribution and, in that connection, on eliminating bad brute luck disadvantage. In part because of this broad focus, it also seems more like a *statement* of the difference between luck egalitarianism and democratic equality and her view that luck egalitarianism is false than an *objection* to luck egalitarianism. More specifically, in response to her points about the proper negative aim of egalitarian justice, luck egalitarians might simply agree that on their view that aim is not distinctively political – e.g. it, like other distributive ideals, can be (un)satisfied in the Robinson Crusoe scenario I mentioned in the previous section – and then request

---

[6] Ironically, Anderson quotes Hayek approvingly later on in her 1999 denouncement of luck egalitarianism. Presumably, then, would the results not have been as damaging had Hayek secretly penned the then-recent academic work defending equality?

an argument for why this view is mistaken. In relation to her positive point, they might say something similar.[7]

There is, however, another way to understand the present passage such that, while it does not state an objection, it sums up her main objections. Anderson gives a number of counterexamples of what intuitively amounts to injustice – namely, situations involving unjust social relations – and these injustices, according to Anderson, make little sense if we assume a distributive ideal of equality, but make good sense if we assume a relational ideal.[8]

Her most quoted counterexample is how luck egalitarians fail to occupy themselves with the unjust unfreedom of gays and lesbians 'to publicly reveal their identities without shame or fear' (Anderson, 1999: 320). According to Anderson, luck egalitarians fail to notice this injustice because it is not a matter of inequality in terms of 'the distribution of divisible, privately appropriated' goods (Anderson, 1999: 319, 288). Rather, it is a matter of unjust social relations – unjust because these are social relations in which people fail to express equal concern and respect for one another (cp. Young, 1990: 19–20).

I agree that it is unjust that gays and lesbians are deprived of the opportunity to publicly reveal their identities without shame and fear. I also agree that luck egalitarians have ignored the relevant injustice as well as many other similar injustices. What I find unconvincing is that luck egalitarians *qua luck egalitarians* must ignore such injustices. Indeed, the situation Anderson describes appears unjust *on luck egalitarian grounds*, since gays and lesbians are worse off in terms of the social good of being able to publicly reveal their identities without fear and shame than others – *in casu* heterosexuals – through no responsibility of their own (cp. Chapter 7.4). While luck egalitarians have focused on the distribution of privately owned 'divisible goods' – at least in their writings on distributive justice – luck egalitarianism as such leaves completely open what is the right metric of egalitarian justice.[9]

---

[7] They might add that there is a difference between desert and responsibility – e.g. I should be consequentially responsible for my loss at the casino, even though I am a morally outstanding person and on that account deserved to win – and that most luck egalitarians think that distributive positions should track responsibility rather than desert (but see Lippert-Rasmussen, 2011). In her later work, Anderson acknowledges this distinction (Anderson, 2008b; 2010a).

[8] Like Scheffler, Anderson emphasizes the putative fact that the concerns of luck egalitarians are strikingly different from those of real-life egalitarians. I discuss this claim in Chapter 6.6.

[9] I need the inserted qualification because Dworkin (2000), for instance, has written extensively on how to 'distribute' goods other than privately owned divisible goods like liberty and political power.

More specifically, the opportunity to reveal one's identity publicly without shame and fear is an important good in the sense that it is very desirable to have it and very undesirable not to.[10] Although you cannot directly distribute that good in the way you can distribute money or land, like welfare it is a good that one can have more or less of. Indeed, Anderson's central complaint about the situation seems to be that there is an *unequal distribution* across homosexuals and heterosexuals of the relevant presentational ability.[11] If *no one* could publicly reveal their sexual identities without fear and shame, no doubt this would be a bad situation, but it is unclear that it might not be one in which everyone relates as equals (cp. Chapter 6.5).[12] Hence, at least in the case of one of Anderson's paradigm examples of a relational injustice, we can naturally translate it into an injustice in terms of the distribution of a certain good.

Consider next Anderson's second main objection – the harshness objection. She imagines an uninsured driver who negligently makes an illegal turn that causes an accident. The driver is rescued and is 'hooked up to a respirator, fighting for his life. A judicial hearing has found him at fault for the accident. According to Rakowski [one of the luck egalitarian theorists whose views Anderson criticizes], the faulty driver has no claim of justice to continued medical care' (Anderson, 1999: 296; cp. Stemplowska, 2011; Arneson 2010, 29–31). This attests to the implausibility of luck egalitarianism, because the faulty driver *has* a claim of justice to medical care.

Why does Anderson think that the faulty driver has such a claim? One answer here, which does not seem to be Anderson's answer, is that citizens lose nothing of comparable importance to what the uninsured driver loses if medical care is discontinued and that it is unjust to let some lose their lives when we – a group of co-citizens – can prevent this from happening at a tiny cost to ourselves. Still, if she does not think the requirement to aid is

---

[10] Welfarist luck egalitarians are indirectly concerned with the relevant unfreedom of lesbians and gays to the extent that it negatively affects their welfare (as, almost certainly, it does).

[11] In his description of the relational ideal, Scheffler (2003a: 22, 23) mentions 'undemocratic distribution of power' and that large 'inequalities of power and status' are incompatible with relations among equals. Power and status are not goods that you can (re)distribute directly in the same way as you can distribute money. Yet, reasonably enough, this does not prevent him from referring to a *distribution* of power and inequalities of status (and what can that mean other than that some have more or the same amount of (/as much) power or status than (/as) others?). Hence, I am not here employing a notion of distribution which is alien to relational egalitarians.

[12] It could do so because *each instance* of 'shameful revelation' involves a short-lived, reversible, hierarchical relation between shamer and shamed person (Chapter 5.3). I accept this point, so strictly speaking I should consider a case where we are shaming ourselves together for being sexual beings. In this case our social relations are certainly non-ideal, but they are not inegalitarian.

in any way conditional on cost, her view seems vulnerable to something similar to the utility monster objection to utilitarianism. That is, we could use almost all of our resources on assisting people who repeatedly act negligently – because they know we will pick up the tab for them – and whose capacities required for democratic equality to obtain can be restored, but only at huge costs to society.

Another answer, which seems to be Anderson's, is that principles – and, thus, derivatively perhaps agents who act on those principles – which would allow discontinuing medical care fail to 'express equal respect and concern' (Anderson, 1999: 289). Presumably, all principles which satisfy this expressive requirement imply that the faulty driver has a claim of justice to continued medical treatment – perhaps not no matter what, but at least in the situation Anderson describes, where his claim does not compete with other equally serious claims. This, or something like it, is what makes the problem of abandonment of negligent victims a problem.

In response, I should like to make three points. First, the present objection is not intimately tied to relational egalitarianism. The locus of justice could be social relations and yet one might deny that the justice of social relations should be assessed in terms of what principles that enjoin, permit or forbid them express or do not express. True, Anderson accepts both an expressive account of claims of justice and a relational account of justice and her acceptance of each of these views colours the other. However, the two views are entirely independent of one another, logically speaking (see Chapters 1.2 and 3.6).

Second, unlike the site objection, although the harshness objection applies to some distribution-focused views of justice, it does not apply to all of them. While it might apply to lifetime versions of sufficientarianism – suppose that the driver has lived a long life, which is much better than any merely sufficiently good life – it does not apply to time-relative sufficientarianism, i.e. the view that justice requires that everyone has enough at any given moment. Also, the objection might apply to luck relational egalitarianism (Chapter 1.2). Together with my previous point, this implies that, whether or not luck egalitarianism is vulnerable to the harshness objection, the objection is not tied to the distinction between distribution- versus relation-focused views of justice.

This brings me to my third and final reply to the harshness objection: namely, that the natural response for a luck egalitarian who accepts it is not to give up luck egalitarianism completely and instead opt for some version of relational equality. Doing so would involve giving up many other moral commitments explained by the luck egalitarian principle which are not threatened by the harshness objection. A better-motivated response to the objection would be to combine luck egalitarianism with a sufficiency view such that justice does not require leaving people in dire straits – at least not when the costs of not doing so are relatively minor.[13]

This might be disputed on the grounds that the response fails to fit what is the problem with failing to assist Anderson's dying motorist. One suggestion is that the problem consists of its being incompatible with our relating as equals qua citizens (Voigt, 2017). But this diagnosis simply does not seem very plausible. Suppose the motorist's wounds are such that whatever we do, he will not be able to act in his capacity as a citizen again, though he will be able to live a normal and good life henceforth in other ways if we help. On Anderson's account as presently interpreted, we have no reason to help him. This is implausible. Another suggestion is that the problem consists of its being incompatible with our relating as equals qua human beings, because of what our failure to help him would express (see Chapter 3.4). That too I think is not a very plausible claim. Surely, what makes it unjust not to help him is in large part the loss he would suffer – his life – if we do not (and the relatively minor costs we have to accept in order to help him) and not something about what failing to help him expresses. If our failing to help him would somehow not express anything objectionable such that our relation to him would not be objectionable from an expressivist point of view if we were not to help him, it would arguably still be unjust not to help him.[14]

Consider finally Anderson's third, and main, objection to luck egalitarianism: the pity objection.[15] This objection concerns the implications of

---

[13] That assumes, of course, that luck egalitarianism actually has the implication which Anderson attributes to it. This is not true of all forms of luck egalitarianism: to wit, it is not true of all-luck egalitarianism, which holds that people who suffer bad option luck should only suffer the expected disvalue of their imprudent choices (Lippert-Rasmussen, 2001; Segall, 2013: 65–8, Stemplowska, 2011: 121–4, 128–31). However, at best this fact softens Anderson's objection, because she can simply shift her focus to cases where the motorist is almost certain to have a traffic accident. If we also believe that, in such a case, justice requires that we help a motorist dying at the roadside, all-luck egalitarianism is equally vulnerable to the harshness objection.

[14] Anderson might respond to the present objection – which, in essence, is a perfectly general objection to the expressivist account of wrongness – that the very fact that we can help him and do not expresses an objectionable attitude. This, however, would be an implausible view of expressive content, though it would cast light on Anderson's suggestion that relational egalitarians do have a subordinate non-instrumental concern, to wit, distributions. Also and in any case, it would not be obvious that any objectionable aspect of the expression pertains to inequality, e.g. because one might think that no one has a claim of justice to assistance in the motorist's predicament.

[15] This objection supplements the harshness objection. The former objection shows that luck egalitarianism has implausible implications regarding victims of bad brute luck, while the latter shows that luck egalitarianism has implausible implications regarding victims of bad option luck.

luck egalitarianism regarding how victims of bad brute luck should be treated. For the purpose of vividness Anderson imagines that the luck egalitarian state sends out 'compensation checks' with an accompanying letter explaining the reasons for compensation. Here is the letter to the stupid and untalented:

> Unfortunately, other people don't value what little you have to offer in the system of production. Your talents are too meagre to command much market value. Because of the misfortune that you were born so poorly endowed with talents, we productive ones will make it up to you: we'll let you share in the bounty of what we have produced with our vastly superior and highly valued skills. (Anderson, 1999: 305)

While this letter might overdo things a bit, Anderson's principled point is that luck egalitarianism 'disparages the internally disadvantaged and raises private disdain to the status of officially recognized truth' (Anderson, 1999: 306).[16] More generally, Anderson believes that the fortunate adopt the attitude of pity towards victims of bad luck when they adopt luck egalitarianism as their guiding principle, and that victims of bad brute luck adopt an attitude of envy of the fortunate when they seek compensation for their misfortune on luck egalitarian grounds. Pity and envy are incompatible with regarding one another as equals and, thus, disrespectful. Accordingly, Anderson concludes that luck egalitarianism 'fails to express concern for those excluded from aid, and fails to express respect for those included among its beneficiaries as well as for those expected to pay for its benefits' (Anderson, 1999: 307).

This objection to luck egalitarianism is flawed. There are at least two reasons why. First, if people can be motivated on grounds other than pity and envy, which are not relevantly objectionable in other ways, when they offer or demand compensation on luck egalitarian grounds, the pity objection is not an objection to luck egalitarianism as such as opposed to an objection to people who offer compensation or claim compensation on certain objectionable grounds. And this seems clearly possible. I might offer compensation simply because I believe in luck egalitarian equality and without having any views on whether people who are due compensation in terms of the relevant metric of justice are to be pitied. If that metric is welfare, for instance, I might admire a person whose welfare level is lower than mine, e.g. because of her artistic achievements, and to whom I offer

---

[16] One might suggest that there is no reason that a luck egalitarian state should communicate its grounds for compensation. However, Anderson might think that this would amount to (a government-house egalitarian) violation of a publicity constraint, which is part of justice.

compensation. The opposite side of this coin is that I might demand compensation without envying those from whom I demand compensation. I might even think that outcome-wise I am better off in every respect than they are, expect for the fact that my opportunities were worse than theirs. It just so happens that I made good use of my opportunities, while they squandered their much better opportunities.

The second reason why the pity objection misses its target is that luck egalitarianism is not a view about on what psychological grounds people should offer or demand compensation. It is, as Anderson emphasizes in other parts of her critique, a view of what the distribution should be, and a just distribution can be brought about through unjust or otherwise morally objectionable motivations.[17] As I concede later (Chapter 7.6), this might show that luck egalitarianism is an incomplete theory of justice, but the vice of incompleteness is different from the vice of falsehood.

I conclude that none of Anderson's three main objections to luck egalitarianism is successful. Before proceeding to take a look at her ideal of democratic equality, which could be perfectly persuasive independently of the unpersuasiveness of her critique of luck egalitarianism, I want to zoom out a bit from the details of Anderson's arguments and point to one noticeable general feature of her critique: namely that it is theorist-focused rather than theory-focused.

A critique is theory-focused if, and only if, it targets one or more claims that are said to be what the theory consists of. A critique is theorist-focused if, and only if, it targets one or more claims that are asserted by individuals who are described as subscribing to the relevant theory.[18] On the first approach, to refute the theory one would define luck egalitarianism and then, say, derive implications from this definition that are implausible.[19] On the second approach, one would group together some theorists whom one regards as and whom others regard as luck egalitarians and then, say, point to implausible claims they make or derive such implications from what they say – not just anything, of course, but things they say that fall within the ballpark of distributive justice – and in this way discredit luck egalitarianism or luck egalitarian theorists.

---

[17] The mere fact that a certain normative view implies that a desirable state of affairs can be brought about through undesirable motivations is not an objection to that view. Presumably, it is possible that democratic equality is brought about through objectionable, unjust motivations.

[18] In drawing this distinction, I am not committed to denying that one will often define a certain theory with the intention, in part, to capture the views of certain theorists whose views one will then criticize once one criticizes the theory as given by one's definition.

[19] Such a definition cannot say that the relevant theory is the set of a subset of beliefs held by a list of named theorists.

Anderson's critique of luck egalitarianism is first and foremost theorist-focused. In her critique, she does not primarily employ her characterization of luck egalitarianism, including the one quoted in Section 2.2. Rather, she tries to identify flaws in the views of philosophers like Richard Arneson, G. A. Cohen, Ronald Dworkin, Eric Rakowski and Philippe van Parijs. This selection is not a bad pick, but even together these excellent theorists hardly exhaust the logical space of possible strands of luck egalitarianism. A manifest example of Anderson's theorist-focused approach comes in the course of her presentation of ways in which luck egalitarianism expresses disrespect towards victims of bad option luck. In the course of doing so, she focuses on Rakowski, whose views, as already indicated, are particularly extreme when it comes to victims of bad option luck. Anderson is aware of this and asks: 'Do other luck egalitarians do a better job than Rakowski in shielding the victims of bad option luck from the worst fates?' (Anderson, 1999: 298). If her critique were theory-focused, rather than theorist-focused, this is not the question she would ask. Rather, she would ask: 'Can one, consistent with luck egalitarianism, do a better job in shielding the victims of bad option luck from the worst fates?'[20]

Another manifestation of Anderson's theorist focus comes out in her objection that luck egalitarian theorists have failed to consider goods that are neither suitably objects of private ownership nor divisible between individuals. This critique is interesting and points to an important omission in the work of luck egalitarians. However, there is nothing in the definition of luck egalitarianism as such that rules out a partial or even an exclusive focus on non-individually ownable, non-divisible public goods. Hence, if Anderson's critique were theory-focused, she would ask whether her definition of luck egalitarianism rules out such goods being (part of) the metric of egalitarian justice, instead of offering examples of luck egalitarian theorists who have ignored such goods.

My point here is not that theorist-focused critiques are somehow deficient (cp. Lippert-Rasmussen, 2012; 2015a; 2015b). Rather, my point is that what follows from the two forms of critique, if successful, are rather different things. Most interestingly: Unlike what Anderson seems to assume, except in exceptional cases a theorist-focused critique – even a highly successful one – cannot rebut a theory. The main reason why this is the case is the already indicated fact that the group of theorists who

---

[20] The realization that critiques can be theory-focused is what lies behind what many think is an epistemic virtue of critics: to wit, that they try to develop the theory they criticize into its strongest form to see if their criticisms apply even to that form.

subscribe to a certain theory might for various reasons far from exhaust the logical space of possible (and even attractive) versions of the relevant theory.

To summarize, Anderson's objections to luck egalitarianism – or at least the three objections that I have considered here – are flawed. (1) They are not directed specifically against luck egalitarianism; (2) insofar as one finds them persuasive it is unclear that this should motivate one to endorse her own democratic equality or, more generally, relational egalitarianism; (3) and, finally, one should not find them persuasive as critiques of luck egalitarianism per se, in part because they are theorist- rather than theory-focused, in part because even when assessed on their own, in different ways, they are not sound objections.

2.4   Democratic Equality

I now move on to Anderson's positive ideal of relating as equals, democratic equality. But before doing so, I should briefly state how I interpret that ideal. As I see it, it pertains both to individual citizens and to the state. Even if every citizen treated every other citizen as an equal, Anderson's ideal would not be satisfied if the state did not treat its citizens as equals as well. Anderson assumes that in a community in which people stand in relations of equality to others, the state (insofar as it exists) acts from principles that express equal respect and concern for all citizens, and to the extent that it does not, the ideal of democratic equality is unsatisfied. For instance, she thinks that a paternalistic state that makes mandatory insurance against various misfortunes acts disrespectfully by, in effect, acting from principles implying that citizens are 'too stupid to run their own lives' (Anderson, 1999: 301). Similarly, she thinks that, in recommending that victims of bad option luck should not be assisted because 'they deserve their misfortune', a luck egalitarian state does not 'treat them with respect' (Anderson, 1999: 301). The interpretative point that I rely on is that the features of a relation between the state and its citizens that make it the case that democratic equality is violated are also features that, to the extent that they characterize relations between individual citizens, violate democratic equality.

With this point in mind, I can state the first positive claim Anderson makes about democratic equality. To the extent that relations between individuals involve paternalistic coercion, contemptuous pity, condescension, envy, demeaning and intrusive judgements of people's capacities to exercise responsibility, or failure to help destitute people on the grounds that their situation is their own fault, the relevant community is not one in which people relate as equals (Anderson 1999: 289, 295, 306–7, 314; cp. Anderson, 2012a: 42–4). Call this Anderson's *no disrespect requirement.*

Perhaps in the case of some disrespectful attitudes, it is straightforward to understand why they are objectionable from a relational egalitarian point of view. Take condescension. One can only condescend to someone whom one regards as inferior to oneself. Thus, assumed hierarchy is built into the nature of condescension.[21] Something similar is true of demeaning judgements of others on the assumption that to demean someone is to lower their status, moral or social, relative to others. However, in the case of other items on the list, it is not clear on what grounds they are included. Consider, for instance, failure to help others because their situation is their own fault. Anderson obviously has in mind cases like the motorist whom I mentioned in Section 2.3, but her formulation is much more general and in such general form it is implausible. If you invest part of your huge fortune in Speculators Inc. and I provide you with very good reason why you should not do so, but you nevertheless proceed and lose a great deal of money such that you have to sell off your yacht, surely I do not fail to relate to you as an equal when I refuse to help you keep your yacht on the grounds that your predicament is your own responsibility.

Second, a community of equals is incompatible with hierarchies where 'human beings' are 'ranked according to intrinsic worth' (Anderson, 1999: 312).[22] Most obviously, a community of equals is incompatible with a society where people are ranked in terms of intrinsic worth on the basis of race, sex or gender, and, thus, relations between citizens are relations between 'inferior and superior persons'. An aspect of this is that equality is incompatible with oppression – that is, 'forms of social relationships by which some people dominate, exploit, marginalize, demean and inflict violence upon others' (Anderson, 1999: 313).[23] Positively, '[the equal moral

---

[21] The same is true of the opposite of condescension – i.e. claiming rights and liberties accruing to people who are superior to oneself. Interestingly, this (unlike condescension) has never been seen as a virtue.

[22] It is not clear what kind of 'intrinsic worth' she has in mind, though intrinsic moral worth seems likely to be at least part of the story (Anderson, 1999: 312; Chapter 3.2).

[23] Anderson says that 'distinct roles in the division of labour' (among other things) never justify the forms of social relationships involved in oppression (Anderson, 1999: 313). While this does not entail, it certainly suggests, the compatibility of distinct roles in the division of labour with Anderson's ideal of democratic equality. Note also that it is unclear that one might not dominate etc. others even if one does not regard oneself as having a superior ranking to one's dominatees in terms of intrinsic worth.

worth of persons] asserts that all competent adults are equally moral agents; everyone equally has the power to develop and exercise moral responsibility, to cooperate with others according to principles of justice, to share and fulfil a conception of their good' (Anderson, 1999: 312; see Chapter 3.2). Hence, every member of the community has a right to take part on an equal footing in the collective self-determination of the community (Anderson, 1999: 313). Call this set of claims the *no-ranking requirement*.

Third, in a society of equals there are certain capabilities – those required for avoiding entanglement in oppressive relationships and those required for participating as an equal citizen in a democratic state and in a democratic civil society – to which citizens must 'have access over the course of their whole lives' (Anderson, 1999: 314, 316). Call this the *time-relative sufficiency requirement*. This requirement does not imply that citizens should enjoy comprehensive equality in the space of capabilities, e.g. in the capability for welfare, but it is incompatible with any group of people being 'excluded from or segregated within the institutions of civil society, or subjected to discrimination on the basis of ascribed social identities by institutions of civil society' (Anderson, 1999: 317).[24] Democratic equality 'guarantees all law-abiding citizens effective access to the social conditions of their freedom at all times' – a requirement the relevance of which comes out in relation to Anderson's harshness objection (Anderson, 1999: 289). Even setting aside non-law-abiding citizens, this proposition suggests that there could be inequalities between groups of people that are compatible with everyone enjoying the social conditions of their freedom (Anderson, 1999: 326). Indeed, it suggests that there could be inequality of opportunity under democratic equality – a possible implication of her rejection of the distributive focus of justice, on which she never takes an explicit stance (cp. Chapter 8.2).

At this point, one might ask whether the time-relative sufficiency requirement shows that democratic equality has a distributive component. Despite appearances – 'sufficiency' is normally associated with a distributive ideal – it does not, because what the requirement says is that, at any given moment, all citizens should have the capabilities that are necessary for their relating as equals. Anderson assumes that, as a matter of fact, what this requires is that citizens have a certain minimum amount of

---

[24] 'Incompatible' here means 'empirically incompatible'. It is conceptually possible, though empirically unlikely, that members of a certain group are subjected to discrimination in civil society on the basis of their ascribed social identity and yet are able to participate as equal citizens, e.g. because they enjoy offsetting advantages relative to those fellow citizens who are not subjected to discrimination.

the relevant capacities, but that is simply an empirical assumption. It could be – indeed Anderson thinks that it is the case – that having too much of certain capacities prevents one from relating to one's fellow citizen's as an equal, e.g. because great wealth corrupts one's mind and, inevitably, one starts to think of oneself as superior to one's fellow citizens (cp. Scheffler, 2003a: 23; Robeyns, forthcoming). Thus, in essence, what the sufficiency requirement says is that citizens should have the amount of resources that their relating as equals requires. But this is not a distributive ideal any more than the following view is a relational ideal: social relations should be such that people have equal opportunities for welfare and, as a matter of fact, this requires that people relate as equals. Unlike distributive sufficientarians, Anderson ascribes an instrumental role to people having enough – instrumental in relation to enabling democratic equality. Hence, Anderson opposes someone having *too much* exactly as much as someone having *too little* for the purpose of realizing democratic equality, so her view might as well be seen as a version of anti-excessivism (cp. Anderson, 2008b: 261–5; 2012a: 54).[25]

Together the no-disrespect, no-ranking and sufficiency requirements capture Anderson's ideal of democratic equality. While satisfying one of the three requirements might render it more likely that the two other requirements are satisfied, each of them can be satisfied even if none of the others is. For instance, the sufficiency requirement might be satisfied even if citizens are often disrespectful to one another and even if citizens are ranked in certain ways, e.g. in terms of looks, that nonetheless do not affect people's ability to avoid ending up being entangled in oppressive relationships or to participate in politics and civil society (cp. Chapter 3.2). Suppose, for instance, that while it is *more difficult* for people at the bottom of the aesthetic hierarchy to do so, they are *able*, expending sufficiently low levels of effort, to do it – it is just that they have to exert themselves more than people higher up the hierarchy have to do.

At this point, we might ask ourselves whether satisfying these three requirements is ('is' of identity) what it is to relate as equals (and whether Anderson proposes the three requirements as the answer to this question). Could we satisfy all three requirements and yet not relate as equals? And can we fail to satisfy one or more of the requirements and yet relate as

---

[25] As I have argued elsewhere (Lippert-Rasmussen, 2015a: 190–1), this also means that Anderson is vulnerable to a *tu quoque* reply, which points to how democratic equality is vulnerable to an objection similar to the harshness objection. Suppose that for some strange reason involving some people's imprudent behaviour, the ideal of democratic equality can only be realized if everyone is very badly off welfare-wise. In that case democratic equality favours insufficiency welfare-wise.

equals? If the answer to either of these two questions is affirmative, it follows that they do not capture what relating as equals is.

In response it might be said that I miss an account of what it is to treat one another as equals which is present in Anderson's article. On this view:

> For two individuals to relate to one another as equals is for them to act in relation to each other only on principles which express equal concern and respect for the two parties involved.[26]

However, it is unclear that this is a satisfactory account of what it is to relate as equals. First, even if it is true, it simply shifts the focus from one difficult question – what is it to relate as equals? – to another and equally difficult question – what is it for principles to express equal concern and respect? – and, thus, it clarifies little. Offhand, it is more straightforward to talk about people's conduct expressing equal concern and respect. For instance, one can say that a person expresses equal concern and respect when she is in part motivated by a commitment to equal concern and respect (cp. Chapter 3.4). But this suggestion appeals to psychological facts and, clearly, there are no psychological facts associated with moral principles as such, so we still need to say something about what it is for a principle to express unequal concern and respect.

Second, arguably, one can relate as equals even if one does not act 'on principles which express equal concern and respect for' oneself and the other party one addresses. Take persons who unreflectively treat others as equals. They are too unreflective to be said to act on principles – they have not reflectively considered their status relative to others – but, instinctively as it were, they nevertheless treat others as equals. Clearly, they do not treat each other as inferior or superior.[27]

Third, there could be cases where one treats others with equal concern and respect even if one does not live in a society which satisfies the relational ideal. Suppose that everyone believes that everyone else is bigoted against women. Suppose a feminist employer does not hire a woman because, given her reasonable but false belief about widespread bigotry

---

[26] Cp. 'equality of fortune fails the most fundamental test any egalitarian theory must meet: that its principles express equal respect and concern for all citizens' (Anderson, 1999: 289). Still, Anderson uses 'test', not 'criterion'.

[27] Perhaps Anderson might say that what this shows is that there is a third category in addition to treating one another as equals and treating one as inferior/superior, namely not doing either, and that relational equality requires that one treats others as equals, not merely that one refrains from treating others as inferior/superior. In Chapter 3.3 I distinguish between treating, regarding and relating as equals. On this view, the unreflective agent in question may treat as an equal even if he does not regard and, thus, does not relate as an equal.

against women, she reasonably thinks that it would be very harmful for this person to be hired for the job and, thus, believes that it would be wrong of her to hire this person. Perhaps what this shows is that relating as equals only suffices for satisfying the relational ideal provided a certain egalitarian background to interpersonal interactions, where that background might include beliefs about the relevant background. The notion of relating as equals has, as it were, an external component, i.e. a component which is external to the dispositions, attitudes etc. of the parties to the relation in question (cp. Chapter 8.2).[28]

This completes my presentation of Anderson's democratic equality. It consists of three main components: the no-disrespect, the no-ranking and the sufficiency requirements. While each of these conditions has certain things to be said for them, it is not clear that they have been satisfactorily articulated. Finally, I have argued that a possible appeal to how principles express equal concern and respect fails to give an account of what it is to relate as equals. An important reason is that it ignores how background factors influence what it is for two people to relate as equals. I now turn my attention to the view of another prominent relational egalitarian: Samuel Scheffler.

2.5 Scheffler's Critique of Luck Egalitarianism

Scheffler's published work on relational egalitarianism dates back to 2003. While he notes that his work is 'indebted to' Anderson's work, he also mentions that his position differs from hers in some ways (Scheffler, 2003a: 7) and, as we shall see, in his more recent work these differences have become more pronounced. In his initial critique of relational egalitarianism, Scheffler focuses on responsibility and what he deems the excessive role that it plays in luck egalitarianism. However, this is only one of four main objections to luck egalitarianism that Scheffler puts forward.[29]

---

[28] Suppose I act on a principle of equal concern and respect, but I would not have done so had I believed that this would benefit members of a certain racial minority that I dislike. Have I not flouted the requirement to relate as an equal, even if I have acted on a principle that expresses equal concern and respect?

[29] One argument which Scheffler discusses extensively and rejects, and which I shall simply mention here, is an argument to the effect that Rawls appeals to a full-blown luck egalitarian ideal, e.g. to show why the laissez-faire is unjust, and then inconsistently ends up defending principles which are inconsistent with luck egalitarianism, to wit, the difference principle (Scheffler, 2003a: 8–31). I do not assess this argument here, in part because doing so requires close attention to various exegetically relevant details in Rawls' work, partly because even if Scheffler's criticisms of the argument are correct that would not amount to an objection to luck egalitarianism but simply to an objection

First, luck egalitarianism does not fit well with our moral intuitions. Scheffler starts from the observation that the core idea informing luck egalitarianism – 'that inequalities . . . are acceptable if they derive from the choices that people have voluntarily made, but that inequalities deriving from unchosen features of people's circumstances are unjust' – 'overlaps but also diverges from prevailing political morality in most liberal societies' (Scheffler, 2003a: 6). Most people think that there are cases where people should not be held responsible for their choices, but where luck egalitarianism implies that they should. For instance, prevailing political morality does not imply that extra income that derives purely (assuming this to be possible) from choices one has made should be exempt from taxation and, possibly, redistributed in favour of those who did not make the relevant choices. Conversely, most believe that there are cases where people should be held responsible for something even if it does not reflect any choices they have made: 'the prevailing political morality . . . is prepared to tolerate significant distributive inequalities deriving from differences of talent and ability' (Scheffler, 2003a: 6).[30] Hence, luck egalitarianism is controversial and, thus, needs independent grounding, which Scheffler thinks cannot be provided. Call this the *counterintuitiveness objection*.

Strictly speaking, in the passages quoted in the previous paragraph Scheffler simply makes empirical claims about the prevailing political morality. But, clearly, Scheffler thinks that the prevailing political morality gets things right here and that the fact that luck egalitarianism in this way diverges from the prevailing political morality amounts to an objection to luck egalitarianism. Moreover, comparing with Anderson we might say that Scheffler's counterintuitiveness objection covers some of the same ground as her harshness and pity objections.

Here are two replies to the counterintuitiveness objection. First, Scheffler is not sufficiently careful in describing cases that support his counterintuitiveness objection. More specifically, some of the cases which he describes are cases where luck egalitarians would say that values

against a certain argument in favour of luck egalitarianism – one which I am not sure I fully grasp and one which, as Scheffler notes, in part consists of an appeal to authority (i.e. Rawls' status as a leading political philosopher). Another set of objections which I disregard are objections directed specifically against Dworkin – objections that I find convincing – to wit, that his 'ethical interpretation' of the choice/circumstance distinction classifies talents and personal character traits differently from how Dworkin wants to classify them according to that distinction, and that Dworkin's wider political ideal of equality is an 'administrative' one, because it is a matter of how the state should treat its citizens (rather than an ideal about how persons should relate to one another). (For an excellent reply to Dworkin, see Scheffler (2003b); see also Chapter 8.5.)

[30] Interestingly, the use of 'tolerate' suggests that the relevant inequality is in one way bad.

other than equality are at least as important, such that it might be morally justified, if not morally required, to do what brings about a more unjust distribution. For instance, Scheffler writes about the principles that people aspiring to a society of equals would endorse: 'reflection of the significance for human relations of practices of forbearance and accommodation might temper [luck egalitarians'] insistence that individuals must fully internalize the costs of all their choices . . . a recognition of the effects on their relations to one another of significant inequalities of income and wealth would almost certainly lead them to limit the extent of such inequalities from any source' (Scheffler, 2005: 22). All of this might be true, but it is entirely compatible with pluralist luck egalitarianism. Such luck egalitarians think that it is *in one respect* objectionable if people's relative distributive positions do not reflect their comparative choices, but that leaves open that in other, and possibly more important, respects this is desirable.[31]

Second, something very much like the counterintuitiveness objection can be directed against the ideal of relational equality. My point here is not just that any moral or political ideal is disputed and thus that, in some sense, any relevant moral or political ideal is in need of justification and that relational egalitarians have not said very much to justify relational equality.[32] Rather, my point is a more specific one. Scheffler contends that luck egalitarians are faced with a dilemma. Either we understand the 'principle of responsibility' – the idea that 'unequal outcomes are just if they arise from factors for which people can properly be held responsible, and are otherwise unjust' (Scheffler, 2005: 7) – abstractly, or we understand it concretely. If the former, it is plausible because it is near tautologous – it amounts to something like 'inequalities are just if, and only if, there is some justification for them' (Scheffler, 2005: 9). But so understood, it is also a principle that does not amount to, nor can serve as a basis for, luck egalitarianism. If, alternatively, we understand it concretely, because we supply a substantive, choice-focused account of what people can 'properly be held responsible for', it might amount to or support luck egalitarianism. But concretely understood, it is controversial and not a widely shared view, since in many cases people reject inequalities which are grounded in choice and accept inequalities that are not. My contention is that relational egalitarianism faces an analogous dilemma.

---

[31] Scheffler is fully aware that luck egalitarians can be pluralists (Scheffler, 2015: 21–22). However, this awareness, I submit, does not manifest itself sufficiently in his articulation of the counterintuitiveness objection.

[32] Scheffler does speak a bit to this issue (cp. Chapter 6).

At an abstract level, it might be quite plausible that people ought to relate as equals. However, at that level, what exactly it is to relate as equals is quite undefined. Specifically, it is unclear why luck egalitarians cannot say that bringing about an ambition-sensitive and endowment-insensitive distribution is relating as equals. Hence, to support relational egalitarianism, the idea of relating as equals must be supplied with a concrete substantive account of what it is to relate as equals. But once we do that, we see that the ideal is controversial – perhaps this is true of any abstract ideal? – in the same way that luck egalitarianism is controversial: to wit, there are many relations in which we think it is entirely proper that people do not in the relevant sense relate as equals.[33] Indeed, Scheffler himself mentions a number of such relations involving 'differences of rank, power and status' without conveying any disapproval (Scheffler, 2005: 18).

Perhaps Scheffler acknowledges that luck egalitarianism and relational equality are in parallel predicaments, because he concedes both that relationships can be valuable without being egalitarian, and that relationships can be egalitarian despite involving 'distinctions of rank or status' (Scheffler, 2005: 18). He infers from this that relational egalitarians must 'characterize in greater detail the special value that egalitarian relationships are thought to have and to consider which differences of authority and status have the capacity to compromise that value' (Scheffler, 2005: 18; see Chapter 6). Scheffler is right about this, but I do not think he offers a characterization of the sort he rightly thinks is needed. That is, it is not clear from his brief remarks on the value of relating as equals why, to use one of his examples, the relation between teacher and student can be valuable without being egalitarian, nor why, alternatively, it can be egalitarian despite involving distinctions of rank and status. Surely, this relation is vulnerable to the danger of distorting 'people's attitudes towards themselves, undermining the self-respect of some and encouraging the insidious sense of superiority in others' (Scheffler, 2005: 19; cp. Chapter 6.3) – a danger which Scheffler thinks is associated with hierarchical relations.

---

[33] Indeed, this is one overall message from Chapters 3, 5 and 6. Arneson (2010, 28), who thinks that equal social relations are extremely valuable but in a purely instrumental way, suggests that 'the difference between the unequal social relations we should reject and the unequal social relations we should accept is that the latter but not the former are effective means to the advancement of prioritarian goals'. This certainly follows from Arneson's desert prioritarian view. However, I find it quite unlikely that this view will imply a sorting of unequal social relations into those to be rejected and those to be accepted which will fit our intuitive sorting. For instance, I suspect many would contend that egalitarian marital relationships should be accepted, even if strongly unequal marital relationships would result in slightly more aggregate value from a desert prioritarian point of view due to the trivial benefits to a huge number of people that, let us imagine, they involve.

Nor is it clear why relations between teachers and students without 'distinctions of rank and status' are not 'a good thing in its own right' (Scheffler, 2005: 19). The situation here is a bit like that of a luck egalitarian who: concedes that in some cases we do not find deviations from the luck egalitarian ideal unjust; concedes that this shows that we must explore the circumstances under which choice-sensitivity is valuable; and then persists in subscribing to the ideal without having provided any account of the sort she concedes she must.

I now turn to Scheffler's second objection to luck egalitarianism: the *fetishism objection*. According to this objection, luck egalitarianism considered on its own is an odd fetishistic ideal: 'unless equality is anchored in some version of [the social and political ideal of equality], or in some other comparable general understanding of equality as a moral value or normative ideal, it will be arbitrary, pointless, fetishistic: no more compelling than a preference for any other distributive pattern' (Scheffler, 2003a: 23; cp. O'Neill, 2008; Scanlon, 2000; Tomlin, 2015).[34]

The claim that a preference for equality is no more compelling than 'a preference for any other distributive pattern' is either extreme or true, but true in a way where it is also true that the preference for relating as equals is arbitrary. Consider a preference for a distributive pattern where people whose names start with an 'S' are twice as well off as anyone else. This seems truly 'arbitrary, pointless, fetishistic' compared to a preference for equality. Surely, Scheffler is not implying the extreme claim that, fetishism-wise, equality is like an S-letter name preference?

Scheffler might respond negatively, but submit that this is only because, lurking in the background of distributive equality, is a 'general understanding of equality as a moral value or normative ideal': to wit, the understanding that fairness requires that people's relative distributive positions must be justified and that the only justifier is differential exercise of choice.[35] However, in that case Scheffler's fetishism objection reduces to the trivially true claim that any distributive pattern will need to be justified and that in the absence of any such justification a preference for a particular distribution appears arbitrary. One might then add that the relevant

---

[34] As Scanlon puts it: equality looks like a 'peculiarly abstract goal – conformity to a pattern' (Scanlon, 2000: 42; cp. Scheffler, 2015: 22; Tomlin, 2015: 8). 'Anchored in' is metaphorical. There are at least two interpretations: first, that distributive equality is shown to be causally conducive to realization of some broader moral or political ideal and, second, that distributive equality is shown to be a constitutive part of the realization of such an ideal, e.g. pertaining to how people relate to one another (cp. Chapter 8.2).

[35] Scheffler could deny that the relevant view here reflects a 'general understanding of equality as a moral value or normative ideal', but if so then I think his claim is false.

general understanding is flawed, because it makes choice play a role which it could only plausibly play if metaphysical libertarianism were true such that we can clearly distinguish between what reflects choice and what reflects circumstances. However, such metaphysical libertarianism is false. This, I take it, is Scheffler's third objection. So construed, the arbitrariness objection does not carry any independent weight. Moreover, Scheffler's use of the fetishism objection makes him vulnerable to a *tu quoque* reply.[36] Luck egalitarians can respond that insofar as the arbitrariness objection, as presently construed, has any bite against them, then it has a similar bite against relational egalitarians. For we can similarly say that, in the absence of a grounding in some more general understanding of the ideal of equality, a preference for relational equality is 'no more compelling' than a preference for any other shape of interpersonal relations, e.g. that some are slightly 'more equal' than others, or that some are 'more equal' than others in some contexts, but 'less equal' than others in other contexts.

To anticipate the next section on Scheffler's deliberative constraint: suppose you and I treat your interests as if they are slightly more constraining on our decisions than mine, and yet we end up making exactly the same decisions as we would have made had we considered our interests to be equally constraining of our decisions. This appears to be a real option in Scheffler's view, since he does not think that the deliberative constraint uniquely constrains what decision people respecting it will make. Is it not fetishistic to care so much about whether the relative weight given to our interests is 1:1, or 0.99:1.01? To anticipate Chapter 4: Why is it so important that we avoid that one person relates to another as if she were slightly superior to that person, e.g. why is it important that a person avoids being slightly hypocritical in that he blames people when his faults are exactly as great as the blamee's, but does not blame people when his own faults are greater, even if only marginally so?

Perhaps relational egalitarians can reply that there is a principled and deep difference between relating as equals and relating to one another as if one party to the interaction were superior to the other, even if only slightly so. Unlike the former, the latter involves (a tiny degree of) hierarchy. Perhaps this is a good reply. But if it is, why cannot – and this is the second horn of the dilemma described three paragraphs

---

[36] In Scheffler (1982: 30–1), he discusses the differential plausibility of different distribution-sensitive forms of consequentialism in a way that does not appear to draw on any understanding of general underlying moral or political ideals, e.g. about how we ought to relate to one another.

above – friends of distributive equality say something similar in response to why it is so important to have an equal distribution as opposed to, say, one that involves a slight degree of inequality? Why cannot they retort that there is a principled and deep difference between a situation in which people are equally well off and one in which some are better off than others: to wit, in the latter case some are better off than others in a way which does not reflect differential choice and that is unfair, unlike the former situation?

I now move on to Scheffler's third objection to luck egalitarianism, i.e. that luck egalitarianism presupposes metaphysical libertarianism and that such a view is false. According to this objection, the view that people should bear the full consequences of their choices or their exercise of control is 'most plausible if those notions are given a "libertarian" or "incompatibilist" interpretation, according to which genuinely voluntary choices belong to a different metaphysical category than do other causal factors. If the distinction between choices and unchosen circumstances is viewed as a fundamental metaphysical distinction, then it may seem capable of bearing the enormous political and economic weight that luck egalitarianism places on it' (Scheffler, 2015: 12; cp. Scheffler, 2003a: 17). Call this the *metaphysical objection*.

As Scheffler concedes, not all luck egalitarians are vulnerable to the metaphysical objection. Richard Arneson (1989) and G. A. Cohen (2011) both leave open that, due to the truth of hard determinism, there are no inequality-justifying choices. Similarly, the way I have formulated luck egalitarianism is neutral on Scheffler's metaphysical question: if hard determinism about responsibility is true, only equal outcomes satisfy that everyone's distributive positions reflect nothing but everyone's compara-tive exercises of responsibility.

Scheffler might reasonably reply, first, that so defined the view stands a better chance of being true, but it is also less interesting because it asserts less and, second, that in some ways it is more counterintuitive than the form of luck egalitarianism he objects to, because in a number of cases where the prevailing political morality embraces choice-based inequalities, the present metaphysically neutral version is non-committal.

The first thing to note about this objection is that Scheffler – in a way which is perfectly legitimate given the fact that the topic is a huge one – does not attempt to show that there is no such thing as libertarian choice. More importantly, he also does not explain why exactly a compatibilist account of choice will not do from the perspective of luck egalitarianism. I am not saying that no such argument can be given, just that he does not give it.[37] Indeed, some of his remarks appear puzzling in this connection. For instance, he hints that, on the libertarian view, 'the ontological distinctiveness of genuine choice gives it a privileged capacity to express our identity and worth as persons, and hence, perhaps, to ground any entitlement we may have to differential reward' (Scheffler, 2005: 12). But, first, assuming that we have libertarian freedom, why cannot one choose to act in a way that does not reveal one's 'identity and worth' – if, for no other reason, than for the trivial reason that many of our choices are trivial choices that in no way express our identity and worth – in which case, on the hypothesized view, luck egalitarians would still hold one accountable for one's choice despite its non-revealingness? Second, if what grounds differential entitlements is differential (expression of) identity and worth, why could not a compatibilist account of (expression of) identity and worth form the basis of differential entitlements? There might be an argument here, but it is difficult to see its contours and, thus, difficult to know whether it is good or bad.

The next thing I want to note in connection with the metaphysical objection is that Scheffler seems to shift from the claim that only if libertarianism is true can the difference between choice and circumstance be very important to entitlement, to the claim that only if libertarianism is true can choice be the only factor which determines entitlements in the sense that people's relative entitlements should be determined completely by their differential exercise of choice.[38] These two claims are different and, in particular, I do not see why libertarian luck egalitarians cannot be pluralists who think that choice is important to entitlements, but that so are other factors, some of which are, in some contexts at least – libertarian luck egalitarians can be contextualists too – more important to people's entitlements, or at least to what distribution we ought to bring about, than facts about exercise of choice.

My third and last point in response to the metaphysical objection is that it in no way motivates shifting the focus from distributions to social relations and, thus, is unclear how it serves Scheffler's overall argumentative purpose. Indeed, the most natural response for luck egalitarians to the objection would seem to be to deny that choice can justify inequality and then shift allegiance to something closer to outcome egalitarianism.

---

[37] So to employ a distinction I introduced in Section 2.3, the present critical point is theorist-focused.

[38] The latter comes out when Scheffler submits that in the absence of a libertarian account of choice 'it is simply not clear why choice should matter so much: why such fateful political and economic consequences should turn on the presence or absence of genuine choice' (Scheffler, 2005: 13).

Consider, finally, Scheffler's fourth objection: that luck egalitarianism is moralistic or encourages moralistic judgements. There are considerable parallels between this objection and Anderson's pity objection.[39] On Scheffler's account moralism is 'a moral failing to neglect the often complex reality of people's circumstances or to subject them to unjustified criticism' (Scheffler, 2005: 14).[40] As he sees it, luck egalitarianism courts moralism by taking the 'sweeping view' that people 'must bear the full costs' of their voluntary choices. This is moralistic on the first disjunct of Scheffler's characterizations because it clashes with 'the more nuanced and context-dependent judgements about the significance of choice that are characteristic of ordinary moral thought . . . In their personal lives, for example, [people] do not insist, as a general matter, that someone who makes a bad decision thereby forfeits all claims to assistance . . . In their personal lives . . . few people have a general policy of refusing to praise their friends and acquaintances for anything other than effort and hard work' (Scheffler, 2005: 15). Call this the *moralism objection*.

My main response to this objection is that, though I agree with Scheffler's observations about how people are disposed in their personal lives, I fail to see the dialectical force of them. First of all, distributive luck egalitarianism is not, nor does it imply, any view about what factors people should focus on in their minds when relating to others – it is a view about which distributions are just. Indeed, Scheffler's own fetishism objection relies on this.[41] Accordingly, the moralism objection is best understood as

---

[39] One element which plays a larger role in Anderson's critique of moralizing than in Scheffler's is the view that the state has no standing to make 'grossly intrusive, moralizing judgements of individuals' choices' (Anderson, 1999: 310; 2008b: 250). Hence, Anderson is not objecting to moralization in Scheffler's sense as such. She is objecting specifically to *the state* making moralizing judgements. One challenge here for Anderson is to explain an apparent exception to this prohibition: punishment. Most agree that punishment involves communication of condemnation of the offenders' choices and Anderson agrees that punishment is an exceptional case without really explaining what sets criminal conduct apart from all other forms of conduct (Anderson, 1999: 327).

[40] To me it is more natural to think of moralism as the flaw of giving too much weight to moral considerations in contexts where one should focus on other concerns, e.g. if in the relation to one's children one deliberates about whether it would be morally permissible for one to play with them or hug them, one is being moralistic. Moreover, surely there are ways of ignoring the complexity of moral situations which are not moralistic – e.g. if one takes a strictly libertarian view of having an affair – and unjustified moral criticisms that are not moralistic – e.g. criticisms that are unjustified because based on obviously false empirical assumptions. I set this terminological point aside, however, since whether or not the flaw that Scheffler addresses is moralism, insofar as it is a flaw, there is a potential objection to luck egalitarianism.

[41] As noted above, a similar reply applies to Anderson's pity objection: luck egalitarianism says nothing about how people should receive information about the grounds on which they have received compensation (Section 2.3). Indeed, it does not say anything about who (or what) should provide compensation for non-choice related disadvantages.

an objection which says that there are morally relevant features in many situations that luck egalitarianism does not acknowledge and that facts about luck are irrelevant in some situations where luck egalitarianism does not imply so.

But, and this is my second reply to the moralism objection, as I have noted several times by now, luck egalitarians can be – indeed, should be – pluralists. Accordingly, luck egalitarians can consistently acknowledge that many moral situations are extremely complex and that assessing them only on the basis of people's choices is objectionably simplistic, and it is unclear, at least, that pluralistic, luck egalitarian thoughts are moralistic. Take the luck egalitarian who helps a 'family member who finds himself unemployed as a result of a poor career choice' (Scheffler, 2005: 15) because he believes that there are duties of special obligation, but also thinks that the family member has no claim of justice to be compensated.[42] At the very least, I suspect that an objection based on the putative unappealingness of the luck egalitarian stance on a case of the present kind is dialectically ineffective, because it is identical, or at least too close, to the issue at stake and, thus, that luck egalitarians are unlikely to see moralism where Scheffler sees it.[43]

To summarize: I have sketched Scheffler's four objections – the counterintuitiveness, the fetishism, the metaphysical and the moralism objections. The first and the last objection are reminiscent of Anderson's objections, whereas the second and the third objections seem unlike any of the objections Anderson makes. As with Anderson's objections, I do not find Scheffler's objections to luck egalitarianism compelling.[44] The fetishism reduces to the metaphysical objection, which is never really spelled out. The moralism objection seems to be misdirected. The counterintuitiveness

---

[42] Luck egalitarians could also say that the value of equality is conditional in the sense that it obtains only on condition that it obtains between people who are related in a particular way, e.g. not as family members.

[43] Scheffler might respond that the pluralist luck egalitarian I discuss here might not be moralistic, but that the luck egalitarian that *he* discusses is. That luck egalitarian holds that 'there is something unjust about inequalities deriving from unchosen aspects of people's circumstances, but nothing comparably unjust about inequalities deriving from people's voluntary choices' full stop (Scheffler, 2005: 6). If so, however, this would merely show that Scheffler fails to criticize the views of some of the most prominent luck egalitarians, e.g. G. A. Cohen, who explicitly embraces pluralism.

[44] Scheffler says that the most 'serious reason for declining to ground egalitarianism in the principle of responsibility is that to do so is to lose touch with the value of equality itself' (Scheffler, 2005: 17). He then proceeds to argue that the value of equality itself consists of the value of living together in a certain way, i.e. as equals. Whether or not these points are true, I do not think they can serve as an objection to luck egalitarianism, because they presuppose the falsity of that view and hence I think Scheffler might misdescribe his view when, in the quoted sentence, he refers to the 'most serious reason'.

objection has some force, but it is unclear to what extent it accommodates the option of pluralist luck egalitarianism. On top of that, it is unclear that the fetishism objection – to the extent that it has any force – cannot be, *mutatis mutandis*, directed against relational egalitarianism as well. None of this, of course, is to say that Scheffler has no point in seeing value in people relating as equals independently of how this affects distributions.

2.6 The Egalitarian Deliberative Constraint

In his early writings on relational equality, Scheffler's description of relational equality is not clearly different from Anderson's. Relational equality, Scheffler writes, is 'opposed . . . to oppression, to heritable hierarchies of social status, to ideas of caste, to class privilege and the rigid stratification of classes, and to the undemocratic distribution of power' (Scheffler, 2003a: 22). As a moral ideal it holds that 'all people are of equal worth'; as a social ideal, that 'a human society must be conceived of as a cooperative arrangement of equals'; and finally, as a political ideal, that one has 'a right to be viewed simply as a citizen, and to have one's fundamental rights and privileges determined on that basis, without reference to one's talents, intelligence, wisdom, decision-making skill, temperament, social class, religious or ethnic affiliation or ascribed identity' (Scheffler, 2003a: 22). While, rightly construed, the ideal of equality is an ideal 'governing the relations in which people stand to one another', it has certain 'distributive implications' (Scheffler, 2003a: 21). For instance, a society in which everyone's basic needs are not met, or in which there are 'significant distributive inequalities' that generate 'inequalities of power and status that are incompatible with relations among equals', cannot be a society of equals (Scheffler, 2003a: 23; cp. Scanlon, 2000: 52).

While Scheffler's early description of relational equality does not clearly differ from Anderson's, he mentions a challenge which he thinks relational egalitarians must face and to which he does not provide any principled solution. It seems that any society will involve social relations between individuals that are not ideal from the perspective of relational equality. Take, for instance, the relation between students and professors, managers and blue collar workers, prisoners and prison guards, and children and parents. In all of these cases, it would seem that in basically any society we can think of there will be such social relations and that they will be deficient in terms of the degree to which they realize the ideal of relational equality when we hold them up against, say, two interlocutors in a town hall meeting who debate the pros and cons of a certain political proposal, seeking to establish what is in the common interest in a spirit of respect and equality (Scheffler, 2005: 17–18; cp. Schuppert, 2015: 108). Call this the *pervasiveness problem*. The pervasiveness problem is to relational equality what Scheffler's counterintuitiveness objection is to luck egalitarianism.

Relational egalitarians might respond to the pervasiveness problem in several ways. First, they might deny there is a problem, because relational equality simply does not apply to the relevant social relations. That, however, is not credible. There is a difference between, say, an authoritarian way of parenting and a non-authoritarian one – a difference where the latter form of parenting is preferable from the point of view of relational equality. Also, the present beyond-scope reply burdens relational egalitarians with the troublesome task of identifying features of the relevant social relations by virtue of which the ideal does not apply – a task I suspect will be difficult to complete (cp. Chapter 5.3).

Second, relational egalitarians might concede that the relevant social relations do fall within the scope of relational equality, but then submit that, despite appearances, the relevant relations are not deficient from the perspective of relational equality. Again this response is not very promising. Take the relation between parents and children. Presumably, it is permissible, if not required, that parents sometimes act paternalistically towards their children. Surely a relation between grown-up citizens, where some act paternalistically towards others is deficient from the perspective of relational egalitarianism? So why is a paternalistic relation between parents and children not?

At this point relational egalitarians might try a third reply: they might say that there are special features of children and the relations that they are capable of having to adults, which, as it were, limits the degree to which the relational ideal can be realized. Thus, insofar as it is realized to the highest degree possible given, say, the fact that (small) children have lesser moral (and prudential) powers than adults, there is nothing deficient about the relation between adults and their children despite its glaring differences from the town hall paradigm case of relational equality.

One problem with this reply is that while it might bear on some of the social relations that I mentioned, it does not bear on all of them. For instance, it is not as if managers and blue collar workers, due to the nature of the parties involved, could not relate as equals. Another problem is this: suppose we could improve the moral powers of children compatibly with retaining the value of childhood and, thus, enable parents and children to relate as equals in the way that parents and children relate later in life, when the children have grown up. Would it not be desirable from the point of view of relational equality to do so, just as it would be undesirable if we were to prolong the period of immaturity such that, in the future, it would be impossible for thirty-year-olds to relate to their parents as equals in the same as way as it is impossible for six-year-olds? This is an important question that takes us straight to the question of what makes egalitarian social relations valuable – a question that I return to in Chapter 6.

A fourth reply to the pervasiveness problem is pluralism. On this view, all of the relevant relations, except perhaps for the relation between children and parents, are indeed deficient from the point of view of relational equality. However, they might be valuable in other ways. Suppose, for instance, that people not getting murdered etc. is valuable independently of how this affects social relations. Assuming that incarceration in ways that involve hierarchical social relations between prisoners and prison guards reduces the number of murders, the value of a reduced murder rate might outweigh the disvalue of inegalitarian social relations.[45] I find this reply plausible. However, it is also one that points to an interesting parallel between relational equality and distributive equality. That is, in response to a number of objections, e.g. the levelling down objection or the harshness objection, friends of distributive equality often respond that while distributive equality matters, it is not all that matters – e.g. welfare and solidarity matter too. Thus, in a number of cases friends of distributive equality will embrace deviations from it because of gains in terms of values other than distributive equality. If the present response is adopted, friends of relational egalitarianism are in a similar position – that is, in some cases they embrace deviations from relational equality because of gains in terms of other values. I do not think this is a particularly bad situation to be in, but, first, it implies that relational egalitarians are in no position to object to the appeal to pluralism by luck egalitarians in response to the pertinent objections and, second, it does not fit well with at least how some see relational equality as a demand of justice, where justice is a special value which is not to be traded off against other values such as welfare and solidarity.

In a recent account of the relational egalitarian ideal, Scheffler takes his point of departure in a simple personal relationship between two

---

[45] One suggestion here is that such relations are compatible with the ideal because prisoners had a choice about whether to be law-abiding, and their being subjected to the authority of prison guards is therefore compatible with relational egalitarianism. This move is promising in some ways but also means that relational egalitarianism, like luck egalitarianism, holds that responsibility and choice play an important role when justifying inequalities (cp. Chapter 1.2).

persons – a marriage – and asks what it is for such a relation to be
a relation between equals. He then later extrapolates, with some mod-
ifications, his conclusions regarding an interpersonal relation between
equals to a political community or a society of equals.

   One component of an account of an egalitarian personal relationship
draws on values other than equality. For instance, in Scheffler's account it
is one in which individuals treat one another with respect and expect to be
treated with respect in return and each sees the other as a moral agent with
the rights and responsibilities accruing to moral agents. These components
do not reflect specifically egalitarian values, but that they do not is one
important point Scheffler makes: to wit, that the ideal of relating as equals
implies that equality is not a 'normatively autonomous value'. To spell out
the relational view, one must draw on values other than equality such as
respect, reciprocity and publicity (Scheffler, 2015: 24).[46]

   Another, and distinctively egalitarian, component of Scheffler's relational ideal is what he dubs the *egalitarian deliberative constraint*:

> If you and I have an egalitarian relationship, then I have a standing disposi-
> tion to treat your strong interests [understood broadly to include the
> person's needs, values and preferences] as playing just as significant a role
> as mine in constraining our decisions and influencing what we do. And you
> have a reciprocal disposition with regard to my interests. In addition, both
> of us normally act on these dispositions.[47] (Scheffler, 2015: 25; cp. Mill, 1972
> [1861]: 33)

---

[46] I am not sure why this is not simply an idiosyncratic feature of Scheffler's account of the relational
ideal. Presumably, one can explain what it is to relate as equals in a way that makes no reference to
other values. True, realizing such an ideal of relating as equals might be far from the ideal way of
relating as equals. Further, presumably one could combine the 'distinctively egalitarian component',
which I address in a moment, with values other than the ones Scheffler espouses and still hold
a combined view which is no less relational (or, as I shall argue in Chapter 7.5, dispositional)
egalitarian than Scheffler's. Finally, why cannot one similarly specify a distributive ideal of equality
that makes essential reference to other values? Specifically, it seems one could similarly tie luck
egalitarianism to reciprocity and mutual respect, or to other values for that matter.

[47] Cp. '[Relational equality] claims that human relations must be conducted on the basis of an
assumption that everyone's life is equally important, and that all members of society have equal
standing' (Scheffler, 2003a: 22). Suppose you and I treat each other's interests as equally important,
but treat our interests as much more important, morally speaking, than those of all others.
On Scheffler's account, we can have an egalitarian relationship. However, some might want to
build into the notion of an egalitarian relationship some requirement about how the interests of
third parties are regarded such that, say, white South Africans under apartheid did not relate to
fellow whites as equals in the way relational equality requires. Second, is the 'just as significant a role'
part satisfied if we do not treat each other's interests as significant at all, or if we treat each other's
interests as equally negatively significant, i.e. can two enemies relate as equals? Third, can two
persons not have an egalitarian relationship if they seek to promote a common cause together, e.g.
saving a certain group of strangers from a certain disease, even if they do not consider each other's

Scheffler explicitly notes that satisfying the constraint is compatible with reaching decisions that do not leave the parties who relate as equals equally well off (Scheffler, 2015: 28–9).[48] Indeed, he thinks that, *pace* a distributive ideal of equality, it is unlikely that participants in egalitarian personal relationships will 'attempt to satisfy the [deliberative] constraint through the self-conscious application of a fixed distributive formula', though the constraint will 'exert pressure in the direction of egalitarian distribution' (Scheffler, 2015: 33, 34).[49] This seems right, if not for other reasons as well, then for the reason that one of the parties to an egalitarian relationship might sacrifice his interests to benefit the other party (and the receiving party might accept the sacrifice) without either party not respecting the deliberative constraint.[50]

In Scheffler's view, this non-association between the deliberative constraint and any fixed distributive formula manifests a deep difference between the distributive egalitarian ideal and the relational ideal: the former, but not the latter, is distributively self-sufficient: 'equality is capable all on its own of generating a presumptively authoritative principle of distribution, albeit one that may have to give way if, from the standpoint of justice, other conflicting values trump equality in some ways' (Scheffler, 2015: 42). The relational ideal tells us what 'kinds of practices and institutions' we must create and 'what attitudes and dispositions' we need in order to live together as equals, but it does not in itself tell us what distribution justice requires or requires us to aim for.[51]

(or for that matter their own) interests as constraining their decision at all – the only thing that they allow to play an influencing role is whatever will help save these people? Finally, how does an agent-relative prerogative play into the deliberative constraint? Can we not have an egalitarian relationship if I am disposed – permissibly so, we might assume – to treat my interests as more constraining of what we should decide to do than your interests?

[48] This is compatible with luck egalitarianism, which, like relational egalitarianism, does not focus on distributive outcomes per se. The more difficult question is whether the deliberative constraint is satisfied in a situation where all parties have the relevant dispositions, but some people have better opportunities than others of having their interests etc. promoted.

[49] In connection with his moralism objection, Scheffler (2003a: 21) observes that luck egalitarianism is 'strongly inward looking', because it rests on judgements about 'different aspects of the self'. Scheffler appears to distance himself from such inward lookingness. However, his deliberative constraint appears no different in this respect. More generally, the egalitarian deliberative constraint sits well with the idea of justice of the ancients, according to which 'justice has to do also with character, with the state of one's soul' (Tan, 2014: 83; cp. Rawls, 1993: xvii ff.).

[50] Perhaps this shows that the constraint is slightly mislabelled, because, strictly speaking, it is not 'interests' that constrain decisions, but the person whose interests it is that does so. The interest-bearer has the authority over which role his interests should play in the parties' deliberations, and if this person insists on promoting his interests, then they should be taken into account in exactly the same way as the interests of any other similarly insisting person.

[51] The mirror image of this, of course, is that, unlike the relational ideal, the distributive ideal is not institutionally and dispositionally self-sufficient – it does not, all on its own, yield a fully determinate

Conversely, even if a strict distributive formula of equality were continuously satisfied, the ideal of relating as equals could fail to be satisfied if one of the parties to the relationship continuously flouted the deliberative constraint. This connects with two more general points that Scheffler makes. First, it makes a normative difference whether we accept the relational view: if we do, we will not aim for any particular distributive pattern.[52] Second, equality, as he construes it, is 'a form of practice rather than a normative pattern of distribution' (Scheffler, 2015: 31). Hence, we cannot helpfully define a certain good, say, social standing, as something that, all other things being equal, two people have equal amounts of if, and only if, they relate as equals, and that one has more of than the other to the extent that the former relates to the latter as superior and the latter relates to the former as inferior (cp. Lippert-Rasmussen, 2015b: 195; Chapter 7.4). Doing so would simply leave out the 'deliberative and practical dimensions' of relational equality. More generally, it shows that there is a deep and genuine difference between distributive views of equality and those subscribed to by relational egalitarians.

We can learn about a society of equals through an extrapolation from this characterization of a two-person egalitarian relationship, Scheffler thinks. The deliberative constraint applies to a society of equals as well: '[E]ach member accepts that every other member's equally important interests should play an equally significant role in influencing the decisions made on behalf of the society as a whole. Moreover, each member has a normally effective disposition to treat the interests of others accordingly' (Scheffler, 2015: 35). So, for instance, in a society of equals, gay marriage laws would be decided in accordance with the egalitarian deliberative constraint on the basis that the interests of gays in being able to marry is just as strong as the interests of heterosexuals. While the deliberative

---

set of institutions and dispositions that people ought to realize. (For the reason expressed just above, I doubt whether the relational ideal is institutionally self-sufficient – might not a certain group of people accept that their interests are satisfied to a lesser degree by the relevant institutions, e.g. because they care more about the interests of others – say, future generations? If so, the relational ideal might recommend different institutions for this case than for cases where individuals are not willing to make sacrifices for future generations.) In any case, Scheffler runs two different distinctions together here. One way of seeing this is by noting two possibilities that Scheffler does not mention: views that are institutionally and dispositionally self-sufficient but where these aim at realizing a certain distribution, and views that are distributively self-sufficient but where the relevant distribution aims at realizing people having certain dispositions and supporting certain institutions.

[52] Scheffler thinks this is more so in personal relations than in political relations between millions of citizens who do not know each other, where because of lack of 'direct deliberative access' some kind of 'output measure' like a distributive formula, indirect though it is, may be the best way of judging whether the egalitarian deliberative constraint has been satisfied (Scheffler, 2015: 39).

constraint exerts a strong pressure in the direction of social and political equality, e.g. it seems incompatible with the huge inequalities generated under laissez-faire, this pressure can give way to other considerations such that it does not issue in a fixed distributive formula, even when interpreted against the broader background of the ideal of relating as equals (Scheffler, 2015: 40). In sum: the deliberative constraint is central to Scheffler's ideal of relational equality. However, it is not the only component, and one of Scheffler's central claims is that to fully flesh out this ideal, one must appeal to ideals that are not distinctively egalitarian.

2.7   A Comparison

Having presented Anderson and Scheffler's positive accounts of their two versions of relational egalitarianism, I will now briefly say something about the relation between them.[53] There are obvious similarities beyond the observation that both imply that the proper focus of egalitarian justice is something other than distribution – social relations – and that both stress mutual recognition and respect. Still, their ideals are different. The satisfaction of Anderson's three requirements neither implies satisfaction of Scheffler's deliberative constraint, nor vice versa.

First, the satisfaction of the deliberative constraint does not imply the satisfaction of Anderson's three requirements. Citizens can comply with the deliberative constraint even if not everyone, perhaps not anyone, has enough to participate as an equal in a democratic state or in civil society, e.g. because there is extreme scarcity. Perhaps the constraint could even be satisfied in the presence of ranking of people, e.g. in a scenario where we take turns being nobles and undoing the relevant changing-places hierarchy would be bad for all concerned (cp. Chapter 5.3). Lastly, it seems citizens might comply with the deliberative constraint and still be motivated in part by attitudes, e.g. pity, that clash with Anderson's no-disrespect requirement. More generally, Scheffler's deliberative constraint is not concerned with what principles, or acting from certain principles, express.[54]

Second, the satisfaction of Anderson's three requirements does not imply the satisfaction of the deliberative constraint. Suppose everyone has a sufficient set of freedoms such that Anderson's sufficiency requirement is satisfied.

---

[53] In this section I draw on work published in Lippert-Rasmussen (2018a).

[54] As noted, Scheffler's deliberative constraint is merely a central component in his ideal of relating as equals, and what I say here leaves open the possibility that the less central, non-distinctively egalitarian components of his ideal imply the satisfaction of Anderson's three requirements.

Suppose, moreover, that people subscribe to laissez-faire whenever everyone is above the required minimum. They do not take any disrespectful attitudes towards one another or act from principles that express disrespect, but they simply disregard the interests of others in such cases, except to the extent that not doing so is instrumental from the point of view of promoting their own interests.[55] Lastly, the no-ranking requirement is satisfied because, let us suppose, it alternates who is harmed by the fact that no one satisfies the deliberative constraint, i.e. of each of us it is true that sometimes we gain and sometimes we lose. We can infer that Anderson and Scheffler's positive ideals of relational equality are quite different.

Another important point at which their accounts differ significantly is this. As we saw, Anderson's ideal of democratic equality incorporates a time-relative sufficiency requirement, which implies that people should have enough to be able to participate as equals in social and political life at all times. This was important for her, because this is her basis for claiming that, unlike luck egalitarianism, democratic equality avoids the harshness objection. Things are different with Scheffler's deliberative constraint, because it appears consistent with the fact that people sometimes decide not to help people with urgent needs. For instance, it appears consistent with adopting a policy of sometimes not helping people with urgent needs that can be helped only at great cost and with little prospect of success, and instead focusing on improving everyone's *ex ante* prospects. By way of illustration: Scheffler's deliberative constraint seems consistent with people deciding not to address the urgent health needs of fragile octogenarians in order to improve everyone's health prospects *ex ante* by focusing on interventions addressing the health needs of young people. I am not saying that this is what people deliberating on the basis of Scheffler's deliberative constraint will decide to do. I am merely contending that nothing in the constraint rules this out, and that this points to an important difference from Anderson, who claims that democratic equality insists that all citizens have a sufficient set of capacities at any given moment. Using terminology that has been coined in relation to discussions about how the ideal of equality applies over time, one might say that Anderson's view implies that people's interests should be treated from a time-relative perspective, whereas Scheffler's implies that it is at least permissible to treat them from a whole-lives perspective. The fact that Scheffler says that 'the egalitarian deliberative constraint is best understood diachronically rather

---

[55] I am assuming with Anderson that indifference to the interests of someone above the minimum threshold is not disrespectful.

than synchronically' suggests that, on his view, interests, when considered on the basis of the deliberative constraint, are best understood from a whole-lives perspective (Scheffler, 2015: 26; Chapter 5.3).

More generally, it is interesting to compare what it is to treat one another as equals – as opposed to what conditions should be met for its being likely etc. that people will relate as equals – in Anderson and Scheffler's accounts, respectively. One striking difference between their accounts is that Scheffler's concerns interests only, while Anderson's does not. Plausibly, Anderson's account pertains to interests, since presumably the requirement of equal concern is a concern for the equal satisfaction of interests. However, Anderson's account also includes a requirement of respect and this, I believe, renders Anderson's account in one respect preferable to Scheffler's, since one can fail to relate to others as equals without displaying any differential concern for the involved parties' interests. Suppose that I am equally concerned with the interests of men and women, but that I systematically commit testimonial and hermeneutical injustices against women.[56] Arguably, this means that I do not treat men and women as equals even though I satisfy Scheffler's deliberative constraint. This seems implausible. Here Anderson's account does better since her account also requires that I act from principles that express equal respect and, plausibly, in the case at hand I will (implicitly) act from epistemic principles ascribing differential credence to the voices of men and women that are disrespectful of women (cp. Chapter 3.2).

In sum: while there are strong affinities between Anderson and Scheffler's positive accounts of the relational ideal, their accounts are also crucially different. Most importantly, they are different when it comes to the core notion of relating as equals.

2.8 Conclusion

In this chapter I have presented Anderson and Scheffer's critiques of distributive accounts of justice as well as their positive accounts of the relational ideal. As we have seen, there is considerable, but far from complete, overlap between their critiques of luck egalitarianism. I have also argued that their criticisms are neither compelling – for all their objections, it might still be the case that justice is concerned with, or at least also concerned with, distributions – nor likely to motivate one to

---

[56] I assume that while, generally, people have a strong interest in not being subjected to epistemic injustices, there are cases where interest-wise they are not affected by them.

adopt some form of relational egalitarianism. Moreover, at least some of their criticisms can be directed in parallel form against relational equality – what I called the pervasiveness problem is quite similar to the counter-intuitiveness objection. We have also seen how they both flesh out their accounts of the relational ideal. As with their critiques, there is no more than significant overlap between their positive accounts of relational equality. For instance, in Anderson's account relational equality is primarily concerned with what the principles that people act on express, while Scheffler's distributive constraint focuses on how people are disposed to regard the normative force of others' interests. Accordingly, it would be a mistake to simply collapse Anderson's and Scheffler's positions under one heading and ignore differences between them (cp. Chapter 7.5). What all this comes down to is that we would like to be more precise about what exactly it is to treat one another as equals. This, after all, is the core of relational egalitarianism, and this is what I shall aim at clarifying in the next chapter, drawing on some of the lessons learned in the present chapter.

CHAPTER 3

Relating to One Another As Equals

3.1   Introduction

As we saw in Chapters 1 and 2, relational egalitarians believe that egalitarian justice is fundamentally about our relating as equals rather than about the distribution of goods. But what exactly is it to relate as equals? This chapter offers an answer to that question and compares it to those that are implicit in the writings of different relational egalitarians. I write 'are implicit' because what it is to relate as equals is curiously undertheorized by relational egalitarians (cp. Wolff, 2015: 214).

One reason why it is important to address the question of what it is to relate as equals is that if we are to have a firm grip on what we subscribe to when we subscribe to relational egalitarianism, we need to go beyond a list of paradigmatic examples of (in)egalitarian social relations. Indeed, to know that the relational ideal cannot be captured by some form of distributive equality with an unconventional account of the metric of distributive justice, we need to know what relational equality is. This connects with another important reason. It is impossible to answer the pressing question of why it is desirable to relate as equals without being able to say what relational equality is. If relational equality is valuable or required, not just instrumentally but non-instrumentally, it is so by virtue of features that characterize relating as equals by definition, and without an account of what it is to relate as equals, we cannot know what these features are. Hence, the present chapter has important implications for what can justify the ideal of relating as equals.

The question of what it is to relate as equals should be distinguished from three different questions with which it can be confused. First, the question of what is causally conducive to people relating as equals is different from the question of what it is to relate as equals. As we have seen, Anderson and Scheffler claim that the ideal of relational equality constrains the amount of distributive inequality that we can allow. This might well be so, but in making this claim Anderson and Scheffler are not making any claims about what it is to relate as equals – on their view, in principle, we could relate as equals despite exorbitant distributive inequalities; it is just that, as a matter of fact, we will not do so (but see Chapter 8.2).

Second, the question of what it is to relate as equals is also different from the question of what makes persons moral equals (Cohen, 2013: 194; cp. Arneson, 1999a; Carter, 2011; McMahan, 2002: 189–266; Singer, 1990; Williams, 1973: 230–49). This question has irked a lot of philosophers, because it seems that what makes persons moral equals must be some property which persons possess to an equal degree, and yet the standard proposals as to which properties give persons their special moral status, e.g. rationality, are properties in terms of which persons vary greatly. However, we can know what it is for people to relate as equals, even if we have no idea regarding the characteristics by virtue of which they should be treated equally.[1] Moreover, knowing what it is to relate as equals – a matter of how one interacts *inter alia* – is different from knowing what it is to be moral equals – a matter of the moral norms that apply to one.

Third, the question of what relating as equals is in an abstract sense is different from the question of what relating as equals involves in some specific context. Take the principle of one person, one vote. Some relational egalitarians think that implementing this principle is crucial for citizens relating as equals in modern democracies. However, it would be odd to say that the principle of one person, one vote is part of the very concept of relating as equals, since presumably, we could relate as equals even if there were no voting institution and we could relate as equals, politically speaking, even if we diverge from the principle of one person, one vote, e.g. if the weight people's vote has is graded on the basis of how affected they will be in terms of their interests on the issue being voted upon.

So much for questions which are different from the one that will occupy us in the present chapter. Section 3.2 notes that 'relating as equals' is really an abbreviation for 'relating as equals in some particular dimension', e.g. morality, social status or our status as knowers. Thus, the first step in our clarification of the relational ideal is to show that 'X and Y relate as equals' is shorthand for 'X and Y relate as equals in terms of Z'. Section 3.3 suggests a two-component analysis of relating as equals according to which X and

---

[1] This is not to say that the two questions are unrelated. Presumably, if rationality is the basis for equal moral status, it would be odd if what it is to relate as equals makes no reference to people's rationality.

Y relate as equals (in whatever dimension is at stake) if, and only if, X and Y regard each other as equals and X and Y treat each other as equals. Having pried apart regarding and treating as equals, Sections 3.4, 3.5 and 3.6 scrutinize each of these two components further. Section 3.7 briefly describes some respects in which my analysis of relating as equals does not capture what relational egalitarians have described as ideal. I argue that relational egalitarians too should be pluralists and concede that there are different ways of relating as equals, and that in order to describe the way in which people ideally should relate as equals we must appeal to values other than equality. Section 3.8 summarizes the result of my analysis.

One main claim of this chapter is that while distributive egalitarians have invested too few resources in showing why distributive equality is desirable, relational egalitarians have invested too few resources in another, and in one way more basic, question: to wit, what it is to relate as equals in the first place. This comes up, for instance, in the different accounts of what makes relational equality desirable, where relational egalitarians sometimes seem to have relating as social equals in mind and in other cases relating as moral equals in mind. The chapter's second main claim is that relating as equals consists of both treating and regarding one another as equals and, roughly, that both can be understood in quite different ways. Specifically, with regard to the latter component I argue that regarding someone as an equal includes more than simply the conscious belief that the persons involved have equal moral status.

3.2 Equals with Regard to What?

I ask: 'Is the book any good?' You reply: 'You mean good qua treatise on political philosophy, or good qua birthday present?' I reply: 'I mean none of that. I just mean: is it good?' At this point, it would be reasonable of you to respond that you do not really know what I am asking. There is a distinction between predicative adjectives like 'red' and attributive adjectives like 'good' (Geach, 1956). Something is not red only qua being of a certain kind, e.g. a car, but something is good only qua being of a certain kind, as your reasonable request for clarification in our imaginary dialogue manifests. Something analogous is true about 'relating as equals'. 'Relating as equals' makes no sense unless we presuppose a certain understanding of the dimension on which we relate as equals. However, there are at least five different dimensions that one might have in mind here.

Moral standing is probably the dimension relational egalitarians most often have in mind. This is manifest in Scheffler's deliberative constraint, which requires participants in egalitarian relations to have a standing disposition to treat each other's interests as being equally constraining in relation to resolving practical matters (Scheffler, 2015: 25; Chapter 2.6). Similarly, as we saw in our discussion of Anderson's no-ranking requirement, she thinks that democratic equality involves a requirement to the effect that people relate as moral equals (Chapter 2.4).

What it is to relate as moral equals depends on one's account of moral standing, but we are roughly familiar with some central elements thereof. So, for instance, we would not be treating one another as individuals with an equal moral standing if we relate to one another as if one party's interests or will inherently count for more than that of others, morally speaking. While, as noted, moral standing is probably the dimension theorists most often implicitly – sometimes explicitly – refer to when they talk about relating as equals, it is definitely not the only relevant dimension. If it were, one might suspect that it is not so clear that the ideal is actually very demanding, since most people nowadays explicitly reject the idea of some people having a lower moral status than others.

Another important dimension is epistemic standing. As is well known from the growing body of literature on epistemic justice, people can fail to relate to one another as epistemic equals through testimonial injustice – giving less epistemic weight to members of a subordinate group's testimony than to others due to prejudice or power – and hermeneutical injustice – the inability of members of a subordinate group to make sense of their experience due to their epistemic marginalization (Fricker, 2007: 28, 158–9; cp. Anderson, 2012b; 2015; Schuppert, 2015: 123). While epistemic hierarchy often goes hand in hand with failing to treat as an equal in terms of moral standing, analytically the two failures are separate, and conceptually it is possible for people to relate as equals in terms of moral standing and yet fail to relate as equals in terms of epistemic standing.

It is natural to suppose that people who cherish that we relate as equals cherish relating as equals in relation to epistemic standing too and, thus, that any general account of what it is to relate as equals cannot simply focus on interests and will, i.e. the sort of things one would focus on if one were to consider relating as equals in terms of moral standing. If so, Scheffler's deliberative constraint is too narrow – people could comply with it and yet not treat one another as equals (Chapter 2.6). It could be that we are both disposed to treat each other's interests equally, morally speaking, but that I dismiss summarily your interpretation of what your interests are and impose my interpretation of those interests on you.

Three, sometimes relating as equals refers to social standing (cp. O'Neill, 2008: 126). Even after having become a world-famous psychologist Freud presented himself as 'Dr Dr . . .'. Presumably, the fact that he did so reflected that he lived in a society which was obsessed with titles and, more generally, a society which was (more so than now) focused on social standing and academic degrees. However, people who treated Freud with deference and admiration might in most cases not have thought – not even unconsciously, I suppose one might add here with particular appropriateness – that they and Freud did not have exactly the same moral standing, e.g. they did not believe that Freud's interests or will counted for more, morally speaking, than their interests or will did.

Perhaps it is hard to draw a clear distinction between cases where relating to one another as individuals with differential social standing is compatible with relating to one another as individuals with equal moral standing, and cases where the two are not compatible, but I assume that there are some cases of the former kind, e.g. the fact that students accept that, within certain constraints, I can decide who gets to speak in my classes does not show that we do not relate as moral equals.[2] Assuming that some such cases exist, it is significant that relational egalitarians object to many cases of differential social standing that clearly fall within this category. As David Miller notes with Michael Walzer: a society in which people relate as equals is one in which people use 'common modes of address' (Miller, 1998: 31), e.g. young people do not call older people 'Sir' and older people young people 'son' etc., even though such a differential mode of address does not signal inequality of moral standing, i.e. that young people's will does not have the same normative authority as that of elderly people or that their interests count for less, morally speaking.[3] Also, one way of our not being social equals is by our not regarding one another as moral equals, though, presumably, in isolated social contexts people who believe themselves not to be moral equals can treat each other as social equals, e.g. a group of racists with different racial backgrounds form a platoon where its members' only chance of survival is to interact in a perfectly cooperative spirit.

---

[2] One reason why this is so is that the arrangement is one that serves everyone's interests best and is one that, presumably, everyone implicitly consents to. Or so I hope.

[3] In a sense, if persons are moral equals, there is nothing we can do about this short of depriving them of the capacities which form the basis of moral standing (as opposed to our believing us to be moral equals, which we can promote or hinder). Things are different with being social equals in that we can influence the degree to which people see each other as social equals and this in turn partly determines whether they are so.

A similar point relates to Cohen's ruminations on the difference between Fellows of All Souls who treat members of staff as equals and those who do not: 'Some Fellows regard scouts as, precisely, servants, that is, as people who do not serve others merely as a matter of fact and circumstance, but as people whose status is such that it is appropriate that their lot in life is to serve others. That sort of regard might show itself, for example, in a certain brusqueness in the instructions as to the desired service that these Fellows give to scouts, and in the nature of the response that the scouts get when they serve well, or badly' (Cohen, 2013: 195).[4] It is not that I disagree with what Cohen writes here. However, in the standard case the mentioned brusqueness etc. might not reflect any beliefs about hierarchy of moral standing, but rather simply beliefs about social hierarchy.

The distinction between moral and social equals also potentially casts light on the pervasiveness problem, which I described in Chapter 2.5:

> Insofar as equality is understood as a substantive social value, which is distinct, for example, from the formal principle that one should treat like cases alike and from the axiological judgement that all people are of equal worth, the basic reason it matters to us is because we believe that there is something valuable about human relationships that are, in certain crucial respects at least, unstructured by differences of rank, power or status. So understood, equality is in some ways a puzzling value and a difficult one to interpret. After all, differences of rank, power and status are endemic to human social life. Almost all human organizations and institutions recognize hierarchies of authority, for example, and most social roles confer distinctions of status which in turn structure human relationships, such as the relationships of doctors to patients, teachers to students, parents to children, attorneys to clients, employers to employees, and so on. If there is any value at all in such relationships, then at least one of the following two things must be true. Either some relationships can be valuable despite having a fundamentally inegalitarian character or else it is not necessary, in order for a relationship to qualify as having an egalitarian character, that it should be altogether unmarked by distinctions of rank or status. The egalitarian need not deny the first point, but, given the ubiquity of the distinctions mentioned, the second point is crucial if equality is to be understood as a value of reasonably broad scope. In fact, both points are almost certainly true. (Scheffler, 2005: 17–18)

---

[4] Recall the quote from Burke about the virtues of submission in Chapter 1.2. Perhaps Burke thought it possible to treat someone as a moral equal whose purpose in life is to serve others, e.g. by treating this person's service-oriented interests as equally important as everyone else's?

The second point makes sense if we think that relational egalitarians subscribe to our relating as moral equals and if we think that there are ways in which people can relate as social unequals which is compatible with their relating as moral equals. No doubt, some ways of relating as social unequals are incompatible with relating as moral equals, but not all ways are.[5] Presumably, some relational egalitarians would argue that even extremely hierarchical social relations can be consistent with relating as moral equals. For instance, the fact that a general can order a private to 'stand in a breach, where he is almost certain to perish', but cannot order the private to hand over a single farthing might be seen as something that manifests the moral equality between the two (Locke, 1960 [1689]: 408).[6]

Four, arguably 'relating as equals' could also refer to aesthetic standing. Anderson, for instance, discusses 'the ugly' and suggests that in a society of equals, 'norms of beauty' are not oppressive. Non-oppressive aesthetic norms are not such that everyone has an equal chance of winning a beauty pageant or of being a 'hot prospect for a Saturday night date'. However, such norms are 'flexible enough' for any person to deem any 'person an acceptable presence in civil society' (Anderson, 1999: 335).[7] One important reason why we care about our aesthetic standing is that it affects our interests considerably, as shown by the present epidemic of eating disorders. However, even in the hypothetical case where it did not, one might still think that in a society of equals people enjoy equal aesthetic standing in some way or other. For instance, even in the hypothetical case where this had no adverse effects on those with lower aesthetic standing, we might still think that a society of equals is one without, say, race- or gender-biased aesthetic norms, e.g. when greater emphasis is 'placed on how beautiful women are' than on how beautiful men are (cp. Fourie, 2015: 100).[8]

---

[5] Cp. Scheffler's remark that a social relational egalitarian 'begins from the question of what relationships among equals are like and goes on from there to consider what kind of social and political institutions are appropriate to a society of equals' (Scheffler, 2003a: 37; cp. Baker, 2015: 69). The basic idea here is that the ideal of moral equals regulates the sort of social relations – hierarchical as well as non-hierarchical – that we should endorse.

[6] Presumably, the idea is that the extreme social hierarchy between the private and the general is strictly limited in terms of the range of ends and means involving the private which the general has authority to employ in pursuit of his goals, and that the private in this sense is not subjected to the general's arbitrary will renders the social hierarchy compatible with moral equality.

[7] To my knowledge Anderson is – to her credit, in my view – the only relational egalitarian who addresses this dimension of relating as equals.

[8] The first non-white to win the title of Miss South Africa, Amy Kleinhans, won the title in 1992, two years after the negotiations between de Klerk and Mandela to end apartheid started (and two years before they culminated in the 1994 election, which brought the ANC to power).

A fifth dimension is the empirical dimension. A teacher who treats her students as if they all have the same learning potential treats them as equals when it comes to learning capacity. Or we might say that a policewoman who disregards contextually relevant crime statistics showing that, for whatever reason, members of some groups are more likely than members of other groups to engage in criminal activities of a certain kind, treats individual citizens as equals when it comes to the probability of their being involved in certain kinds of crime. While some egalitarians might think that, at least in certain contexts and with regard to certain matters, relational equality requires that we treat one another as equals in the relevant empirical dimensions, as a general matter I suspect relational egalitarians would want to say that complying with the relational ideal is compatible with letting nothing but epistemic evidence determine whether we relate as equals when it comes to empirical dimensions.[9]

An important aspect of Anderson's democratic equality pertains to people being equals empirically speaking. This comes out, for instance, in her description of democratic equality as involving the idea that 'all competent adults are equally moral agents: everyone equally has the power to develop and exercise moral responsibility, to cooperate with others according to principles of justice, to shape and fulfil a conception of their good' (Anderson, 1999: 312; see Chapter 2.4). On a natural reading, this suggests that all competent adults have the same level of powers to develop and exercise moral responsibility etc. Whether this is so is an empirical question. Suppose we learned from psychological studies that some agents are much better than others at developing and exercising moral responsibility. If so, we are no longer able to relate as equals on the present reading. On another reading, no such thing is being asserted. Rather, what is being asserted is that all competent adults have at least a certain threshold level of power to develop and exercise moral responsibility etc.[10] This is consistent with the level of relevant powers of competent adults varying hugely above that threshold level. Since, by definition, it is part of what it is to be competent to have the relevant threshold level, it follows that all competent adults have the relevant powers. Adding that they all have it 'equally' is superfluous – it is like saying that all lions are equally lions. My suspicion is that the fact that Anderson inserts this

---

[9] Though relational egalitarians might say that the degree of evidence we require in order to have an epistemically justified belief about a certain matter might vary with its moral importance.

[10] Admittedly, this too involves a certain, though much weaker, empirical assumption.

superfluous 'equally' attests to the attraction of the idea that people are equals empirically speaking in the former, more demanding, sense.

The present five-item list in relation to dimensions in which people can be treated as equals is not intended to be exhaustive. The following four points are this section's main points. First, to say that:

X and Y relate as equals

is always shorthand for:

X and Y relate as equals in terms of Z

where 'Z' denotes some specific dimension, e.g. one or more of the five dimensions that I have identified above.

Second, while the dimension that relational egalitarians often have in mind is moral standing, there are other kinds of standing which could be at stake. Arguably, in a society in which people relate as equals they also do so in relation to social, epistemic, aesthetic and possibly other forms of standing as well. It is important to be clear about the dimension along which persons are said to relate as equals, especially in relation to the value of doing so. Presumably, the value of relating as equals will depend very much on the dimension one has in mind. Take the difference between moral and social standing. Assuming that all persons have equal moral standing, then relating to one another as moral unequals, because we do not regard one another as equals, is to relate on the basis of a false assumption. If we believe that it has value that we do not relate to one another on the basis of false assumptions, it follows that our relation has disvalue. However, the same argument cannot – at least not in the same way – be made with regard to social standing. For social standing is socially constructed through how we relate to one another. Hence, if we are generally regarded as unequals in terms of social standing, then the fact that we relate to one another as social unequals does not imply that we relate to one another on the basis of false assumptions – quite the contrary, since, regrettably, that is the way we are. Hence, our relationship does not involve any disvalue of the sort I am talking about here (though, of course, in all likelihood it will involve other disvalues).

Third, luck egalitarian accounts of justice differ in terms of which equalisandum they endorse. Similarly, different accounts of relational egalitarianism differ in terms of the dimensions along which people should treat one another as equals. To put it differently: just as distributive egalitarians must answer the question 'Equality of what?', relational egalitarians must answer the question 'Equals along what dimensions?'. And just as distributive egalitarians differ among themselves in terms of how they answer the 'Equality of what?' question, relational egalitarians differ – or, perhaps more appropriately, could differ if they were to address the question systematically – among themselves in terms of the relationendum question. In this section, I have identified at least five different dimensions in terms of which people could be treated as equals. These can be combined such that we have more than five different answers to the 'Equals along what dimensions?' question. But there are further possibilities for variation. Even if we agree, say, that people should relate as moral equals, there are different views about what relating as equals involves relationendum-wise. On some accounts, it is a matter of expressing equal respect (Anderson, 1999; Wolff, 1998). A different – but related – view says that relating as moral equals is a matter of equal recognition (Fraser & Honneth, 2003). A third view focuses on equal concern for each other's interests (Scheffler, 2015: 25–31). A fourth view focuses on freedom understood as non-domination (Pettit, 1997; cp. Garrau & Laborde, 2015).[11] And there are other possibilities. In short, the 'Equals along what dimension?' question is no less daunting than the 'Equality of what?' question.

Fourth, we can distinguish between a one-dimensional form of relational egalitarianism, according to which all that matters from a relational point of view, fundamentally speaking, is that people relate as moral equals, and a multidimensional form, according to which relating as equals in other dimensions also matters fundamentally. Anderson's ideal of relating as equals is multidimensional. While Scheffler's ideal might pertain to more than the dimension of equality of moral status, e.g. social status, it is fair to say that the former is its main focus.

3.3   Relating, Regarding and Treating

Setting aside for the moment the issue of the dimension of relating as equals, what is it for people to relate as equals? To work our way towards an answer to this question we might look at a similar question about a simpler, more concrete case. We might ask, say, 'What is it to relate as brothers?' By saying of two people that they relate as brothers one might convey that they treat each other in ways which are typical, descriptively speaking, of the ways in which brothers treat each other, e.g. they might frequently seek

---

[11] Hausman and Waldren (2011: 579–84) argue that relating as equals refers to a plurality of different and separable egalitarian concerns. Their taxonomy cuts across mine.

each other's company, or they act in ways that brothers are normatively expected to act towards one another. Or one might convey that they have certain attitudes towards one another and their relations, e.g. that they feel strongly connected to each other, and that they believe that they ought to act towards one another in certain ways, e.g. that they ought to help each other out in difficult situations.[12] Extrapolating this analysis to the case of relating as equals we might say:

> X and Y relate as equals if, and only if:
>
> (1) X and Y treat one another as equals;
> (2) X and Y regard one another as equals.[13]

On this analysis relating as equals has two components: a behavioural component – how one treats another – and an attitudinal component – how one regards another (Cohen, 2013: 193–200; cp. Fourie, 2012: 107, 112).[14] Together they are sufficient for relating as equals and each of them is necessary. By way of analogy: if brothers both treat one another as such and regard themselves as brothers, then they relate as such. However, if they do not treat one another as such, or if they do treat each other as such, but they do not regard each other as brothers, they do not relate as brothers (though it may seem as if they do).

While the way in which one regards another tends to be manifested in the way one relates, and while it might also be true that, in some ways, one's knowledge of how one regards another derives from one's observation of how the one treats the other (and is not simply based on

---

[12] One might add a – to my mind plausible – third condition: they treat each other as brothers, *because* they regard each other as brothers, i.e. it is not just accidentally and, say, for purely selfish reasons that they often help each other out. Applied to the analysis of 'relating as equals' below, this line of thought suggests adding: (3) X and Y treat one another as equals, because X and Y regard one another as equals. The reason I have not included this (equally reasonable) requirement, apart from a concern to keep things relatively simple is that I do not find textual evidence that relational egalitarians in general think that this is a necessary condition of relating as equals or that this is necessary for its being desirable to treat and regard one another as equals (but see the discussion of Scheffler's deliberative constraint in Section 3.4). On the motivational notion of treating as, which I will discuss in Section 3.4, if X and Y treat one another as equals (i.e. (1) is satisfied), then it follows that X regards Y as an equal and that Y regards X as an equal (i.e. (3) is satisfied).

[13] There is a difference between two individuals relating as equals over a period of time, and their doing so in a particular interaction. If, for instance, a couple who stay together over a long period of time occasionally do not relate as equals on particular occasions, we would not on that account say that, in their marriage as a whole, they do not relate as equals. Here I focus on individuals relating as equals on a particular occasion. There is a similar distinction between relating as equals in one particular dimension of interaction or over a broad range of different interactional contexts.

[14] Miller (1998: 23) specifies the nature of social equality in such a way that it involves both that people 'regard and treat one another as equals'. If he thought treating one another as equals implied regarding one another as equals, it would be superfluous to include 'regard' in that statement.

introspection), these two components can come apart.[15] Two people can treat each other as equals even if they do not regard each other as such. Suppose two racists of different racial backgrounds must interact with one another under the scrutiny of their strongly anti-racist employer. In that case, they might well – in behavioural terms at least and for opportunistic reasons – treat one another as equals, i.e. their behaviour towards one another might be indistinguishable from what it would have been had they not been racists. Conversely, two people can fail to treat one another as equals even if they see each other as such. Think of a case where two anti-racist but opportunistic friends of different racial backgrounds have to interact under the scrutiny of their strongly racist employer.

At this point, some might note that some of the social relations that relational egalitarians object to – e.g. Young's five faces of oppression (exploitation, marginalization, powerlessness, cultural imperialism and violence) and domination – seem to be defined by the way in which people treat each other. While they might often be accompanied by an objectionable self-elevating way of regarding oneself relative to those whom one exploits etc., it is certainly possible to exploit people whom one regards as one's equal (or even to exploit people whom one regards as one's superior – think of a group of slaves who, tragically, see themselves as natural slaves in the Aristotelian sense, but who have overpowered their masters and have strong egoistic reasons for exploiting their former masters). Some might infer from this that relating as equals *simply is* treating one another as equals.

While I agree that some social relations to which relational egalitarians object are defined independently of the way in which the parties involved regard one another, I want to resist the suggested inference for the following three reasons. First, we can respond to the observation in the previous paragraph differently. We can say that while relational egalitarians object to treating as unequals, even when this does not involve relating as unequals in my sense, this is not denying that failing to treat as equals people whom one does not regard as equals is even worse.[16] Second,

---

[15] As Cohen puts it: 'the regarding is a reason for the treating, which it could not be if it were not distinct from the latter' (Cohen, 2013: 197). Perhaps it could be the other way round as well: The fact that I treat someone as an equal could be thought of as an indirect reason for why I should regard him as an equal, e.g. if I have independent reason to think that people normally are as I treat them to be. Huckleberry Finn could see his refraining from reporting Jim as a reason why he should regard him as an equal.

[16] I critically assess this claim in (Lippert-Rasmussen, 2006; but see Lippert-Rasmussen, forthcoming). On one version of the suggested view, treating as an unequal and regarding as an unequal interacts such that the wrongness (or badness) of the resulting whole – relating as unequals – is greater than the wrongness (or badness) of the sum of two components – treating and regarding as unequals.

relational egalitarians object to belief sets, e.g. ideologies such as racism or sexism (Anderson, 1999: 312), at least in part because of how those who subscribe to such belief sets regard others, independently of how their subscription to the relevant belief set manifests itself in the way in which they treat others. Hence, unlike oppression, domination, etc., at least some social relations to which relational egalitarians object, e.g. sexism and racism, by definition involve a certain non-egalitarian way of regarding others. Third, the mere fact that people do not relate in the ways e.g. that Young and others identify as oppressive is not enough to show that things are as good as they could be from a relational point of view. Moreover, perhaps the reason relational egalitarians have failed to notice this is precisely because, as noted in the previous paragraph, objectionable ways of regarding one another tend to go hand in hand with oppression etc. and, thus, relational egalitarians may have failed to note, or noted but simply found unlikely and, for that reason, unimportant, situations in which oppression etc. is non-existent, but in which people fail to regard one another as equals.

In view of this, the main claim of this section is that we can analyse what it is to relate as equals as being a matter of both treating one another, and regarding one another, as equals. The next three sections expand on what each of these two components amounts to.

3.4 Treating As

To treat someone as an equal is a matter of how one treats that person in one's interactions with that person, e.g. a matter of whether one casts this person in a subordinate position. It follows that one cannot treat someone as an equal when one neither interacts with this person nor unilaterally affects this person in any way. I might regard Martians – suppose they exist – as moral equals and they might regard me as such, but we cannot treat each other as equals:

> *The causal condition*: X and Y treat each other as equals only if X and Y can affect their respective situations in a relevant way.

The reason for the qualification 'in a relevant way' reflects that the situation would be no different if Martians and Earthlings could, say, marginally affect each other in ways that are irrelevant to their concerns, e.g. if Earthlings can unnoticeably affect the Martian atmosphere's composition.

The next step in analysing what it is to treat as an equal is to distinguish between 'treat as __' and 'an equal'. There is a general question about what it is to treat someone as __, e.g. as a brother, which is independent of whatever it might mean to treat as an equal. Hence, a natural way to proceed is to break the question of what it is to treat someone as an equal into two questions: what it is to treat as if __, and what it is to be equals. First, I address the 'treat as __' issue, and distinguish between different senses of that notion, and next I turn to the notion of 'equals'.

Here is a common notion of treating as __, i.e. the *normative notion*:[17]

> X treats Y as __ if, and only if, (X believes that) X's treating in the way X treats Y would be permissible (not against Y's rights, appropriate etc.) only if Y is __.

Suppose I am a doctor and you seek my advice about some medical problem. During my examination of you, I sedate you and perform whatever medical procedure on you that I think is best. Suppose that this procedure happens to be, and that we agree *ex post facto* that it is, the best procedure and the one which you would have asked me to perform had I presented you with the relevant medical facts. Still, you can complain that I treated you as someone who did not have the right to decide over her own body, since only if that were the case would what I did have been permissible.[18] I could deny that I treated you as such, if, say, due to the urgency of the situation there was no time to ask for your informed consent. But the fact that I can deny having treated you as someone who has no right to decide over her body on these grounds attests to the relevance of the normative notion of 'treating as if __'. That reply is one that enables me to argue that my action is permissible. Even if you have a right to decide over your body, such a right is defeasible, and in cases where it is reasonable to believe that the right-holder would have consented to one's infringing that right and where that infringement would save the right-holder's life, it is permissible to do so.

The normative notion involves different moral concepts, e.g. *permissible, having a right to* and *being good*, as well as others that I do not list here.

---

[17] I say 'normative' not 'moral' because 'as' should also cover the other dimensions that I distinguished between in Section 3.2.

[18] There is a possible problem of regress here. Presumably, relational egalitarians want to say that whether it is permissible for me to φ depends on whether in φ-ing I would be treating others as equals. However, on the moralized version of the normative notion, in order to know whether I treat someone as an equal when I φ, I first need to know whether φ-ing is permissible. The regress arrives because that in turn depends in part on whether φ-ing is treating as an equal – that which we initially wanted to know. One way to avoid regress is to insert 'setting aside whether X treats Y as __' between 'only if' and '(X's believing that)'.

To see that, in addition to permissibility and having a right to, we also need the notion of goodness, consider a case where, as a member of some literary prize committee, I praise a particular author's book as being the best literary work of the year. We might say that in doing so I treat the author as being the author of the best book of the year, where the relevant standards in question are literary standards, since it is only fitting to do what I did, if, in fact, the author is the author of the best, aesthetically speaking, book of the year.

I should also explain the need for the parenthesized '(X believes that)'. The need for this reflects the fact that 'treating as __' can be defined objectively or subjectively. In an objective account, I treat someone as __ only if I act in the way that would be permissible if Y is __.[19] In a subjective account, I treat someone as __ only if I act in the way that *I believe* would be permissible if Y is __. Suppose I believe falsely that to treat my friend as an equal, I must give much more weight to her interests than to my own. I fail to do so, instead giving our interests equal weight. In so doing, I act, let us suppose, exactly the way I ought to act, objectively speaking, given that we are moral equals (setting aside my beliefs about what treating as an equal requires). On a subjective account, I have failed to treat my friend as an equal, but not so on an objective account. Relational egalitarians have not explicitly addressed the issue of whether one should embrace a subjective or objective or, indeed, (as I suspect that, on reflection, many of them would favour) a conjunctively subjective and objective account of 'treat as __'.

On the subjective notion of the normative conception of 'treating as __', the agent must hold a certain belief about the normative properties of the way in which she treats the other person. However, it is not required that this belief is motivationally efficacious – in principle, I could treat you in a way that I believe is morally required only if you are my moral equal and yet not treat you as such *because* I have this belief. If we add the requirement that the belief motivates the treating, we get a subspecies of the normative conception, which I think is sufficiently important to merit a label of its own, the *motivational notion*:

---

[19] Suppose we adopt a slightly modified account of the objective normative notion of treating as __ such that X treats Y in a certain way which is permissible if, and only if, Y is __ and, as a matter of fact, Y is __. In that case, it is entailed that X acts permissibly. Treating as __ is obviously desirable in the sense that if Y is __, then in treating Y as __, X acts permissibly. Applying this lesson to treating as equals, if X treats Y as an equal and Y is an equal, then X acts permissibly. But presumably, treating each other as equals is desirable for reasons other than the fact that we are treating each other as such entails that we act permissibly.

> X treats Y as __ if, and only if, (1) X believes that X's treating in the way X treats Y would be permissible (not against Y's rights, appropriate etc.) only if Y is __; and (2) this belief is part of X's motivational state in relation to how he treats Y.

Unlike the normative notion, the motivational notion requires that the agent acts on normative beliefs of a certain kind and that these beliefs are what determine how the agent treats others. Some such notion might be close to what Scheffler has in mind. His deliberative constraint implies that parties to an egalitarian relation have 'a standing disposition' to treat each other's strong interests as equally constraining of 'our decision and influencing what we will do' (Scheffler, 2015: 25). While Scheffler does not mention normative beliefs and focuses on dispositions, the best way to understand him here involves imputing to the parties the normative belief – if not occurrent, then dispositional – that each others' interests *ought to* influence equally what they do together.[20] For suppose he intends the deliberative constraint to be understood differently. In that case, two people who, against their own judgement or for purely selfish reasons, are disposed to take each other's interests equally into account comply with the deliberative constraint. Perhaps there is a sense in which they relate as equals, but I suspect that relational egalitarians will want to say that, ideally, relating as equals involves more than what the present relationship involves.

A third way in which one can treat as __ comes out in the *communicative notion*:

> X treats Y as __ if, and only if, X by his treatment of Y intends to communicate the message that Y is __.

Suppose that as chairperson at a meeting I ask if anyone has objections to a certain proposal about which several persons have expressed a positive opinion. No one raises any objections and I say: 'OK, then the issue is settled and we move on to the next item on the agenda'. In doing so, I treat the issue as one that has been settled in accordance with the positive opinions of several participants in the meeting. The grounds for this being the case could be that in saying what I said I intended to communicate to the participants in the meeting that the issues had been settled in

---

[20] While, typically, the best explanation of why an agent conforms with the deliberative constraint is that she believes that the parties to the relevant egalitarian relation's interests ought to be accommodated equally, in principle it is possible for an agent to be disposed to conform with the constraint in the absence of any such belief.

the way that several participants in the meeting had expressed a positive opinion about.

A fourth way in which one can treat as __ is captured by the *expressive notion*:

> X treats Y as __ if, and only if, X's treatment of Y expresses that Y is __.

On this notion, what is crucial is not X's communicative intentions, but what the relevant act expresses. Suppose I am unfamiliar with the language in which the meeting described just above is conducted and believe that my utterance really means 'I disagree strongly with the opinions voiced so far and am deciding to postpone the decision until later', and that this is the message I want to communicate. There is a sense in which, despite my communicative intentions, I have acted as if the issue was settled in favour of the view that some participants expressed their preference for. If I proceed in the way I intended to communicate, other participants can complain: 'But you acted as if we had decided to proceed with the option that people had expressed views in favour of'. And once they learn that I did not know the meaning of the words that I uttered, they need not retract their complaint as unfounded.

What determines what an act expresses is a big question which might be answered in different ways. One view says that what one's conduct expresses is determined by how others might reasonably understand it given the relevant social and cultural context which is shared by X and those relative to whom X's treatment has the relevant expressive meaning (cp. Hellman, 2008: 59–85). On this view, if I fly a Confederate flag over an official building in southern US states I might express racist attitudes, even if I am not in any way racist – I am simply unaware of the cultural meaning of the flag – and have no intentions to communicate anything else.[21] Also, communicative intentions might matter on the expressive account in the sense that what it is reasonable for others to see a given treatment as expressing might depend on what communicative intentions (they reasonably believe) the agent has (cp. Scanlon, 2008: 53).

The communicative and the expressive notions are related, though different. In a nutshell, the communicative notion is subjective, because it is tied to X's communicative intentions in a way that the expressive notion is not. Hence, although the communicative and expressive notions

---

[21] Suppose everyone knows this fact about me. I suppose that, on the relevant expressive notion, I do act as if I have racist views and, thus, fail to treat everyone as equals.

often overlap, I can treat someone as __ in the expressive sense without
doing so in the communicative sense, and vice versa.

At least two relational egalitarians explicitly embrace the expressivist
notion of treating as equals: Anderson and Schemmel. I return to the
latter's position in Section 3.6, so here I will focus on Anderson's position.
In a number of places, she suggests that 'the most fundamental test any
egalitarian theory must meet' is 'that its principles express equal respect and
concern for all its citizens' (Anderson, 1999: 289).[22] Moreover: 'equality of
fortune, in attempting to ensure that people take responsibility for their
choices, makes demeaning and intrusive judgements of people's capacities
to exercise responsibility and effectively dictates to them the appropriate
use of their freedom' (Anderson, 1999: 289).[23] Strictly speaking, equality of
fortune is a moral principle and moral principles do not – it is metaphysically impossible for them to – make judgements (cp. Chapter 2.3). Hence,
what Anderson must mean is that, in many cases, an agent who tries to
bring about a distribution favoured by equality of opportunity must make
'demeaning and intrusive judgements' – something which involves
a failure to express equal respect and concern. But in that case the objection
is not that equality of fortune in itself fails to express equal respect and
concern. Rather, the objection is that, in some/most/all cases, to inten-
tionally bring about the distribution favoured by equality of fortune an
agent must make judgements that/the making of which fail(s) to express
equal respect and concern (or better: express unequal respect and unequal
concern) and that any principle of which it is true that, in some/most/all
cases, to realize that principle agents must make judgements that fail to
express equal respect and concern is false.[24]

---

[22] The requirement that a principle expresses equal respect and concern is more demanding than the
requirement that a principle does not express unequal respect or unequal concern on the plausible
assumption that some principles neither express one nor the other.

[23] Elsewhere Anderson writes that it is 'the reasons luck egalitarians offer for coming to the aid of the
victims of bad brute luck' that are disrespectful (Anderson, 1999: 295; cp. Anderson, 1999: 303). Also,
she asks whether paternalist 'policies', which luck egalitarians might favour to avoid the harshness
objection, 'express respect for citizens' (Anderson, 1999: 301). And in yet other places Anderson
observes that her question is not with the consequences of expressing certain attitudes, but 'with
what attitudes' a certain 'theory expresses' (Anderson, 1999: 306n61).

[24] However, this cannot be right. Suppose that to implement democratic equality we need information
about people's level of basic capabilities, which can only be obtained from a certain whiz kid
statistician who is more than willing to provide us with that information, but only on the condition
that we make some demeaning and intrusive judgements about one another. Given the general
premise underlying Anderson's reconstructed objection, this example shows that democratic
equality is false (unless, implausibly, Anderson can argue that judgements about people's capacities
to exercise responsibility are not disrespectful when made in the pursuit of the democratic
egalitarian cause).

So construed one might wonder why Anderson's basic test is not simply whether citizens are *actually* treated with equal concern and respect. Suppose that it is possible for an agent to treat fellow citizens with equal respect and concern, even though the principle from which he acts does not express equal respect and concern. It seems odd to say that this agent violates egalitarian justice, whereas an agent who acts from principles that express equal concern and respect, but does not actually treat with equal concern and respect, does not. Perhaps Anderson's view makes best sense if we assume:

> X treats Y with equal concern and respect if, and only if, X treats Y on the basis of principles that express equal concern and respect.[25]

Anderson might think this claim is true, because to treat people with equal concern and respect is, in part or in full, to treat them in a way that expresses equal concern and respect. In any case, it seems clear that Anderson's notion of 'treating' is different from Scheffler's. Scheffler does not in his account of the ideal of relational equality emphasize what people express. Rather, his main notion of 'treat' is the motivational idea of treating as equals.

A fifth way in which one can treat someone as __ is the *presuppositional notion*:

> X treats Y as __ if, and only if, X's treatment of Y makes (best) sense only if X presupposes that Y is __.

Suppose I make a criticism of someone's philosophical work. I do so in an extremely kind way, overemphasizing whatever virtues one can point to, and go on at length about why the mistakes that my interlocutor has made are very natural mistakes to make. In this case, it might be right to say that I treat my interlocutor as someone who lacks self-confidence, because the way in which I formulate my criticisms (which are not very damaging

---

[25] One bit of textual support for this interpretation is that Anderson moves straight from a claim about what principles (she uses the term 'theories') express to a claim about principles treating people as inferiors (Anderson, 1999: 306n61). Still, there are other passages which suggest otherwise. She thinks having access to no other sources of nutrition than 'pet food or the dumpster' relegates people to a 'subhuman status'. Suppose I am starving and for some reason the only source of nutrition you can provide me with is pet food. Suppose also that you provide me with the food because you think this is the only way I am able to participate in civil and political life on an equal footing. Presumably, you do not, according to Anderson, act on disrespectful principles. Still, it might be thought that your action expresses disrespect, because of the cultural meaning of serving pet food to people – a cultural meaning of which, let us suppose, I am unaware. If so, there is a sense of disrespect – one that Anderson draws on in the present example – in which one can act disrespectfully even if one does not act from a principle which expresses disrespect (cp. Hellman, 2008: 75).

anyway) makes best sense if I presuppose that this person lacks self-confidence (and I do not want to make this person feel bad).

This notion is different from the four previous notions. It might well be that it would be permissible etc. for me to put forward my objections in a much more straightforward way, and thoughts about this being permissible etc. might be completely absent from my motivational set. Further, I might have no intention to communicate my beliefs about my interlocutor's lack of self-confidence. Finally, it might be true that the way in which I put forward my criticism complies with the relevant conventions about how one should put forward one's criticisms, but that people know that I often ignore etiquette and, accordingly, that the way in which I put forward my criticisms does not make sense as an attempt to conform to conventions.

So much for the five notions of treating as __: the normative, the motivational, the communicative, the expressive and the presuppositional notion. I do not put forward this list as an exhaustive list of relevant ways of 'treating as __'. I do think, however, as we shall see in Section 3.6, that the notions that I have covered here are those that relational egalitarians typically employ. Note also that relational egalitarians might think that equality requires that we treat one another as equals in more than one – indeed in all – of the senses above. Note, finally, that the two main proponents of relational egalitarianism – Anderson and Scheffler – employ different notions of treating as __: the expressivist and the motivational respectively.

3.5   Equals

Turning next to the notion of equals – an issue that also bears on what it is to regard as equals, to which I turn in the next section – consider the following formal account of what it is to be equals:

> X and Y are equals if, and only if, the same basic normative rules and axiological principles apply to them.

While formal equality might be part of what it is to treat people as equals, it does not fully capture what relational egalitarians have in mind. Consider: 'Everyone is required to bow before the Queen if they are not royal themselves, and required not to bow if they are royal'. This same rule applies to commoners as well as to royals and in that sense it applies to everyone. Yet people who comply with this rule clearly do not treat one another as equals.

So what is required to make a standard one that, metaphorically speaking, treats people as equals? To answer this question I will first propose an account of what it is to be moral equals and then see if we can use that account to explain what it is to be equals in the other senses that I identified in Section 3.2. In light of the failure of the previous account, I propose:

> X and Y are moral equals if, and only if, the same basic normative rules and axiological principles apply to them and if, in accordance with those rules and principles, X and Y are equally important in whatever respects are fundamentally morally significant (other than the fact that people relate to one another as equals).

This formulation leaves open what the fundamentally morally significant respects are. Hence, it leaves open whether people's welfare-based interests or their will is what is fundamentally morally significant about them. Or both. Or neither. The reason I stick with this relatively open phrase is that, presumably, people who have quite different views on what is fundamentally morally significant about persons can agree that it is important that people are treated as equals.

Moreover, the present account only requires that the relevant rules etc. specify that people are equally important in whatever respects are fundamentally morally significant. This leaves open the possibility that people can be not equally important in whatever respects are not fundamentally morally significant. Suppose we believe that people's interests are what are fundamentally morally significant about them. On that view people are equals only if, at a fundamental level, people's interests are equally morally important. However, that leaves open the possibility that, at a non-fundamental level, some people's interests are more important than other people's interests in the sense that we can permissibly give priority to their interests over the interests of others. Suppose, for instance, that we can save either a renowned scientist, who is about to have a breakthrough in her research on a cure for cancer, or a philosophy professor, of whom nothing comparable is true. In this case, we can permissibly save the scientist compatibly with the two persons in question being moral equals.[26]

The present account of what it is to be moral equals is also compatible with a considerable amount of agent-relativity. Suppose we believe that parents are required to give greater weight to the interests of their children than to the interests of children of other parents, such that 'being the child

---

[26] I am not saying that this is required by moral equality of persons. Hence, I leave open the possibility that the fact that they are moral equals implies that it is permissible to draw (possibly weighted) lots between them.

of' is a relation which is fundamentally morally significant. This is consistent with the present account, because the requirement in question is not grounded in everyone's interests not being fundamentally, equally important, and parents can acknowledge that other parents have reason to give priority to their children.[27]

So much for what it is to be moral equals. Can the present account be extended to what it is to be equals in some of the other dimensions that I identified in Section 3.2? Let me start with the epistemic dimension:

> X and Y are epistemic equals if, and only if, the same basic epistemic rules and axiological principles apply to them and if, in accordance with those rules and principles, X and Y are equally important in whatever respects are fundamentally epistemically significant.

With one exception, this is a plausible extension of the notion of equality in the moral dimension to the epistemic dimension. The exception is that I have omitted the parenthesized 'other than the fact that people relate as equals', since while it might be morally significant that persons are epistemic equals, or at least that they treat each other as such, I am not sure that it makes sense to say that it is fundamentally important, epistemically speaking, that people relate as epistemic equals. That being said, the analysis is attractive and structurally analogous to the analysis of being moral equals. For instance, it allows that, non-fundamentally speaking, people are not epistemically equals, e.g. that some people are experts and that we have more reason to defer to their views on the areas on which they are experts than we have to defer to the views of non-experts.

The present analysis also allows for epistemic agent-relativity. Suppose you and I both observed the same car under similar circumstances. You saw it as green and I saw it as red and we both know this. Suppose I persist in believing the car is red, despite the fact that I can tell no story about why my observation is somehow more reliable than yours. On the present account, I do not treat you as my epistemic superior provided that I see no epistemic flaws in your similarly persisting in believing that the car is green. Things would be different if I persist in believing that the car is red and blame you, epistemically speaking, for not suspending judgement on the matter given that you know that I saw the car as red and can tell no story about why my observation is less credible than yours.

A similar extension gives the right result when it comes to social equals:

---

[27] Similarly, treating as equals is compatible with co-citizens giving priority to their co-citizens' interests over the interests of other co-citizens.

> X and Y are social equals if, and only if, the same basic normative social rules and axiological principles apply to them and if, in accordance with those rules and principles, X and Y are equally important in whatever respects are fundamentally socially significant (other than the fact that people relate to one another as social equals).

One natural objection to this account of what it is to be social equals is that for people to be social equals in this sense, social hierarchies, relations of authority, division of decision-making capacities etc. would have to be completely absent, and that seems completely utopian. There are two reasons why this objection does not defeat the present analysans. First, people who subscribe to the ideal of our being social equals might stress that, obviously, a state in which everyone is social equals is an ideal situation which we can strive to come as close to as possible, but that in light of other values, e.g. efficiency, we must compromise with social equality and accept relations of hierarchy etc. (cp. the pervasiveness problem, Chapter 2.6). However, this does not contradict the claim that whenever we can do without hierarchy and organize our social lives on a strictly egalitarian basis that is better. Second, friends of our being social equals might emphasize that the present formulation only pertains to those aspects that are fundamentally socially significant. Hence, they might say that at least some forms of derivative hierarchy etc. are compatible with social equality. For instance, it is compatible with social equality that a group of people, all of whom have equal decision-making power, (reversibly) delegate that authority to an agent who then has superior decision-making power.

Consider next being aesthetic equals:

> X and Y are aesthetic equals if, and only if, the same basic normative aesthetic rules and axiological principles apply to them and if, in accordance with those rules and principles, X and Y are equally aesthetically valenced in whatever respects are fundamentally aesthetically significant.[28]

I have substituted 'aesthetically valenced' for 'important', because the latter term seems tied to interests etc. in a way which aesthetic valence is not naturally seen to be. So qualified, the present account delivers the right results. It implies, for instance, that we relate to one another as aesthetic equals if men and women are judged in accordance with the same rules, e.g. that male and female bodies are both judged on the basis of how fit they

---

[28] I have omitted the parenthesized 'other than the fact that people relate to one another as equals' for a reason which is similar to why I omitted it in my account of being epistemic equals.

look, for instance. Also, it implies that racist norms of beauty are incompatible with our being aesthetic equals.

One might object to this account in a way which is similar to the way in which some might object to my account of our being social equals: everyone relating to everyone as being equally aesthetically valenced is utopian. Recall, for instance, Anderson's sufficientarian view in relation to the issue of ugliness: 'An alternative [to state-funded cosmetic surgery] would be to persuade everyone to adopt new norms of acceptable physical appearance, so that people with the birth "defect" were no longer treated as pariahs. This is not to call for the abolition of norms of beauty altogether. The norms need only be flexible enough to deem the person an acceptable presence in civil society. They need not entitle such a person to claim equal beauty to others, since successful functioning as a contestant in a beauty pageant, or as a hot prospect for a Saturday night date, are not among the capabilities one needs to function as an equal citizen' (Anderson, 1999: 335).[29] One might continue: to aim for anything more ambitious than that certainly goes much beyond anything that real-life egalitarians have ever had an interest in.

My response to this challenge is similar to my response to the related challenge to my account of being social equals. Everyone being aesthetical equals is utopian. However, people who successfully decide to adopt aesthetic norms that would realize such an ideal seem to realize the ideal of relating as equals to a higher degree than those who do not. Indeed, certain strains of the pansexual community do aim for attraction being based on personality (though, presumably, they allow for some people having more attractive personalities than others). In any case, little follows from what real-life egalitarians have been concerned with. For them it is important to be seen as non-utopian, and that alone suffices to explain why aesthetic equality is outside their focus.

Consider, finally, empirical equality. Here my analysans needs to be modified in light of the fact that it focuses on rules and principles. Instead I propose:

> X and Y are empirically equals if, and only if, they have the same, relevant empirical properties and to an equal degree.

---

[29] One might of course be sceptical of whether, in order to function as an equal citizen, it might not have to be the case that one has to be roughly as hot a 'prospect for a Saturday night date' as others, e.g. if people respond differentially to people on the basis of their looks even in political settings. It is unclear what Anderson's basis is for her view that once one is deemed to be 'an acceptable presence in civil society' that suffices for functioning 'as an equal citizen'.

As a matter of fact and possibly setting aside range properties, people are not empirically equals. However, this does not mean that it is irrelevant to define the notion. As I have already indicated, at least in some contexts and with regard to some matters, some people think that we have significant reason to relate as equals, empirically speaking. For instance, some people think that we ought to relate to one another as being equally talented, or at least not being unequally talented along the dividing lines between different, socially salient groups.

Together with the previous section, this concludes my analysis of 'treating as equals'. I divided the analysis into an analysis of 'treating as' – arguing that we can distinguish at least five different senses thereof: the normative, the motivational, the communicative, the expressive and the presuppositional notions – and an analysis of 'equals' – proposing definitions along the lines of all five dimensions identified in Section 3.2.

3.6   Regarding As Equals

Having analysed in Section 3.5 the first component – treating one another as equals – in what it is to relate as equals, I now turn to the second component – regarding as equals. This component in turn can be analysed into two components: regarding as equals, and being equals. Since I analysed the latter in the previous section, I can focus on what it is for someone to regard someone as something.

Initially, this seems simple – I regard X and Y as equals if, and only if, I consciously believe that X and Y are equals. However, this is not so, and to explain why not, I want to introduce two different distinctions. The first distinction is between cognitive and non-cognitive attitudes. Consider two different kinds of misogynists. The first kind believes that men have a higher moral status than women. The second kind believes that men and women have the same moral status, but would have liked things to be otherwise. Arguably, both misogynists do not regard men and women as equals, though for different reasons and in different ways. If so, the purely cognitive understanding of regarding as equals is inadequate. Whether we relate as equals is not just a matter of what we believe, but it is also a matter of how we respond non-cognitively.[30]

---

[30] In fact, this shows that my analysis of 'treat as __' is probably incomplete, because it needs to be extended to cover cases where '__' refers not to how the world is, but to how the world ought to be. For the purpose of understanding relational egalitarian theorists, this omission is less important, since their focus has been on cognitive conceptions of regarding as equals.

The second distinction I want to introduce is the distinction between explicit and implicit beliefs, as it were. Suppose someone asks me about whether I believe that a certain gender stereotype is accurate, e.g. that men are more assertive than women are, and I sincerely reply that I do not think it is and cite numerous psychological studies which show the stereotype to be inaccurate etc. Suppose, however, that in a psychological test I am much more inclined to pair the word 'assertive' with male faces and 'insecure' with female faces. Thus, while, at some level, I regard men and women as equally assertive, at another I regard men as more assertive than women. If so, regarding someone as __ is not merely a matter of conscious belief. It is also a matter of how, as it were, we implicitly regard people. This observation is important if for no other reason than for the reason that, as many psychological studies have shown, people's explicit and implicit beliefs can diverge quite significantly (Holroyd, 2017: 385–9).

Assuming that how people explicitly and implicitly regard one another can be separated, the question arises as to whether relational egalitarians care about how people regard others in only one of the two senses or whether they want people to regard one another as equals in both senses. Here I think the answer is pretty clearly the latter. Take for instance racism, which surely is a paradigm of the sort of thing that relational egalitarians oppose qua relational egalitarians (cp. Anderson, 1999: 312; Anderson, 2010b: 59). Generally, relational egalitarians oppose not just explicit racism, but also things like implicit racist biases. In her discussion of epistemic injustice, Anderson puts emphasis on cognitive biases which are 'difficult to control even by the most conscientious and well-intentioned agents. We usually are not aware of when our credibility perceptions are affected by prejudice. Even when we suspect ourselves to be affected by prejudice and take measures to block its discriminatory effects, the virtue of testimonial justice is largely forced to operate in the dark: we do not know how much we are prejudiced against a speaker, and so do not know how much to correct for this bias' (Anderson, 2012b: 167–8). In any case, suppose we move from a state in which people explicitly regard one another as equals but implicitly do not, to one in which they do both. It would be odd to say that this involves no improvement as far as the ideal of relating as equals goes.

This almost concludes what I have to say about different ways of regarding as __. One additional point that should be mentioned is a way in which regarding as equals is different from treating as equals. As I noted in Section 3.4, treating each other as equals presupposes that people can causally affect one another. This is unlike regarding one another as equals, since two people can regard one another as equals, even if they are unable to affect each other. On the plausible assumption that being socially related requires being able to affect one another, it follows that, taken in isolation, the latter of the two components in the ideal of relating as equals is not really a relational ideal.[31] Hence, to the extent that relational egalitarians are concerned with how people regard one another, part of what they are concerned about does not in a strict sense pertain to social relations.

I have now offered an analysis of what it is to relate as equals. My basic points are that relating as equals is a rather complex notion, and that it can be analysed in two different components: treating as equals and regarding as equals. When it comes to the 'as __' part, I argued that there are at least four different ways in which one can treat someone as __ (in relation to one of which I introduced a subspecies, the motivational notion). As far as the 'equals' part is concerned, I suggested that this involves ascribing equal authority and significance to the perspectives of different people. Finally, as far as 'regarding' is concerned I argued that non-cognitive and implicit attitudes also matter from a relational point of view. Eventually, we will see how this analysis of what it is to relate as equals helps us assess the claim that egalitarian justice requires that we relate as equals.

3.7 The Ideal of Relational Equality and Ideal Ways of Relating As Equals

While the account of what it is to treat one another as equals that I have proposed above captures much of what relational egalitarians care about, it does not capture everything. My general view here is that relational egalitarians often set themselves the task of not merely describing the ideal of relating as equals, but the more demanding task of describing the ideal way of relating as equals. In describing the latter, in effect they appeal to values other than the relational ideal.[32] This is unproblematic as long as we are clear about what we are doing, e.g. so that we do not, say, contrast the ideal way of relating as equals with the ideal of distributive equality (as opposed to the ideal way in which this ideal might be realized) and

---

[31] One could reply that whether one treats another as an equal depends on whether one regards another as an equal and that the requirement to regard one another as equals only applies in situations where one relates to another and, thus, potentially, could relate as equals, i.e. there is no obligation on the part of Earthlings to regard Martians as equals.

[32] Take for instance the following passage: 'social egalitarians are mainly concerned with the protection of every person's free and responsible agency *and* how people relate to each other' (Schuppert, 2015: 108 [my italics]).

conclude on that basis that the latter ideal is impoverished, abstract, soulless etc. Just as friends of distributive equality can and should be pluralists and concede that distributive equality is far from everything that matters, so can and should friends of relational equality. Hence, the present section is a plea for pluralist relational egalitarianism. Its substance consists of three examples of how relational egalitarians in effect appeal to values other than people relating as equals when they describe their ideal.

My first example is Jonathan Wolff's (2010: 337) notion of a socialist ideal of a society of equals. In such a society, 'each individual can think of themselves as valued as an equal'.[33] On my account of what it is to relate as an equal, it does not follow from the fact that people relate as equals that they can 'think of themselves as valued as an equal'. At most, what follows is that, in some relevant fundamental respect, all can think of themselves as valued no more and no less than others. So even if relating as equals in my sense is part of what Wolff has in mind, it is clearly not all of it. Does this show that my analysis does not capture everything that goes into relating as equals, or does it show that Wolff packs into the (socialist) ideal of relating as equals more than simply that people relate as equals?[34] I believe the latter is the case.

First, Wolff's concern that we can all think of ourselves as valued as equals does not directly pertain to social relations – whether an individual thinks of herself as being valued as an equal is not in essence a matter of her social relations to others. They might bear indirectly on this possibility in that social relations determine (in part) causally whether people can think of themselves in this way. However, Wolff's non-instrumental concern is with a certain individual capability and it is not clear why this concern cannot be captured within a distributive ideal.

Second, in describing his preferred socialist ideal of a society of equals, Wolff describes a particular way in which people can relate as equals and which allows us to realize other values as well. Consider a society in which everyone must think of herself as pretty worthless, but no more and no less worthless than everyone else, and relate to

---

[33] Much here hangs on what exactly Wolff means by 'can think'. Does he mean that it is warranted in light of how each individual relates to others and others relate to him or her? Or simply that it is not impossible for them to think of themselves as such? Also, as I read the passage it implies that everyone is valued *and* that everyone is valued as an equal. These two elements can come apart as when someone, who likes no kind of fruit, says that he values all fruits equally.

[34] Wolff might not disagree. The adjective 'socialist' might signal that he describes a specific ideal of relating as equals – one that differs from other ideals by virtue of which other ideals of relating as equals it encompasses. Also, in later work Wolff (2015: 220) distinguishes between 'a theory of social equality' and an ideal of social equality.

others on that basis. Such a society is far from ideal, but it is better in
one respect than a society in which everyone thinks of herself as pretty
worthless, though there are hierarchies of worthlessness. That respect is
that the former society is, for all its faults, at least one in which people
relate as equals.

Christian Schemmel is another relational egalitarian whose description
of the ideal of relational equality draws on values other than people relating
as equals. On his view, justice requires that the state express appropriate
attitudes in its dealings with individuals. To illustrate the inadequacy of
luck egalitarianism, Schemmel considers the following five scenarios
described by Thomas Pogge:

> [Now distinguish five] different scenarios in which, owing to the arrange-
> ment of social institutions, a certain group of innocent persons is avoid-
> ably deprived of some vital nutrient V – the vitamins contained in fresh
> fruit, say, which are essential to good health. The [five] scenarios are
> arranged in order of their injustice, according to my preliminary intuiti-
> judgment. In scenario 1, the shortfall is officially mandated, paradigmati-
> cally by the law: legal restrictions bar certain persons from buying food-
> stuffs containing V. In scenario 2, the shortfall results from legally
> authorized conduct of private subjects: sellers of foodstuffs containing
> V lawfully refuse to sell to certain persons. In scenario 3, social institutions
> foreseeably and avoidably engender (but do not specifically require or
> authorize) the shortfall through the conduct they stimulate: certain per-
> sons, suffering severe poverty within an ill-conceived economic order,
> cannot afford to buy foodstuffs containing V. In scenario 4, the shortfall
> arises from private conduct that is legally prohibited but barely deterred:
> sellers of foodstuffs containing V illegally refuse to sell to certain persons,
> but enforcement is lax and penalties are mild. In scenario 5, the shortfall
> arises from social institutions avoidably leaving unmitigated the effects of
> a natural defect: certain persons are unable to metabolize V owing to
> a treatable genetic defect, but they avoidably lack access to the treatment
> that would correct their handicap. (Schemmel, 2012a: 127; Pogge, 2008:
> 47–8)

On the assumption that all five scenarios involve the same distributive
inequality (something which, by the way, we cannot assume just because it
is stipulated that all five scenarios involve the same distribution of nutrient
V), luck egalitarianism is unable to explain why the first scenario is more
unjust than the later ones, and why the second scenario is more unjust than
the third, and so on and so forth.

This, Schemmel contends, is explained by the fact that the attitudes
expressed by state (in)action in the five scenarios are objectionable to

different degrees (Schemmel, 2012a: 133).[35] For instance, in the first scenario the state expresses 'open hostility', whereas in the last one it expresses 'mere neglect' (Schemmel, 2012a: 134). The important point here is that not all objectionable attitudes need to clash with having an egalitarian attitude, and Schemmel appeals to ways in which expression of attitudes by the state can be objectionable, even if not objectionable from the point of view of relational equality. Take hostility. For the sake of argument, grant Schemmel that expressing hostility, at least in a range of cases, makes an action unjust (and not just morally impermissible or *pro tanto* morally impermissible). However, hostility as such is not an inegalitarian attitude.[36] While it might be rare for a policy to express hostility to all groups within a certain logical space – say, men, women, transgendered people etc. – such a policy might well be objectionable, but it does not appear objectionable by virtue of the way in which the expression of hostility constitutes hierarchical social relations etc.[37] Hence, to the extent that we find it objectionable for the state to express (universal) hostility to its citizens, we have moved beyond setting out the ideal of relating as equals.

There is also reason to believe that Schemmel's account does not work as an account of relational justice even if that account is not egalitarian. The state can express attitudes towards a certain group of people even if there are no social relations which this group of people and the state are parties to. Suppose, for instance, that Turkey had killed all Armenians (and not 'just' 1.5 million Armenians) during the Armenian genocide and that Turkey refused to apologize more than a century later. In that case, there is no social relation between those individuals for whom contempt is expressed and the present state that expresses this attitude. The lesson to learn from this is that a concern for the expressive dimension of actions does not perfectly overlap with social relations and this, in turn, shows that

---

[35] Schemmel (2015: 159) seems to distance himself from the view that expressive concerns form the core concerns of relational egalitarians: 'the primary concern of liberal relational egalitarians is to rule out dominatory relationships, that is, relationships exposing some to the capacity of others to exercise arbitrary influence over them'.

[36] Schemmel claims that other things being equal, 'treating people with hostility is more unjust than displaying contempt for them, which in turn is more than neglecting them' (Schemmel, 2012a: 136). (Despite the wording here I believe that in all three cases Schemmel has the expressing of a certain attitude in mind, e.g. expressing neglect, and not just neglecting.) I am not sure I follow Schemmel here and, at any rate, he does not defend this claim. If in defending myself against a culpable aggressor I express hostility towards the aggressor, this seems less objectionable than expressing contempt.

[37] A similar point applies to the two other attitudes Schemmel (2012a: 134) mentions: contempt and neglect.

Schemmel's concern is not tied specifically to the nature of social relations.[38]

Consider, finally, my third example of a description of an ideal way of relating as equals: Samuel Scheffler's account of relational equality. Prior to presenting his deliberative constraint, Scheffler notes that

> [a] natural first thought is that the participants in an egalitarian relationship will have a reciprocal commitment to treating one another with respect. Each sees the other as a full-fledged agent who has the capacities associated with this agential status. Each expects the other to bear whatever responsibilities are assigned to a person in virtue of this status and, similarly, each sees the other as entitled to make whatever claims accrue to a person in virtue of this status. Moreover, neither participant is seen by either of them as possessing more authority than the other within the context of the relationship, and each sees the other as entitled to participate fully and equally in determining the future course and character of the relationship. (Scheffler, 2015: 24)

No doubt relating to one another in this way is valuable. However, people can relate as equals even if one or more of the components just mentioned is absent. Two conflicting parties can relate as equals even if they do not 'have a reciprocal commitment to treating one another with respect', e.g. they find it permissible that on some occasions they are not treated with respect by the other and permissible that they themselves sometimes do not treat the opposing party with respect.

In saying this, I do not believe myself to be in any substantive disagreement with Scheffler. He notes that 'the ideal of an egalitarian relationship draws on values other than equality itself. It draws on values such as reciprocity and mutual respect, and on a conception of the rights and responsibilities of agents . . . the ideal of an egalitarian relationship is a complex one, and . . . several of its elements draw on values other than equality per se . . . At the same time, the ideal also includes some distinctively egalitarian elements [of which Scheffler describes one – the egalitarian deliberative constraint]' (Scheffler, 2015: 24–5). The way I would describe this is by saying that the ideal of relational equality can be realized in various ways, i.e. the egalitarian deliberative constraint can be realized in different ways. Scheffler thinks that some of these ways are

---

[38] One might try to retain such a connection by saying that only when the state expresses attitudes about individuals to whom it relates can such expressions of attitudes be objectionable. This would be analogous to the suggestion on behalf of Scheffler's deliberative constraint that only when people have social relations to one another is it objectionable if they do not comply with the deliberative constraint (Chapter 7.5).

better than others and to specify those, we must appeal to values other than relational equality. Or to put this differently: the relational ideal, specified in such a way that it articulates a desirable way for people to relate to one another, draws on ideals other than relational equality. While Scheffler might think that relating as equals is only desirable once specified in a certain way, where it draws on values such as respect and reciprocity such that there can be no tragic conflicts between relating as equals otherwise specified and other values, my basic point in this section stands. That is, it is not an objection to my account of what it is to relate as equals that relating as equals in a way which is best involves more than my analysans. Scheffler might be a sophisticated pluralist, in that certain things are valuable – or, one might suggest, more valuable (Moore, 1989 [1903]: 27–30) – only when specified in ways that draw on other values, but my aim in this chapter has simply been to analyse what he refers to as being 'distinctively egalitarian'.[39]

   In sum: a number of relational egalitarians have offered descriptions of what, ideally, it is to relate as equals that go beyond my analysans. However, this is not an objection to my analysis, since its main aim is to articulate what it is to relate as equals, not to articulate what is the best way to relate as equals. For that purpose, we need to appeal to other values and in doing so we must concede that relational egalitarians, like distributive egalitarians, must be pluralists.

3.8   Conclusion

The overall ambition of this chapter has been to offer an analysis of relational egalitarianism that, ideally, is as precise as those that have been offered of distributive egalitarianism. Such an analysis serves to separate distributive and relational egalitarianism from one another, to lay the groundwork for an attempt to explain what is valuable about relational equality, and to display the fact that relational egalitarianism is a large family. In Section 3.2, I argued that 'relating as equals' is an abbreviation for 'relating as equals with respect to __' and identified five different dimensions along which people can relate as equals. I then argued in

---

[39] Scheffler expresses this point by saying that the distributive view postulates 'a normatively auton-omous value' – an equal distribution – whereas relational egalitarianism does not. However, while this might be true as a characterization of what actual proponents of distributive equality have proposed, it is not true as a characterization of distributive egalitarianism as such. Logically speaking, one could subscribe to a distributive view according to which an equal distribution is valuable only when realized in a social context that realizes other values too.

Section 3.3 that relating as equals combines two different components: treating one another as equals and regarding one another as equals. Sections 3.4, 3.5 and 3.6 then proceeded to analyse these two components. Section 3.4 analysed what it is to 'treat someone as __', and Section 3.5 what it is to be 'equals' along the five dimensions identified in Section 3.2. In relation to the first analysandum, I argued that there are at least four different senses in play regarding what it is to 'treat someone as __': the normative, the communicative, the expressive and the presuppositional notion senses. Section 3.6 analysed the notion of regarding as equal, emphasizing both implicit and non-cognitive attitudes in addition to explicit and cognitive attitudes. One main claim of this chapter is that relational egalitarians have not said enough about what it is to relate as equals, and I have employed some of the conceptual apparatus introduced in this chapter to cast light on the notions of relating as equals employed by a few relational egalitarians. In the course of doing so, I take myself to have shown that relational egalitarians might have quite different things in mind when they subscribe to the relational ideal. Finally, drawing on the works of three relational egalitarians in Section 3.7 I addressed the worry that my analysans does not capture everything relational egalitarians care about. My basic response to this worry has been to distinguish between relating as equals and relating as equals in the way that is desirable all things – values other than the value of relating as equals – considered. The wider upshot of this is to draw attention to the fact that, like distributive egalitarians, relational egalitarians can and probably should be pluralists about value.

CHAPTER 4

Equality and Being in a Position to Hold Others Accountable: A Case Study

4.1 Introduction

In 2007 Al Gore won an Oscar for the documentary *An Inconvenient Truth*, in which he calls on his fellow Americans to reduce their greenhouse gas (GHG) emissions. It only took one day before the Tennessee Center for Policy Research put out a press release accusing him of climate hypocrisy. According to the think tank, Gore's luxury mansion used roughly 'more than twenty times the national average of gas and electricity'. It submitted: 'As the spokesman of choice for the global warming movement, Al Gore has to be willing to walk the walk, not just talk the talk, when it comes to home energy use'.[1]

In response, Gore's spokesperson, Kalee Kreider, did not deny the consumption figures. Rather, she pointed out that the fact that Al Gore and his wife work from home boosted their home energy consumption and that they were in the process of installing solar panels. Moreover, Kreider noted that it was predictable that opponents of Gore's political agenda would 'go after him' in this way.[2] Imagine that instead Al Gore had responded personally to the criticisms as follows:

> True, my gas and electricity consumption is much larger than permitted by the principles that I subscribe to and exhort others to comply with. However, as former Vice President I have an elevated standing. While the same first-order moral principles apply to all of us – we all ought to reduce our GHG emissions significantly – different second-order principles regulating moral exhortation, blame etc. apply to us. As an elite person

---

[1] http://news.bbc.co.uk/1/hi/6401489.stm [last accessed 17 March 2017]. On some accounts, being willing to 'talk the talk' but not 'walk the walk' does not deprive one of the standing to advise people to 'walk' in the relevant way (Wallace, 2010: 317). In some cases, advice from someone who does not 'walk the walk' is better advice, epistemically speaking, since such a person knows what she is talking about. However, Gore was not simply advising people to reduce their GHG emissions, but also conveying the message that they were blameworthy if they did not do so.

[2] http://news.bbc.co.uk/1/hi/6401489.stm [last accessed 17 March 2017].

championing a good cause, I can hold you ordinary folks to account for your failure to comply with the relevant first-order principles. But you, average Americans, cannot hold me accountable for failing to live up to those same principles. In short, I am not accountable to you, but you are accountable to me.

Ms. Kreider's timid response did not make Gore's problems disappear, but one does not have to be a spin doctor to see that the present imaginary response would have been an outright disaster. This reflects a very deep way in which we relate to one another – even to good-cause, elite politicians like Al Gore – as equals. Perhaps the nobility in feudal societies could get away with, say, blaming commoners for their vices without the expectation that they themselves would be held to account for their comparable or even worse vices by commoners. But these societies were permeated with the view that people were not each others' equals and that, say, it would be presumptuous for a commoner to criticize a nobleman for failing to live up to shared standards, but not presumptuous the other way round.[3] Similarly, in a feudal society a virtuously non-patronizing, but otherwise faulty, nobleman might supererogatorily take a commoner's charge of hypocrisy seriously, but average Americans would not see Gore as exceedingly virtuous had he publicly taken the charge of climate hypocrisy seriously despite the lowly standing of his critics. Anderson puts it well: 'Social equals live on terms of reciprocity with one another, none imposing conditions on others that they would reject for themselves' (Anderson, 2008b: 265).

This egalitarian norm does not just reflect the relation between citizens. It is also a norm that regulates the relation between states (cp. Fabre, 2018). In its 2017 annual report on human rights, the US State Department criticized China for human rights violations, e.g. 'torture, executions without due process, repression of political rights and persecution of ethnic minorities, among other issues'. The main reply of China's State Cabinet was not to deny that these human rights violations took place. Rather, it was the following: 'With the gunshots lingering in people's ears behind the Statue of Liberty, worsening racial discrimination and the election farce dominated by money politics, the self-proclaimed human rights defender has exposed its human rights "myth" with its own deeds'.[4] In short:

---

[3] Elsewhere I have argued that praise can be hypocritical in a way similar to blame (Lippert-Rasmussen, 2012: 307–8). For present purposes, I limit myself to blame. Moreover, one can be hypocritical in ways other than by blaming or praising, e.g. one can do, like Al Gore, openly or in secret, what one urges others not to do.

[4] www.reuters.com/article/us-china-usa-rights-idUSKBN16G11N [last accessed 17 March 2017].

US criticisms of China should be dismissed, because in light of its own tainted record the United States has no standing to hold other states accountable for their human rights violations. To the extent that it nevertheless proceeds in so doing, it is acting hypocritically.[5]

None of this implies that China is not blameworthy for its human rights abuses. More generally, denying that one's blamer (or exhorter) has a standing to blame (or to exhort) is not denying blameworthiness (or that one really should do what the hypocrite exhorts one to do). Compare Al Gore to Saint Gore. Saint Gore is like Al Gore, except for the fact that despite his high income and wealth, he lives in a modest house, which, at significant cost, is designed to be GHG neutral, he never flies a jet, etc. Suppose Saint Gore had appeared in *An Inconvenient Truth* saying exactly what Al Gore did. Despite both Gores making the same exhortations, we would respond very differently to them. Saint Gore, unlike Al Gore, has, as one might put it, earned his right to urge us to change our ways – in that respect, he would be a much more effective critic, because climate change deniers etc. would find it harder to ignore the substance of what he says by focusing on how his own conduct diverges from what he is urging other people to do. Since there is no difference between what Al and Saint Gore are saying, the explanation for that fact cannot lie in *what* they are saying. The explanation lies in their being differently positioned to say what they are both saying.

This egalitarian view of the standing to blame is so deeply entrenched that we find it hard to imagine living in a society in which the second-order principle regulating blame were different. Perhaps in part for this reason, the idea of standing to blame is largely undertheorized in contemporary moral and political philosophy.[6] Specifically, no one has really addressed the issue of the egalitarian norms surrounding the standing to blame in the context of relational egalitarianism (cp. Cohen, 2013: 115–42; Dworkin, 2000: 182–8; Scanlon, 2008: 122–214; Smilansky, 2007: 90–9). The aim of

---

[5] Direct replies to blame include denying that one performed the action that one is being blamed for, and agreeing that one did it, but arguing that one's doing it was justified or excusable. Indirect replies do not address these matters, but involve a denial that the blamer has the standing to blame (Cohen, 2013: 119). Accusing the blamer of hypocrisy is one indirect reply to blame, but there are many others, e.g. one might respond that the blamer does not herself believe in the principle to which she appeals, as when a fundamentalist Islamist blames the state that imprisons him for violating his human rights; that the relevant blameworthy action is none of the blamer's business; that the blamer is complicit in the action; that the blamer has done something similar. The latter reply is the so-called *tu quoque* reply, which I distinguish from the hypocrisy reply below.

[6] Another reason might be that the notion of standing is a foundational notion, which cannot be analysed further (cp. Todd, 2017).

this chapter is to explain why this is a mistake and to make some progress in understanding why it is very fruitful to think of having a standing to blame in the context of relational egalitarianism. Relational egalitarianism can derive considerable support from the egalitarian nature of our norms regulating blame, and we can learn more about this ideal using the case of hypocritical blame as a case study. One important lesson we can learn from it is that the relational egalitarian ideal informs relations between persons in general and is not restricted to how the state should relate to its citizens (cp. Chapter 5.4). Another important lesson pertains to the nature of the value of relating as equals (cp. Chapter 6.5).

Section 4.2 characterizes hypocrisy and having a standing to blame. Section 4.3 takes a critical look at R. J. Wallace's egalitarian account of what makes hypocrisy morally wrong. While it is inadequate in a number of ways, its egalitarian focus is spot on. Section 4.4 considers wherein the value of anti-hypocrisy norms lies. I argue that while, generally, absence of hypocrisy is good for us, anti-hypocrisy norms are best understood as reflecting a basic deontic requirement to relate as equals. Or to put the last point differently: anti-hypocrisy norms conform to a basic deontic requirement to relate as equals. Section 4.5 connects the anti-hypocrisy stance with more common relational egalitarian themes and then moves on to note that, ironically, one prominent luck egalitarian, whom some see as inherently opposed to relational egalitarianism, G. A. Cohen, devoted considerable attention to the issue of hypocrisy-free social relations.

4.2   What Is Hypocritical Blame?

What is it to blame someone hypocritically? There are two distinctions which I need to draw attention to initially. First, there is a distinction between believing that someone has acted in a blameworthy way and actually blaming someone (Bell, 2013: 265–7; Sher, 2006: 112; Wallace, 2011: 366–9). I can blame someone without believing that they have acted in a blameworthy way, e.g. because I believe that blaming them for something which is in fact not blameworthy has certain good pedagogical effects that render my blaming them justified, all things considered. Similarly, I can believe that someone has acted in a blameworthy way without actually blaming them. I might deem that my daughter is blameworthy for being rude towards an annoying acquaintance, even though I find that I do not blame her, e.g. because I do not have any of the reactive emotions – resentment for instance – that are normally associated with or even constitutive of blame, and because I do not deem our relation to be impaired as a result of her blameworthy action. In merely judging someone to be blameworthy even when one is at greater fault oneself, one is not being hypocritical.[7] Similarly, had Al Gore not exhorted anyone to reduce GHG emissions, but simply expressed his belief that this is what we ought to do, nothing about his own conduct would have deprived him of the standing to express this view.[8]

There is a huge discussion about what exactly it is to blame someone. Some philosophers, e.g. R. J. Wallace (2010, 323; 1994: 18–83; Wallace, 2011; cp. Strawson, 1962), emphasize the having of certain reactive emotions, while others emphasize seeing one's relation to the blamee as one that has been impaired and thus revising the expectations and intentions that one has pertaining to the relationship (Scanlon, 2008: 122–214).[9] For the purpose of this book, I can largely set aside these differences. All I need to assume is that there is a distinction between merely judging someone to be blameworthy and actually blaming that person.

The second distinction to which I need to draw attention is between public and private acts of blaming. There is a difference between openly holding someone to account by venting one's anger and demanding that one's blamee apologize etc., and secretly bearing a grudge against someone. I shall focus on public acts of blaming, even though one can blame privately in a hypocritical way as well, and relating to someone as an equal might be incompatible with privately engaging in hypocritical blame too. The reason for the latter is that doing so involves not regarding the target of one's blame as an equal (cp. Chapter 3.3).

Having drawn these two distinctions, we can now ask what it is for someone to blame someone in a hypocritical way:

X blames Y for φ-ing in a hypocritical way, if and only if:

(1) X blames Y for φ-ing;
(2) X herself believes or should believe that she herself has done something which is relevantly similar to φ-ing;[10]

---

[7] Some deny that. If you do, think of my topic as a subclass of blamings.
[8] While it is irrelevant for present purposes what explains this asymmetry between blaming and judging in a merely cognitive sense, one might conjecture that the latter, unlike the former, involves no interpersonal demand for a certain uptake, e.g. an apology, on the part of others and that the right – or standing – to demand such an uptake is what hypocrisy undermines.
[9] One problem for Scanlon's account is that one can blame dead people and yet there seems to be no (non-contrived) way in which this involves a modification of my relation to the deceased. In some contrived sense it is possible to 'adjust one's intentions' regarding a deceased, e.g. one might decide no longer to lay flowers regularly on this person's grave. Wallace's account stands up better against the case of dead people, since, clearly, one can have reactive feelings towards dead people.
[10] φ-ing itself, of course, is relevantly similar to φ-ing, but so might other actions be.

(3)   X does not to a suitable degree or in a suitable way blame herself for her conduct which is relevantly similar to φ-ing;

(4)   it is not the case that X believes there are morally relevant differences between her own conduct relevantly similar to φ-ing, on the one hand, and Y's φ-ing, on the other hand, that justifies her blaming Y for φ-ing and not blaming herself for her own conduct relevantly similar to φ-ing to the relevant degree or in the relevant way (or it is the case that X has a belief to this effect but then X has so for insufficiently good reasons).[11]

Suppose that while up until now I have always done more than my fair share of household chores, for once I do not. Suppose my wife blames me for this. Here it seems natural for me to respond to her blame indirectly. Rather than (or in addition to) denying that I have not done my fair share, e.g. because given my previous greater efforts my fair share now is lower than what it would otherwise have been, and rather than conceding that I have not, but arguing that there are excusing conditions, I can respond that *she* has no standing to blame me for *that* and that insofar as she does so (ad. 1), she is being hypocritical. This is the case if, in addition to blaming me, she is well aware that while I have not done my fair share this week, there are many more weeks where she has not done her fair share (ad. 2); she does not blame herself for not having done her fair share these other weeks (ad. 3); and it is not the case that my wife believes that there are special reasons that make it more wrong not to do one's fair share of the household chores this week – e.g. none of us has to prepare for an important job interview – than not to do one's fair share in the weeks where she did not – or she believes there are such reasons but on insufficient grounds – e.g. that I mind doing household chores much less than she does, despite the overwhelming evidence suggesting this is not the case (ad. 4).

Before proceeding to the issue of what makes hypocritical blaming wrong, I should like to highlight some features of the present definition of hypocritical blame. First, in the standard case of hypocritical blame I engage in the very same behaviour as that which I blame others for. However, as (2) reflects, I can engage in hypocritical blame by blaming

---

[11]   One implication of this definition is that hypocritical blame need not involve any deception at all (cp. Wallace, 2010: 315). Perhaps one of the worst forms of hypocrisy is where powerful people blame oppressed people for faults everyone knows are dwarfed by the comparable faults of the blamers, but where these powerful people can rely on fear of their reprisal as something that will stop the oppressed people from drawing attention to the greater faults of their oppressors.

someone for, say, shoplifting even if I have never shoplifted myself. I can do so if I have, say, engaged in other forms of activity that are at least as wrong given the standards on the basis of which I condemn shoplifting (cp. Lippert-Rasmussen, 2012: 303–4). Suppose, for instance, that I condemn shoplifting on the grounds that it harms the interests of innocent people and that I have often been engaged in unprovoked, violent assaults on people. In that case, the charge of hypocrisy seems no less warranted than if I were a shoplifter rather than a violent assaulter myself.[12]

Note also that (2) takes a subjective form. Whether I blame hypocritically when I blame someone for shoplifting does not depend on whether I actually have shoplifted myself, but on whether I (have good reason to) believe that I have shoplifted myself. Suppose I have honestly and excusably forgotten about my own past shoplifting, but that my blamee is well aware of it. In that case, she can indirectly respond to my blame by denying that I have any standing to blame her – not because my doing so involves hypocrisy but simply because, as a matter of fact, I have done the very same thing for which I hold my blamee to account. This response is known under the label *tu quoque* (or 'you too'). It often goes hand in hand with the charge of hypocrisy, because usually people are (or ought to be) aware of their own wrongdoing. But sometimes they are not (nor is it the case that they should be) and in those cases the *tu quoque* reply might be appropriate, because it is not sensitive to the blamer's epistemic situation in the same way that the charge of hypocrisy is.[13]

---

[12] The morality of blame takes an interpersonal form which, in a certain important sense, rules out aggregation (cp. Chapter 6.3). Suppose my faults are much smaller than Ronald's. I blame him. Now comes along Ronald's twin brother, who is exactly like Ronald, and I blame him too. The same happens with Ronald's triplet and so on and so forth. Yet we will not reach a number of Ronalds such that the Ronalds can say to me that I am no longer in a position to blame *them* given that I am somewhat blameworthy too and that I have done a lot of blaming already. All that matters for standing to blame someone (not: its being permissible to blame someone) is that *relative to each of them* my faults are smaller. Suppose instead that I can either prevent a small loss in terms of welfare to Ronald or prevent a somewhat greater loss for myself. Many would say that it is permissible for me to prevent the greater loss to myself. Now comes along Ronald's twin brother, and it turns out that I can either prevent a small loss of welfare for both of them or prevent the somewhat greater loss for myself. Perhaps it is still permissible for me to prevent my somewhat greater loss. However, most think that, given that the losses in question are different in size but not radically so, there is a number of Ronalds such that it would no longer be permissible for me to prevent the greater loss to myself than to prevent the aggregatively much greater loss for the Ronalds. This is so despite the fact that *relative to each of them* my loss is greater.

[13] Suppose I have forgotten all about my own similar faults and could not reasonably have been expected to remember. In that case, I am not being hypocritical for not engaging in self-blame even if I can properly be silenced as a critic – or, at least, as one who merely criticizes others – once my own similar faults are pointed out to me *tu quoque*-style (cp. Todd 2017: 5–11).

Second, (3) reflects that I can blame others for conduct that I have myself engaged in without hypocrisy provided that I blame myself to a degree which is commensurate with the severity of my other-directed blame relative to the severity of the wrongness of my blamee's wrong. If my wife starts by conceding that, in the past, she did not do her fair share and sincerely blames herself for not having done so, I can no longer accuse her of hypocrisy for blaming me for not doing my fair share this week. To see why I need 'in a suitable way' in addition to 'to a suitable degree' in condition (3) consider a shoplifter who blames herself for shoplifting time and again. However, now she blames an occasional shoplifter without addressing her own shoplifting. Here it is not the ample degree to which she blames herself which is deficient, but the way in which she does so.[14]

Third, (4) reflects the fact that blame is situated in a wider network of normative beliefs and that many moral factors influence the wrongness of actions. Accordingly, even if the blamer has engaged in exactly the same kind of behaviour narrowly described, it might be that, from the perspective of the blamer, the two instances of blame are relevantly different. For instance, suppose that, unavoidably, I am much more sensitive to blame than the blamee is and believe that the justifiability of blame depends on the degree to which the blamee is harmed by being blamed. In that case, I might not be hypocritical when I blame my friend for shoplifting, but do not similarly burden myself with self-blame for exactly the same conduct. Another possible difference pertaining to otherwise similar actions are cases where the blamer and blamee stand in a certain hierarchical relation. Suppose a professor blames a student for being sloppy with the student's references in his writing. The student retorts – correctly – that so is the professor. The professor might correctly deny that she is blaming hypocritically provided that she believes that it is her job to educate the student and not the student's job to educate her (cp. the pervasiveness problem, Chapter 2.6, and the Al Gore example in Section 4.1). This is not to say that the professor's blame is appropriate. Blame can be inappropriate for many other reasons than that it is hypocritical.

The present definition focuses on cases where the hypocritical blamer believes that she has done something relevantly similar conduct to φ-ing. This is too narrow, as the following case – call it *illa quoque* (Lippert-Rasmussen, 2012: 297) – brings out. Suppose I blame Bertie for some

---

[14] I am grateful to Kartik Upadhyaya for clarification at this point as well as several others in this chapter.

action which is perfectly similar to one performed by Celia, yet I do not blame Celia for her perfectly similar action. Given certain additional assumptions, that Bertie, Celia, and I are all relevantly related, Bertie might dismiss my criticism as hypocritical.[15] Suppose, however, that Bertie and I are married and I blame Bertie for adultery, whereas Celia is a colleague of mine, whom I have just met once at a cocktail party at which others told me about her adultery. In that case, Bertie cannot dismiss my blame as being hypocritical on the grounds that I do not blame Celia. Celia is a stranger to me, whose misconduct is in general none of my business (cp. Lippert-Rasmussen, 2012: 308; Smith, 2007: 478, 483; Todd 2017: 2–4).[16]

Finally, note that my definition makes sense of the commonsense idea that hypocritical blame involves some sort of incoherence (cp. Wallace, 2010: 307) – namely, the incoherence of treating two cases, which from the perspective of the blamer are relevantly similar, differently. This concludes my discussion of the definition of hypocritical blame.

4.3   Wallace's Egalitarian Account of the Distinctive Wrongness of Hypocrisy

One question is what it is to blame someone hypocritically. Another question is what makes hypocritical blame morally wrong. This question presupposes that there is something wrong about hypocritical blame. I believe that there is and that most believe that there is. While I know of people who deny that there is anything wrong *as such* about hypocritical blame, I do not *think* I know of anyone who does not act *as if* they believed there is something wrong about hypocritical blame – at least when they, or people they care about, are subjected to hypocritical blame.[17] This is not to say that hypocritical blaming is always morally impermissible, all things considered. For instance, it might be permissible, all things considered, that Al Gore holds us to account for our irresponsible GHG emissions, if that would motivate us to reduce our GHG emissions. Still, this does not

---

[15] In a political context, indirect responses to blame often take this form, e.g. friends of Palestinians respond to those who blame Palestinians, or the relevant Palestinian organizations, for terrorism by pointing out that the blamer does not blame Israel for its putatively similar or worse acts targeting Palestinians or relevant Palestinian organizations in Gaza or the West Bank (or the other way round, if sympathies are reversed).

[16] Here I am not offering an account of which individuals are contextually relevant to blame. I am simply pointing to the fact that there is such a phenomenon as contextual irrelevance to blame.

[17] Some of my good, consequentialist friends say that their being disposed to act in these ways is justified because it has good consequences.

imply that there nothing wrongful about hypocritical blame. Or, at least, this is how one would describe a case like Gore and *An Inconvenient Truth* from a pluralist perspective.

Recently, R. J. Wallace (2010) defended an account of the wrongness of hypocritical blame which explicitly appeals to the equal moral standing of persons, which is interesting from the perspective of an inquiry concerning relational egalitarianism – a view which he does not address in his insightful article.[18] While central elements of his account of the wrongness of hypocritical blame must be rejected – in particular, Wallace's view that such an account can be based on the moral requirement to treat different persons' *interests* equally – I want to build on it to provide an account of the wrongness of hypocritical blame which, like Wallace's account, involves the ideal of equality and, more specially, crucially involves the ideal of relating as equals, but which has a broader scope than just interests and moral standing (cp. Chapter 3.2).[19]

According to Wallace, the core of the wrongness of hypocritical blame lies in the blamer not treating the interests of different persons as being equally morally important.[20] A hypocritical blamer fails to do so in two ways. First, he treats his own basic interest in avoiding blame as more important than the similar basic interest of his blamee. My complex stance when I am hypocritical 'attaches to my interests greater importance than it ascribes to yours, affording my interests a higher standard of protection and consideration than it affords yours. This offends against a presumption in favour of the equal moral standing of persons that I take to be fundamental to moral thought' (Wallace, 2010: 328). Second, a hypocritical blamer treats the victim of her own wrongdoing's interest in not being subjected to the relevant wrongdoing as less important than the interest of the victim of the blamee's wrongful action in not being subjected to the relevant wrongdoing. Because persons have equal moral status and because equal moral status implies that, presumptively at least, the equally important interests of people are equally morally important, in effect the

---

[18] Wallace (2010: 317) also submits that a hypocrite has no, or less of a, standing to blame. However, Wallace appears to believe that considerations about lack of standing do not provide the fundamental explanation of what makes hypocritical blame wrong.

[19] Interests are important, but they are not all that matters.

[20] Or, as Wallace puts it: the objection to hypocrisy is 'grounded . . . in the victim's interest in equal consideration and regard, an interest that is both second-order and essentially comparative in nature' (Wallace, 2010: 332). Wallace connects this concern with a 'system of social sanction and constraint that essentially involves the distribution of esteem and disregard' (Wallace, 2010: 333), thus connecting what it is to treat one another as equals with the distributive concern about the social goods of 'esteem and disregard'.

hypocritical blamer is committed to impermissibly denying the moral equality of persons.[21]

While there is something to this account, it cannot be right as stated here. Consider the second way in which Wallace contends that a hypocritical blamer fails to treat people as moral equals. Clearly, it is not true of hypocritical blame as such – nor does Wallace say so – that it involves unequal weighting of the interests of third parties. This is so for the simple reason that the victim of the hypocritical blamer and the victim of the blamee could be one and the same person (cp. Upadhyaya, forthcoming).[22] This means that it is the first way in which Wallace contends that a hypocritical blamer fails to treat people as moral equals that is crucial to his account.

However, a morally relevant interest in avoiding blame is also only contingently related to instances of blaming and, thus, cannot account for what makes hypocritical blaming *pro tanto* wrongful. There are three reasons why this is the case. First, as I noted at the end of the previous section in relation to the *illa quoque* reply, hypocrisy might lie in failing to blame some third party for that person's fault, which is similar to that of one's blamee. In this case, one is not giving any greater weight to one's own interest than to that of anyone else.[23]

Second, consider a case where, generally, I am a self-effacing person who gives the interests of others greater weight than my own interests. Hence, even if on this particular occasion I give greater weight to my interest in

---

[21] Arguably, on the normative, expressive and presuppositional notions of 'treating as __', the hypocritical blamer treats the blamee as well as the victim of her own wrongdoing as moral inferiors, thereby in effect denying moral equality (Chapter 3.4).

[22] Upadhyaya argues that it is not as if a hypocritical blamer whose victim is different from that of the blamee acts more wrongly, or blames with a less appropriate standing, than a hypocritical blamer whose victim is identical to that of the blamee's, as one would expect if Wallace were right and that the distinctive wrongness of hypocrisy is an additive function of the two wrong-making features of hypocrisy that Wallace identifies.

[23] Admittedly, the fact that I turn a blind eye to flaws of my friend might be an epistemic reason for thinking that I would turn a blind eye to similar flaws of my own if I had such flaws. However, it does not warrant an accusation of hypocrisy that one would give one's own interest in avoiding blame greater weight if, counterfactually, one had performed a relevant, similarly blameworthy action. In any case, Wallace might say that a blamer who is vulnerable to *illa quoque* fails in a non-egocentric way to give equal weight to the interests of different others. Admittedly, such differential blame might be completely accidental. But in that case, arguably, it is not hypocritical. If it is not completely accidental – say, I sympathize with the culprit I do not blame and do not sympathize with the culprit I blame – then my differential blame is hypocritical. However, in that case it also involves a culpable failure to give equal weight to the interests of others. *Pace* Todd (2017: 24–5), one's blamee might even have no duty (corresponding to one's right to blame) to apologize, make plans to avoid similar wrongdoing in the future etc. in response to (or on account of) one's blame expressed (or one's internally blaming the blamee) in the presence of someone who is a much greater sinner, albeit a sinner whom one sympathizes with.

avoiding blame than I do to that of my blamee, taking into account the wider context, it is not true in general that I give greater weight to my interests than I do to the interests of my blamee. Indeed, it might be true that, on the whole, I give greater weight to the interests of others. Still, my blaming could be wrongfully objectionable, in which case we must reject Wallace's account or refine it such that it becomes instance-relative, i.e. we should on each and every occasion treat people's interests as equally important. Such an account, however, might not be very plausible, since, presumably, whether, in a given instance, I treat another as an equal is in part determined by my pattern of actions in general.

Third, Wallace assumes that persons have a basic interest in avoiding blame. However, it is not clear that this is so (cp. Upadhyaya, forthcoming). Indeed, one might think that one has an interest in avoiding acting in a way that is wrongful, or wrongful and blameworthy, and that being blamed provides useful information and motivation in this respect. Suppose I believe that my interest in avoiding acting in a way that is wrongful or blameworthy is stronger than my interest in avoiding being blamed (where the latter derives from the unpleasantness that often comes with being the target of blame). Suppose, moreover, that I blame someone for something where I have done something similar myself. Here I could be engaged in wrongful hypocritical blaming even if, in light of the fact that I actually believe that I have an all-things-considered interest in being the object of blame whenever appropriate, it is not true of me that I treat my interest in avoiding blame as being more weighty than the similar interest of others. If so, Wallace's account must be rejected.

4.4 Why Not Hypocrisy?

In the previous section, I assessed R. J. Wallace's account of what makes hypocrisy wrong. His account is interest-based in that he thinks hypocrisy is wrong because it involves not treating people's interests as being equally morally weighty. Appealing to various cases which seem to amount to wrongful hypocrisy in the absence of differential treatment of different people's interests, I rejected this account. Still, Wallace is right to base his account of the wrongness of hypocrisy on the value of equality, even though I believe an egalitarian account of the wrongness of hypocritical blame should take a different shape.

Instead of a narrow focus on persons as interest-bearers, we could see them as interest- as well as attitude-bearers, i.e. as people who hold beliefs and emotions and do so in part in response to reasons. Arguably, in hypocritical blame one does not respect persons equally as attitude-bearers. That is, one blames someone else ignoring that one has reasons for blaming oneself on the very same or relevantly similar grounds. Since demanding the response one demands when one blames someone is inappropriate when one is the proper target of the same kind of blame, one in effect subordinates the perspective of the other attitude-bearer in hypocritical blame (cp. Frick 2016: 246).[24]

Here is an analogous situation involving disrespect for people as knowers. Suppose that you and I agree that one of us should do the cleaning today and that the person who should do it is the person who did not clean the house last time around. However, we have different recollections of who this is – you seem to recall that you did it last time around, while I seem to recall that I did. Neither of us can offer the other reasons why his memory of the matter is more reliable than the other's, and no issue of strategic misrepresentation of memories is at stake. If you nevertheless proceed to declare that since you did the cleaning last time around, now it is my turn, you treat me disrespectfully as a knower.[25] The only way in which I could accept your argument for why I should do the cleaning requires that I disregard my own status as a knower – one who happens to disagree with you – and simply take your word for what are the matters of fact (cp. Chapter 3.2).[26]

Something analogous takes place in the case of hypocritical blame. When I blame you hypocritically, in effect, I treat you disrespectfully as someone who forms attitudes about how you should respond to others on the basis of reason.[27] That is, I know that, since I have a similar or even worse fault than the one I blame you for, from your perspective it is no less fitting that you hold me to account than that I hold you to account. Hence, in demanding the uptake that follows from accepted blame, I ignore that

---

[24] No doubt this account requires elaboration beyond what I provide here. One example: suppose I blame you for some act, where I myself have committed relevantly similar acts on a much worse scale. However, I also know that you are unaware of this and do not even have any evidence available to you of my wrongdoing. Question: in what sense do I subordinate your perspective? I suspect the answer here must be that I ignore how I know things would look like from your perspective, if you were informed of the relevant facts.

[25] Things would be no different with regard to relating as epistemic equals, if we both recall that the other did the cleaning last and you proceed to declare that since I did the cleaning last time around, you will do it this time around.

[26] It seems that in accepting your decision and its motivation I both treat and, assuming that my treatment reflects how I regard you, regard you as my epistemic superior. Any, even several, of the five notions of 'treating as' that I identified in Chapter 3.4 could be at play in this example.

[27] This might not be the case when I know that you do not know that I am no less of a sinner myself. Here my hypocritical blame might be wrong for other reasons, e.g. the way in which I deceive you.

from your perspective, it is equally reasonable for you to make the same demand against me.

At this point you might ask where relating to one another as equals comes into the picture (cp. Frankfurt, 1999: 146–54; Raz, 1986: 217–44). Could we not simply say that justice requires that we respect each other as reasons-responsive bearers of attitudes and that the requirement of equality is a by-product in the sense that since we are all reasons-responsive persons, if we all treat each other as reasons-responsive persons, it follows that we relate as equals? I do not think so. The inequality is a necessary part of what makes the relevant hypocritical blame or the ignoring of your standing as a knower disrespectful. If, in my example involving conflicting memories, I ignore not only your recollection, but my own as well, I might disrespect you as a knower, but I do so in a different and, to my mind, less objectionable way than if I simply ignored *your* recollection. Similarly, if I invite a group of sinners to hypocritically blame someone else, I disrespect their status as reasons-responsive persons, since I simply presume that they accept my invitation to unreasonably exonerate themselves from blame. While this might be disrespectful, in a way it is disrespectful in a different and less objectionable way than in the case where I blame someone despite my being no less of a sinner. It is less disrespectful because it does not involve my treating them as less than an equal.

Some might object that there are two ways of not relating as an equal. First, one can treat the other as inferior. No doubt this is the standard case, e.g. I hypocritically blame someone in a way that presupposes that the target of my blame has no standing to hold me to account for my worse faults. However, one can also fail to relate as an equal by treating the other as superior. In the blaming case, we can imagine someone who condemns herself for a minor wrong and invites a much greater sinner to join her in condemnation of herself. Call such blame hypercritical. In the knowing case, we can similarly imagine someone who immediately accepts the other person's recollection as truthful. People might think that there is something objectionable about cases such as these – perhaps it is a vice to diminish oneself in these ways, perhaps one even wrongs oneself by not respecting oneself as a knower – but few will think that it involves wronging one's interlocutor (cp. Lippert-Rasmussen, 2012: 296, 302).[28]

---

[28] No doubt, in some cases one could argue that one wrongs one's interlocutor in various indirect ways, e.g. we have a duty to assist others in not deluding themselves about their own moral standing and in being hypercritical towards ourselves, we fail in relation to this duty.

So hypocritical – like hypercritical – blame is one way of not relating as equals. Yet people regard these two forms of blame quite differently – specifically, they think of the former, and more usual, form of blame as worse. One suspicion here is that this reflects that when people embrace the ideal of relating as equals, what they really embrace is something slightly different: that people do not relate to others as superiors. One motivation for this view is that one wrongs one's interlocutor when one relates to this person as a superior, but need not wrong anyone when one relates to others as an inferior – one could, but typically does not, wrong others by relating as an inferior, and one cannot wrong oneself. Or alternatively, people might embrace an ideal which is more demanding than that, but which still incorporates a self-other asymmetry: that people do not relate to others as superiors and, but to a lesser degree, not as inferiors either. Call the former view the asymmetric view and the latter the weakly symmetric view.[29] Call the view that the hyper- and hypocritical views are equally condemnable relative to the ideal of relating as equals the symmetric view.

One plausible suggestion here is the following. Hypercritical blame is much more rare than hypocritical blame. Hence, there is a temptation to move swiftly from the ideal of relating as equals to a condemnation of hypocritical blame without taking any notice of hypercritical blame. However, this is not because people do not subscribe to the symmetric view. It is simply because the former issue seems much less pressing in view of its rarity.

There are other reasons that speak in favour of the symmetric view – reasons that will be expounded more fully in Chapter 6, where I address the more general question of what makes relating as equals desirable. For one thing, both hypo- and hypercritical blame are undesirable in that, typically, they make people's lives worse. Both go hand in hand with having a deficient self-conception, to wit, over- or underrating oneself or, as one might put it, having too much or too little self-respect relative to the degree of merited self-respect.[30] Both things can certainly be extrinsically bad for us. Individuals' relations to others often fail, and in ways that are bad for all parties involved, because of people's deficient self-conceptions. Some might even take a perfectionist view on deficient blame and say that knowledge, especially self-knowledge, is an important aspect of well-being and that a deficient self-conception as reflected in deficient blame:

---

[29] In Lippert-Rasmussen (2012) I embraced the asymmetric view.

[30] 'Go hand in hand with' is a vague expression. It is meant to be consistent with the fact that a person can engage in hypo- as well as hypercritical blame without having a deficient self-conception, i.e. the mispositioned blame is simply a one-off not reflecting any self-conception deficiency.

to wit, hypo- as well as hypercritical blame – embodies lack of self-knowledge which, other things being equal, means that the deficient blamer's life goes less well than it otherwise would.[31]

At this point I should return to the self-other asymmetry. That is, suppose hypo- as well as hypercritical blame is bad for people. Are they equally bad for people? And if so, are they equally wrong?[32] I do not have much to say in response to the first question, which in part has an important empirical component. I want to emphasize, however, that hypercritical blame can harm not only the deficient blamer herself, e.g. by undermining her self-confidence, but it can also harm others, e.g. by luring them into indulging in mistakes about their own self-importance. This helps me in addressing an aspect of the second question: I do believe that hypo- and hypercritical blame are equally wrong per se. The most obvious reason for thinking otherwise is the belief that the former only involves harming others while the latter only involves harming oneself, but as we have seen, the two forms of blame do not differ per se in this regard. Yet even if they did, this would not make them differ per se morally speaking. That is, I am happy to say that agents have a moral option to sacrifice their own well-being, when that promotes the well-being of others, even when the well-being of others is promoted to a lesser degree than the well-being of the self-sacrificing agent is reduced. This supports what I called the symmetric view, i.e. the view that hypo- as well as hypercritical blame is bad from the point of view of the ideal of relating as equals and, thus, expressing that ideal as a matter of relating as equals (as opposed to, say, not relating to others as superior) really does capture the relevant relational value.

Let me end this section by considering a different challenge to the account that I have given. Suppose I know that a person takes an impersonal view of blame, i.e. he thinks that anyone can blame anyone for any blameworthy conduct and that a sinner can blame a (near-)saint no less than anyone else. Suppose, moreover, that I hypocritically blame this person, ignoring my own greater flaws, but that I would not have done so had this person held standard views about the standing to blame. Can I say that in blaming this person, I do not subject this person's perspective to my own, in which case not all cases of hypocritical blame involves

---

[31] This is not to deny that hypocrisy can come in handy in some respects and perhaps even in some cases result in the hypocrite living a better life, all things considered, than she would without a deficient self-conception.

[32] When it comes to well-being, arguably, if hypo- and hypercritical blame are not equally harmful, they are not equally wrong.

subordination of the blamee's perspective? I do not think so. For even if this person thinks that he is open to blame from me, from his perspective, it is also the case that, from his perspective, I am open to blame from him. In simply ignoring this fact, I subordinate his perspective to my own and, thus, violate equal standing.[33]

In sum: in this section I have proposed, first, that a plausible account of the wrongness of hypocritical blame points to how it subordinates the blamee's perspective to that of the blamer, where 'perspective' is broader than interests. Second, I have embraced a symmetric version of this view, suggesting that hypo- and hypercritical blame are equally wrongful.

4.5   Hypocrisy and Relational Equality

Typically, blaming someone involves a social relation between the blamer and the blamee and possibly others as well, e.g. bystanders to the blame. This is most obviously so in the paradigmatic case where one person publicly blames someone in that person's presence. However, blame need not involve social relations. If I blame another person in private and never express this, nor let how I behave towards anyone reflect my blaming this person, perhaps this is a case where blame does not involve or affect social relations.[34] However, such cases are rare. But whether or not I am right about this, because paradigm cases of blaming do involve social relations, then insofar as one cares about the egalitarian nature of social relations, one also cares about relations of blaming having an egalitarian character.

Suppose I am right that blame often involves social relations and that hypocritical blame is objectionable in part because of how it clashes with the ideal of relational equality. If so, it is interesting to note how hypocrisy

---

[33] Wallace correctly observes that 'there is nothing necessarily problematic about failing to care equally about all items that one takes to instantiate evaluative properties of a given type' (Wallace, 2010: 327). Suppose that it so happens that all of us are only interested in blaming one particular person (say, our partner), even though everyone is equally blameworthy. Perhaps there is nothing wrong about such a situation. However, at the very same moment the blamee turns attention to the fact that others have a case to answer as well, then brushing aside or ignoring this response is hypocritical and wrong. Rarely in cases of hypocritical blame is it true that the blamee is simply only interested in their own faults and not exercised about similar or worse faults of others. I write 'rarely' and not 'never' because there are some such cases, e.g. parents with a strained relation with their children might simply not care about their children's blameworthy behaviour, even if they care a lot about their own failings in relation to their children. Also, perhaps it is wrong for blamers not to be concerned about their own blameworthy actions.

[34] Perhaps this shows that relational egalitarians care about more than social relations. They also care about how we regard one another independently of how this manifests itself in our behaviour (cp. Chapter 3.6).

plays an important role in the work of G. A. Cohen (2013: 115–42). Despite his impeccable luck egalitarian credentials, Cohen was very alert to this egalitarian aspect of blame and moral exhortations, whereas, to my knowledge, social relational egalitarians have yet to address hypocritical blame and related phenomena. The ironic twist to this point serves as an important qualification to Anderson's theorist-focused critique of luck egalitarianism (Chapter 2.3). An additional ironic twist is that Cohen himself never elaborated the connection between his ideas about being in a position to blame, on the one hand, and relational egalitarianism, on the other. There are two features of Cohen's account that I want to draw attention to: first, his discussion of who can condemn the terrorists and, second, his discussion of the incentive argument for inequality.

In relation to the former issue, Cohen distinguishes between two ways in which one can fail to be in a position to blame others. First, one can have committed the same, or equally bad or even worse, act as the one for which one blames someone else. This is the *tu quoque* reply, which I have already mentioned. Second, one can be relevantly involved in the blamee's blameworthy action, either by having somehow been involved in causing that action or by depriving the blamee of reasonable alternatives to that action for which one blames the other. Call this the *complicity-based reply*. Both indirect responses to blame attest to the egalitarian nature of norms regulating blame.

Consider first the *tu quoque* reply, i.e. that one is not in a position to state the truth about someone's blameworthiness with 'vehemence and indignation . . . and in the posture of judgement' (Cohen, 2013: 116) when one's own faults are at least as bad. In blaming you for a fault which is similar (or worse) than my own fault, I imply that you are accountable to me for your fault, e.g. that you are under a normative requirement to explain yourself to me. However, by in effect brushing aside that I have a relevantly similar case to answer for to you, I am acting as if the relevant normative principles regulating blame somehow put me in a superior position relative to you (recall the Anderson quote in Section 4.1).[35] In this sense, hypocritical blame is incompatible with relating to one another as moral and social equals and to the extent that individuals, or institutions, or individuals in institutional roles, blame hypocritically, they instigate inegalitarian social relations.

---

[35] The relevant exception need not involve a denial that the relevant first-order normative principles apply to oneself too. Our hypocritical blamer says: 'What I did was at least as wrong as what you did. Still, I don't have to justify myself to you, but you have to justify yourself to me'.

Second, consider the complicity reply. It too reflects the egalitarian nature of norms regulating blame and for much the same reasons. That is, relations are symmetrical in the sense that if you are answerable to me for φ-ing, then I am similarly answerable to you for, e.g. assisting you in φ-ing, or for making φ-ing the only reasonable option for you. To use Cohen's example and setting aside a lot of controversial issues, if Palestinians have a case to answer for terrorist atrocities, then Israelis have a case to answer for occupying the land on which Palestinians live and for preventing them from forming a state and, thus, any conventional military option for resisting their oppression. Hence, if my blame reflects that I only acknowledge one side of the situation, I am in effect treating your different perspective as subordinated to my perspective. Or, to put things in a way which is more recognizable from the perspective of relational egalitarianism, I am in effect subordinating you or, as some feminist philosophers put it in the debate about pornography, silencing you (cp. Langton, 1993).[36]

Some might challenge this analysis as follows: suppose we lived in a world in which hypocritical blame is universally accepted. No one dismisses hypocritical blame and no one thinks that they are entitled to dismiss hypocritical blame – even (near-)saints have a case to answer to sinners. Would not that too be a world in which we relate as equals, albeit in a different way from how we in fact do, such that to the extent that we deem our way of relating as equals better than this way, this reflects some value other than the value of relating as equals?

I think this reply is correct at one level – that is, in some abstract sense this social world is one in which we relate as equals. We do so in the sense that the same norm regulating blame applies to all of us. However, it is an abstract sense that allows for a multitude of instances of giving and receiving blame which are inegalitarian in the sense that they all involve the parties subordinating their interlocutor's perspective to that of the blamer's own perspective. Admittedly, things can be reversed immediately thereafter in that the former recipient of hypocritical blame can blame her former hypocritical blamer and have her blame accepted. Indeed, we can imagine a world of sinners in which blame is always reciprocal – whenever X blames Y for an act, Y will, cacophonously, blame X for another act – and

---

[36] Something of the reverse kind happens when, say, well-intentioned British people blame British colonialism for the violent conflicts in the Middle East, but refrain from (proportionately) blaming (any or some of) those Middle Eastern agents who commit violent acts, or any other perpetrators of relevant historic injustices. This sort of submissive self-blame too is incompatible with relating as equals.

always hypocritically. We can even imagine that individuals in this world are reflective and egalitarian to the extent that they fully accept that they are the targets of hypocritical blame and that they recoil at the thought of someone blaming hypocritically without accepting being hypocritically blamed. This world, while, *ceteris paribus*, certainly better than, say, one in which some groups of people, e.g. clergy and nobility, are not answerable to others, e.g. commoners and slaves, is still not ideal from the perspective of relational equality. This is the case, first, because of the many instances of blame in which some people's perspectives are subordinated to those of others, and, second, because of the universal disposition to subordinate the perspectives of others in acts of blaming. For this reason, our norms regulating blame embody a fuller and more plausible understanding of what it is to relate as equals (cp. Chapter 6.5).

I now move on to Cohen's critique of the incentives argument, in which hypocrisy plays an important role, though one which Cohen foregrounds to a lesser degree. In that critique, Cohen explores what a Rawlsian incentives-based justification of inequalities looks like if we imagine talented people addressing untalented people, urging the latter to embrace inequalities.[37] In the course of so doing he likens the situation to one in which a kidnapper offers the parents of the child whom he has kidnapped an argument along the following lines for why the parents should pay the ransom: 'Kids should be with their parents. Unless you pay me the ransom, little Hank won't be with you. Thus, you should pay me the ransom'. As Cohen points out, kidnapping-cum-offering-this-argument manifests many vices and one of them is hypocrisy. 'Why', the parents might reasonably well ask, 'did you kidnap little Hank in the first place and why do you not simply return him given that you yourself believe that kids should be with their parents?' Appealing to this principle without being willing to put one's money – *in casu*, one's prospect of a ransom payment – where one's mouth is by not kidnapping other people's children is hypocritical.

According to Cohen, once we imagine talented people defending incentive-based inequalities to untalented people appealing to the difference principle, we see that something similar is going on. Imagine talented people arguing: 'You should be as well off as possible. Unless we get handsome incentives for our efforts, you will be less well off than you could be. Thus, we should get incentives'. According to Cohen, untalented people can respond in a way reminiscent of how Hank's parents can

---

[37] Cohen mentions the interpersonal test in relation to his discussion of who can condemn the terrorists in Cohen (2013: 119n8).

respond to their child's kidnapper: 'Why, if you think that we should be as well off as possible, do you insist on incentives for your efforts?' Cohen believes that, in the standard case and like the kidnappers, talented people can give no good answer to this question. Moreover, given that talented people are aware of the fact that they could make worse-off people better off by refraining from demanding incentives, their attempt at persuading untalented people to accede in their demand for incentives is hypocritical.[38]

Cohen connects his critique of incentive-based justifications for inequality with what he calls the interpersonal test: 'This tests how robust a policy argument is by subjecting it to variation with respect to who is speaking and/or who is listening when the argument is presented . . . If, because of who is presenting it, and/or to whom it is presented, the argument cannot serve as a justification of that policy, then whether or not it passes as such under other dialogical conditions, it fails (*tout court*) to provide a comprehensive justification of the policy' (Cohen, 2008: 42).[39] This test shows that an incentives-based justification of inequality is not robust, because even though it might serve as a justification from a third-person perspective, it cannot do so once talented people utter it to untalented people. Talented people must relate differently than mere bystanders to premises about what they will do in the absence of incentives: to wit, they cannot see this simply as a matter of prediction but must see it as a practical matter, i.e. a matter of deliberation for them about what they should do. The fact that, according to Cohen, talented people, in the standard case at least, argue hypocritically if they were to appeal to the difference principle shows why an incentives-based justification for inequality from within a Rawlsian perspective cannot pass the interpersonal test.[40]

In a critique of luck egalitarianism in which Anderson constructs a multidimensional dichotomy between luck and relational egalitarianism, Anderson embraces the interpersonal test and connects it with Darwall's

---

[38] It, and the disposition itself as opposed to their stating it, might be bad, even worse, in other ways as well.

[39] Suppose we seek to justify a certain policy, P, and one premise in that justification is a premise about how a certain group of people will act when P is in force. Then P is comprehensively justified only if it is justified for these people to act in this way. Often policies, e.g. crime prevention policies, are at most non-comprehensively justified, since they address the fact that people act in ways which are unjustified.

[40] One aspect of the standard case is that talented people do not believe that it is something like a law of nature that holds independently of their wills that worse off people will be even worse off in the absence of incentives.

idea of a second-person standpoint (cp. Chapter 7.3).[41] Some might try to explain what is wrong with hypocritical blame by appealing to Darwall's idea of a 'second-personal address'. To use his illustration of the idea: if I stand on your foot you can address me in two ways in order to give me a reason to remove my foot. You could give third-person reasons, e.g. that we have reason not to cause harm. Or you could simply demand that I remove my foot (unless, perhaps, if, at the same time, you are standing on my foot). In so doing, your demand would in itself give me a second-person reason to remove my foot. This is something you can do because it is your foot – it would not give me a second-person reason to move if you simply told me to do so assuming I was standing in a public space not causing you any form of suffering etc. – and this gives you second-person authority over the matter. On this account, unlike a non-hypocritical blamer who is suitably related to the blamee, a hypocritical blamer has no second-person authority to blame and accordingly the fact that *she* blames the blamee gives the blamee no reason to feel and express remorse, to apologize, or to promise improvement. Still, third-person reasons of the relevant sort still apply, which explains why people other than the hypocritical blamer are in a position to blame and, presumably, also explains why the hypocrite can still think that the blamee acted in a blameworthy way.

This account is, while suggestive, problematic. First, we can imagine cases of hypocritical blame in which the blamer cancels any implicature to the effect that there are second-person reasons involved or that she is relying on second-person address. Imagine a blamer who says: 'You should not feel ashamed, express remorse, apologize etc. because *I* say you ought to or because *I* point out how blameworthy your act is. In short: don't answer to me. You should feel ashamed because that is how in fact you should think about yourself in relation to this case. And you should not apologize or justify or explain yourself to me, but you should do so to your victim'. This person blames hypocritically even if, by her statement, she explicitly distances herself from any claims to second-person authority and, thus, on the relevant account, does not do anything that she does not have a standing to do. Even the act of pointing to Darwallian third-person reasons requires a moral standing not undermined by hypocrisy etc.[42]

---

[41] While Anderson appeals to Darwall, she largely borrows her description of second-personal justifications from Cohen, who according to her dichotomous map of the landscape of egalitarian political philosophy is supposed to subscribe to a third-person mode of justification.

[42] Perhaps this is tricky because, arguably, her very act of blaming the person claims second-personal authority despite disavowing it (cp. Kukla and Lance, 2009: 109).

Second, it is difficult for the Darwallian account to make sense of why one regains one's standing to blame, once one accompanies one's blame of another with an appropriate dose of self-blame. Why cannot one respond to a suitably self-critical blamer that it is fine that he blames himself for his greater faults, but this does not restore his second-person authority to blame others?[43]

The main lesson for our purposes to take away from Cohen's views of who has a standing to blame terrorists and his view about having the standing to justify inequalities in a certain way is the following: while Cohen is probably *the* paradigmatic luck egalitarian, he was very much alert to issues that are best characterized as issues of relating as equals.[44] In fact, as his discussion of the incentives-based justifications of inequality shows, even his discussion of which distribution of goods is required by justice is influenced by his idea of mutual justification in a way which arguably reflects a second-person standpoint. This means that if, like Elizabeth Anderson, we are in the business of drawing a distinction between different *theorists* of egalitarian justice, we have the problem that some theorists, like G. A. Cohen, belong to both camps (Chapter 2.3). This might not say much about *theories* of justice as such: perhaps the right way to see the fact that Cohen subscribed to both a distributive and a relational ideal of equality is to infer that there was some deep tension in his position. However, it should alert us to the fact that distributive and relational ideals of justice might be perfectly compatible and, in fact, might both be grounded in some deeper moral truth (Chapter 7.6).

4.6 Conclusion

In this chapter, I first defined hypocritical blame. Crucial to this definition is a certain kind of incoherence between the fact that one condemns others for failing to comply with certain principles which one oneself similarly, or to an even greater degree, fails to comply with. I then scrutinized Wallace's interest-focused egalitarian account of what makes hypocritical blame distinctively wrong. I argued that his focus on interests is too narrow,

---

[43] Perhaps Darwall might say that the relevant second-personal authority is constitutionally egalitarian and that once the blamer acknowledges through a suitable degree of self-blame that answerability is symmetrical between blamer and blamee, he has not resigned membership of the community of people with equal moral standing, as it were. Alternatively, one might say that, precisely because the agent makes no second-personal address, the agent does not engage in blaming as opposed to something which is closely related to blame.

[44] I return later to his views on other topics (Chapters 8.3 and 8.7), which also attest to the truth of this claim.

but endorsed his basically egalitarian approach to the topic. I suggested, more broadly, that what makes hypo- and hypercritical blame wrong is that it involves subordinating one person's perspective to that of another's. The ideal of avoidance of such subordination, I suggested, is best construed such that it requires that hypo- and hypercritical blame be avoided at any given moment. Since the relation of blaming someone is – at least in paradigmatic cases – a social relation, I argued that these claims about blame bear on how, more generally, we should understand the ideal of relating as equals (cp. Chapter 6.4.). Then in Section 4.5 I drew attention to how the idea of having a standing to blame or even assert certain truths – an idea which is central to the notion of hypocritical blame – plays a prominent role in the work of a paradigmatic proponent of a distributive ideal of justice, i.e. G. A. Cohen. This fact should alert us to the possibility that the distributive and the relational ideals of justice are consistent, perhaps even deeply connected.

Suppose that part of what it is for people to relate as equals is for them not to engage in hypo- or hypercritical blaming. In that case a question arises which is analogous to a question that relational egalitarians have asked in relation to distributions of goods. A number of them – Anderson, Scanlon and Scheffler – have argued that while distributive inequalities per se are compatible with relational equality, as a matter of fact relational equality is incompatible with large distributive inequalities, which thus, for purely instrumental reasons, are undesirable from a relational point of view. Are there similarly other features that society can have which are not in themselves objectionable from the relational point of view, but which in a similar way should be avoided for instrumental reasons because of how they induce hypo- and hypocritical blame?

I conjecture that there are at least two such features. First, segregation facilitates hypocrisy because it isolates people from the perspective of others and thus eases the pressure they face in the direction of having to justify themselves to others. Since segregation, geographical as well as social, often goes hand in hand with economic inequalities, there seems to be at least one important instrumental reason for why, if we want live in a non-hypocritical society, we should reduce economic inequalities or, alternatively or additionally, prevent them from translating into segregation.

Second, power asymmetries, I conjecture, have a similar effect. The mere presence of others, of course, does not make one aware of the perspective of others. Hence, if power asymmetries allow us to count on not being confronted with the perspective of others, this in itself might render us more hypocritical. Since relational egalitarians are explicitly preoccupied with power asymmetries even though it is unclear why this concern cannot in part, at least, be perfectly well articulated within a distributive paradigm (cp. Chapter 7.4), interestingly, the present discussion suggests that one aspect of the relational ideal gives us an instrumental reason to promote certain states of affairs in the interest of realizing other aspects of the relational ideal. In short, perhaps the important political implication that follows from this chapter is that in relating as equals it is important to a truly egalitarian society that it is an integrated one, i.e. that its citizens are often confronted with the perspectives of others.[45]

---

[45] Something similar might be true of a global egalitarian community. I should add that I am not suggesting, optimistically, that with a large amount of awareness of the perspectives of others, we will get rid of hypocrisy etc. completely. However, I do think it is one important means of reducing the degree to which we relate as unequals.

PART II

Site, Scope and Justification

CHAPTER 5

Egalitarian Relations: Time, Site and Scope

5.1 Introduction

According to relational egalitarians, we ought to relate as equals. Often they have in mind an exemplar of the sort of relations to which this ideal applies: political relations between normal, rational adult co-citizens debating public affairs in the town hall. However, many relations unavoidably, or perhaps unproblematically or even preferably, involve some form of hierarchy (cp. Chapter 2.6). Hence, it is important to delimit the scope and site of the ideal on principled grounds. For instance, does it speak to the relations between people in the private sphere, such as child–parent relationships? One would expect relational egalitarians to favour non-authoritarian family relations over authoritarian ones. However, it is difficult to see how the relationship between five-year-olds and their parents could fully realize the ideal of relating as equals without a problematic watering down of the requirements of this ideal. This constitutes what I shall call the *problem of relational equality at the margins*, so to speak. More generally, this chapter discusses a number of different dimensions along which relational egalitarianism might be specified in different ways.

Section 5.2 raises the problem of intergenerational justice. Does the ideal of relating as equals extend to past and future generations? Because, by definition, the social relations that normally embody treating one another as equals are absent in our relations to past and future individuals, relational justice appears to have little to say about obligations to future (and past) generations.[1] Hence, if relational egalitarianism is meant to replace luck egalitarianism as a complete account of egalitarian justice, it had better

---

[1] According to my analysis of relating as equal, X and Y relate as equals only if they treat one another as equals and that again requires that X and Y can affect their respective situations in a relevant way (Chapters 3.3 and 3.4). Such reciprocal treating as equals never obtains between past and future generations, since future generations can never relevantly affect the situation of past generations.

provide some account of how the ideal can be extended to an intergenerational context. Section 5.3 turns to another issue about relational equality and time: the relation between different age groups. Some distributive ideals take a whole-lives perspectives on distributive equality, while others take a sub-whole-lives perspective in addition to that. On this view egalitarian distributive justice requires not just that people's lives as a whole are equally good, but also that different corresponding segments, perhaps even particular moments, of their lives are equally good (cp. Bidadanure, 2016; McKerlie, 1996; 2012; Temkin, 1993). I argue that there is a similar distinction between different relational accounts of justice, some of which focus on whether people relate as equals when we take into account their relations over their entire lives, and some of which also, or simply, require that people relate to others as equals at any given moment in their lives. I argue that there is something to be said for both ways of specifying the ideal and that Anderson's and Scheffler's accounts have different implications regarding this matter.

Section 5.4 turns to the site of relational equality. In connection with distributive justice there has been a debate, especially in relation to the difference principle, about whether distributive principles apply only to the basic structure of society, as Rawls thinks they do, or whether they govern people's actions in their daily lives as well, as Cohen believes (Chapter 4.5). There is a similar question to be asked about relational equality and, as we shall see, different relational egalitarians answer it differently. I argue that a broad-scoped account – one which says that the ideal of relational equality applies to any social relation – is the more plausible one, even if what it means to relate as equals will vary across different kinds of social relations. Section 5.5 turns to the issue of the scope of relational equality, or, more precisely, to the issue of cosmopolitan versus non-cosmopolitan accounts of the ideal of relational equality. Again, we are familiar with this issue about scope from debates about distributive equality, where friends of distributive equality divide into those who think that the requirements of egalitarian justice are limited by state borders, and those who think that they extend further and reach out to all of humanity (and possibly beyond). To date, relational egalitarians have tended to take the former view. Anderson's democratic equality, for instance, is an ideal that pertains to co-citizens who exercise political self-determination through their state. However, cosmopolitan relational egalitarianism is a possible, though presently less well-explored, position. I will suggest that it might cohere better with the underlying rationale for the ideal (cp. Nath, 2015: 186–208; Nath, 2011; Schemmel, 2012b). In the course of motivating this suggestion, I say more about the question of the proper relationendum of relational justice.

This chapter makes three main claims. First, it argues that relational equality comes in many different versions, a fact which has not received the attention that it deserves. One driving motivation here is to develop the strongest possible form of relational egalitarianism. Second, the ways in which different relational theories differ are strikingly similar to the ways in which different ideals of distributive equality are different. The proverb has it that there is nothing new under the sun. I will not say that, but I will say that the issues considered in this chapter suggest that relational equality represents less of a break with, if for a moment I may use Iris Marion Young's phrase, the 'distributive paradigm' than some think it does. Third, because justice extends beyond the reach of social relations, justice needs to have, in part at least, a distributive focus. Relational justice does not extend to the margins of justice, as it were. This claim means that those who think the relational ideal can replace the distributive ideal are mistaken, and it provides some support for the efforts expended in Chapter 7 to defend a pluralist version of egalitarian justice, which includes relational as well as distributive elements.

5.2   Intergenerational Justice

In this and the next section I discuss two questions pertaining to relational equality and time which, really, are two specific questions regarding the scope of relational equality: the question of justice between different generations of persons who live lives that do not overlap in time, and the question of justice between people belonging to different birth cohorts but whose lives overlap, e.g. what justice requires regarding co-existing young and old people. The first question is often called the question of inter-generational justice. The other question, which I will address in Section 5.3, I shall refer to as the question of justice between age groups. My main aim in bringing up the question of intergenerational justice is to defend the claim that not all requirements of intergenerational justice can be grounded in a concern for egalitarian social relations.

Here is a simple argument:

(1)   Intergenerational justice pertains to justice between different genera-tions whose lives do not overlap.
(2)   Different generations whose lives do not overlap do not have any social relations.

(3)   If relational egalitarianism provides a complete account of the requirements of justice, then justice does not pertain to relations between groups of persons who do not have any social relations.

(4)   However, justice pertains to the relations between different non-overlapping generations (i.e. intergenerational justice is at least a part of a complete account of the requirements of justice).

(5)   Thus, relational egalitarianism does not provide a complete account of the requirements of justice.[2]

This argument strikes me as compelling. The first premise is definitional and incontroversial – it simply states in a pretty standard way what the topic of intergenerational justice is. The second premise is uncontroversially empirically true, e.g. when philosophers discuss matters of intergenerational climate change, it is – regrettably, for us at least – true that those who belong to the present cohort of people emitting GHG will not exist when the cohort of people who will be born in 2097 come into existence. The fourth premise is not indisputable, e.g. some Hobbesian contractarians argue that since there can exist no cooperation for mutual benefit across non-overlapping generations – later generations cannot benefit earlier generations – norms of justice do not apply to the relation between different generations. However, the view that there is such a topic as intergenerational justice is the dominant view and while this does not make it true, I shall allow myself to take it for granted, believing that most readers of this book will share it (cp. Barry, 1989: 189–203; Gosseries & Meyer, 2009: Rawls, 1999: 283–93).[3] This leaves me with the third premise.

Relational egalitarians could deny the third premise, if they can either show that relational egalitarianism does not imply that relations of justice cannot obtain between people who are not socially related, or if, alternatively, they can show that, despite what may seem to be the case, non-overlapping generations do have social relations.[4] Let me start with the first

---

[2] Similar arguments can be made with regard to animals and to human beings who are so cognitively impaired that we cannot have social relations with them. For simplicity, I restrict my attention here to intergenerational justice.

[3] O'Neill (2008: 134) thinks that there is nothing unjust about Inca peasants being worse off than we are because this involves neither stigmatization, domination, reduced self-respect on the part of the worse off, servility nor prevention of fraternal relations. It is not clear if he similarly thinks that there is nothing unjust about our reducing distant future generations to the level of Inca peasants given that so doing will not involve stigmatization, domination etc.

[4] In Chapter 3.3 I argued that relating as equals covers both treating and regarding one another as equals. Obviously, non-overlapping generations can know about each other and, thus, regard each other as equals – perhaps they can do so even if they do not know about each other, e.g. I can be agnostic on whether there lived human beings more than 100,000 years ago and yet think that if so, they would have been my equal. Hence, what is at stake here is the *treating as equal* component.

possibility. Relational egalitarians might say, correctly, that what grounds relations of justice obtaining between people might be different from what the object of justice is. Hence, there is nothing inconsistent about holding the view that what grounds that relations obtain between a set of people is that, say, they can causally affect or be causally affected by other members of that set, even though the relevant norms of justice that then obtain between them only concern the nature of their social relations and not how they causally affect or are affected by each other in general.

This reply is unsatisfactory for at least two reasons. First, it is pretty clear that for relational egalitarians what makes it the case that relations of justice obtain between people is the fact that they are socially related in a certain way.[5] Both Anderson and Scheffler stress that the relevant norms of justice that obtain between people are grounded in their taking part in a cooperative arrangement. Scheffler (2003a: 22) writes about relational equality as a social ideal, which admittedly is not the only aspect of the relational ideal in his view, that it assumes that 'a human society must be conceived of as a cooperative arrangement among equals, each of whom enjoys the same social standing'. It is hard to see how this could be true if relations of relational justice obtain between people in virtue of some fact other than that they take part in a cooperative arrangement.[6]

Even if I am right about what actual relational egalitarian theorists believe, this, of course, does not speak to what relational egalitarians are committed to qua relational egalitarians (cp. Chapter 2.2). This is where my second reply becomes relevant. For even if what grounds the requirement to relate as an equal is not being socially related, this just brings to attention that what people who think that there is such a thing as intergenerational justice believe is that what justice concerns is more than just relations. That is, people who discuss intergenerational justice in relation to climate justice, say, think that justice pertains to the distribution of goods across generations. So even if the grounds and the content of justice come apart in the way I have entertained, the present objection stands – it just applies directly to the content of justice.

---

[5] Admittedly, this might not be so for those relational egalitarians who think that it is impersonally valuable that people relate as equals and the more the better (see Chapter 6.4).

[6] As we have seen, Scheffler thinks that relating to one another as equals can also be understood as a moral ideal. So construed 'it asserts that all people are of equal worth and that there are some claims that people are entitled to make on one another simply by virtue of their status as persons' (Scheffler, 2003a: 22). This suggests that justice might obtain between a set of people who are not socially related, since the claims that they make upon one another reflect entitlements that they have simply qua persons.

Relational egalitarians could adopt a move which some Hobbesian contractualists have adopted to argue that despite the absence of any hope for cooperation for mutual advantage between present and distant future generations, relations of justice still obtain between us. They might say that relations of justice obtain between two groups of people who are not directly socially related, but who are chain-related social relations-wise, e.g. members of the first group are socially related to members of an 'intermediate' group that in turn is socially related to members of the third group, and so on and so forth. On the present suggestion, relations of justice do after all obtain between the first and the third group despite their members not being socially related. Applied to the topic of intergenerational justice, we are then related to future generations in such a way that relations of justice obtain between us because we are socially related to members of our children's generation; in turn they are socially related to members of our grandchildren's generation and so on and so forth. However, this move is deficient for a number of reasons. Suppose that, due to some weird twist of evolution and techniques of cultural transmission, in the future generations will not overlap at all. In that case, the relevant chain connections would not exist. Yet we would still stand in relations of justice to future generations. If so, these relations are not grounded in the existence of serially overlapping sets of social relations.

Moving on to the second relational egalitarian reason for denying the third premise, the first thing to note about this possibility is that a lot here hangs on what it involves to be related socially. One might suggest:

> X and Y are socially related only if: (1) X is socially related to Y and Y is socially related to X; and (2) X can causally affect Y and Y can causally affect X.

The first condition reflects the idea that social relations are symmetric – it cannot be the case that I am socially related to someone who is not socially related to me. The second condition seems a very weak requirement and an intuitively compelling idea. Suppose there are people on Venus (cp. Pogge, 2008: 204–7). We cannot causally affect them in any way, although we can observe them, something of which they are completely unaware. Surely, we are not socially related to them. Why not? One plausible suggestion is that being socially related involves being able to affect causally those to whom one is so related in certain ways and since, *ex hypothesi*, we cannot affect Venusians causally in any way, a fortiori we cannot affect them causally in the way that being socially related involves.[7]

Suppose that, contrary to my view, in the hypothetical scenario Venusians are socially related to Earthlings. In that case, we can reframe my argument and still reach the same conclusion. For, under the present assumption, relational egalitarians do not believe that *any* social relation will suffice for relations of justice to obtain; rather, only a subset of social relations – relations which are not instantiated in the Venusians example – are bearers of relations of justice. To put this point differently: if the notion of social relations is so thin that non-overlapping generations can be socially related, then a lot of the things that relational egalitarians say make little sense. Take for instance Anderson's characterization of the positive claim of democratic equality:

> Positively, egalitarians seek a social order in which persons stand in relations of equality. They seek to live together in a democratic community, as opposed to a hierarchical one. Democracy is here understood as collective self-determination by means of open discussion among equals, in accordance with rules acceptable to all. To stand as an equal before others in discussion means that one is entitled to participate, that others recognize an obligation to listen respectfully and respond to one's arguments, that no one need bow and scrape before others or represent themselves as inferior to others as a condition of having their claim heard. (Anderson, 1999: 313)

Clearly, we are not related to non-overlapping generations in such a way that it makes sense for us to strive to 'live together' with them, collectively determining what we do.

At this point, some might deny that being socially related is a symmetric relation – that is, they might suggest that X can be socially related to Y even if Y is not socially related to X. Suppose Bowman and Hal interact. Bowman falsely believes that Hal is a cleverly designed, mindless robot, while Hal is aware that Bowman is a person. On the assumption that one cannot have a social relation to something one believes is mindless – after all, I cannot be socially related to my mobile phone even if it is a means of sustaining many, if not most, of my social relations – Bowman has no social relations to Hal even if, plausibly, Hal, who, let us suppose, is a non-human person – a *2001: A Space Odyssey* supercomputer-cum-consciousness – and unaware of Bowman's false belief about her nature,

---

[7] In the example they can causally affect us – what they do causally affects what we observe – but they cannot causally affect us *knowingly*. We cannot causally affect them. I am inclined to say that neither party is related to the other socially. If so, perhaps we can say that being able to knowingly causally affect some other party is necessary for being socially related to that person.

might be socially related to Bowman. On this asymmetric view of social relations, the present generation might be socially related to future generations, since they can knowingly causally affect them, even if future generations cannot, once they come into existence, causally affect the present generations, whose members will have ceased to exist by then. Relational egalitarians might add that because, in practice, intergenerational justice is about how present generations treat later generations, relational egalitarians *can say* something about intergenerational justice.

In response to this suggestion, let me first note that I am not sure that the example provided in the previous paragraph shows that social relations can actually be asymmetric. I see the plausibility of Hal responding to the discovery that Bowman has been thinking of her as a mindless robot all along by concluding that even though she *thought* they were socially related, *in fact* they were not. I am also not sure that there is no such thing as requirements on justice in relation to past generations (Lippert-Rasmussen, 2015a: 156–61). However, I do not want to put any argumentative weight on this claim in the present context for there is another and probably much less controversial reason why the present suggestion does not work.

Being able to causally affect, or being able to causally affect knowingly, are, I suggested, necessary conditions for being socially related. However, it is also clear that this is far from a sufficient condition. Consider again an archipelago of small islands, each of which is inhabited by a lonesome Robinson Crusoe-like person (Arneson, 1999b: 225–7). Each of these persons can read in a book, one copy of which has washed ashore on each of the islands, about the conditions of all the other Robinson Crusoes, and while the sea is such that travelling between the islands is impossible, each Robinson Crusoe can put foodstuff on a raft and put it into the sea where it will then drift to the next island, affecting the conditions of the person living on that island. Relational egalitarianism does not speak to this situation – recall the quote from Anderson in the previous paragraph – since the relevant Robinson Crusoes are not socially related. They are not socially related because they cannot interact, i.e. they cannot adjust their conduct in light of each other's conduct, and they cannot communicate, not even by non-vocal deeds. These are further necessary conditions for being socially related, and while we can knowingly causally affect future generations, we cannot interact or communicate with them. Thus, we are not socially related to them.

At this point, relational egalitarians might concede that relational justice simply does not speak to the issue of intergenerational justice and that this is an issue to which distributive principles of justice apply, but then contend that whatever these principles are, they are not principles of distributive equality. After all, when applied across generations, such principles imply absurdly that there is something unjust about us being better off than people living in ancient Rome, and people ten generations into the future being better off than we are.

In response, I note that I think the relevant implication is not absurd and that the idea that it is fails to take into account is the fact that friends of distributive equality can be pluralists and appeal to other values and, thus, might think that levelling down is rarely, if ever, morally required, all things considered. However, more importantly, even if relational egalitarians are right that distributive equality is not the right distributive principle for distributions across generations, conceding that a non-egalitarian distributive principle, e.g. sufficiency or prioritarianism, applies to intergenerational justice is a huge concession. For one thing, many of the objections that relational egalitarians put forward against distributive equality have a much broader target, e.g. distributive principles in general (Chapters 1 and 2). Hence, if relational egalitarians concede that such principles apply to intergenerational justice, these criticisms must be withdrawn in the absence of an explanation of why they only apply outside an intergenerational context. Moreover, if distributive principles apply *across* generations, it then becomes a challenge to explain why they do not apply *within* generations as well. It would seem ad hoc to say that they do not simply because the relational ideal applies to people belonging to the same generation and, if anything, one would suppose that there is a stronger case for believing that distributive principles apply within generations than that they apply across generations.[8]

In sum: relational egalitarianism cannot account for how relations of justice can obtain between generations whose lives do not overlap. On the (to my mind) plausible assumption that relations of justice do obtain between generations, it follows that relational equality does not provide a complete account of egalitarian justice.

---

[8] For instance, this is true of the typical Hume or Hume-inspired circumstances of justice reasons (cp. Rawls, 1999: 109–12) that are offered (though not by Rawls) for why justice does not pertain to non-overlapping generations.

Table 5.1 *The Weird Scenario*

	0–15	15–30	30–45	45–60	60–75
Adrian	Young	Middle-aged	Old	Middle-aged	Middle-aged
Beatrice	Middle-aged	Old	Middle-aged	Young	Middle-aged

5.3 Age

I now shift my attention to justice between overlapping generations, e.g. young and old people. According to relational egalitarians, justice requires that people relate as equals. But what exactly is it to relate as equals when it comes to age?

To see that there is a real issue here, let me start by considering a very simple but also somewhat weird scenario – though not more weird than something that at least two of my children imagined to be real, when they were three-year-olds – involving two persons and two persons only. These two people – Adrian and Beatrice – are born at the same time, and each live years consisting of the same and equally long phases of life. Suppose Adrian is born young, is a child for fifteen years, after which he is middle-aged for fifteen years, old for another fifteen years, and then, amazingly, is middle-aged – not chronologically speaking of course, but bodily and experientially – for another thirty years before he dies. Beatrice is born middle-aged and lives for fifteen years as such, is old for fifteen years, then spends another fifteen years as middle-aged before turning into a child for fifteen years. In her final fifteen years she reverts to being middle-aged. Table 5.1 offers a schematic representation of the scenario.

When Adrian is a child and when he is old, Beatrice is middle-aged and looks after him. When Beatrice is a child and when she is old, Adrian is middle-aged and looks after her. Except for the last fifteen years of their lives, they do not relate as equals – at least not in the way that the paradigm town hall model involves. However, in effect Adrian and Beatrice take turns being dependent on each other and having the other making paternalistic decisions on his or her part, e.g. because bodily immaturity or impairments prevent them from being active citizens in civil society. Suppose that at any stage in their lives they know these facts.[9] One line

---

[9] In discussions of distributive justice, a similar example – changing-places egalitarianism – has been used to cast doubt on the whole-lives view of distributive equality.

of thought here is that this situation involves no relational injustice. Because Adrian and Beatrice know that they will take turns being dependent upon the other before enjoying the last fifteen years of their lives being simultaneously mature and independent, their situation is in *no way* deficient from the point of view of relational equality – the problems that unequal social relations involve are not present in this case (cp. Chapter 6.4).[10]

More generally and in the world of ageing as we know it, all of us – except for those who die young – pass through the relevant age groups, and, arguably, because of this dynamic aspect relating as equals is compatible with our being dependent on others and on others acting paternalistically towards us during some part of our lives. At the least, these kinds of relations between age groups seem different and less objectionable than similar relations between groups without a similarly dynamic group membership structure, e.g. men and women, able-bodied and disabled people, and different racial groups.[11]

Consider the following two views on how time bears on what it is to relate as equals:

> *The complete-lives view*: X and Y relate as equals in their dealing at *t*, if (1) when considering how X and Y relate to one another over the course of their whole lives, it is defeasibly true that X and Y relate to one another as equals; and (2) at *t*, X and Y are both aware that (1).
> *The time-relative view*: X and Y relate as equals in their dealing at *t*, if (1) when considering how X and Y relate to one another at *t*, it is defeasibly true that X and Y relate to one another as equals; and (2) at *t*, X and Y are both aware that (1).

To see the difference between these two views, return to my example of Adrian and Beatrice. Consider them at a point in time where Adrian is a child and Beatrice is middle-aged, effectively running Adrian's life at that time. On the time-relative view, the sufficient condition for Adrian and Beatrice relating as equals – as opposed to the last fifteen years of their lives (hopefully) – is not satisfied. However, this is different on the complete-

---

[10] For instance, Scanlon (2000: 204) thinks that one objectionable feature of relational inequality is that 'it is an evil for people to be treated as inferior, or made to feel inferior'. Arguably, neither Adrian nor Beatrice treat each other as such, nor need feel inferior, in the scenario described.
[11] Still, relational equality might constrain distributive inequalities between age groups. Suppose young people are so badly off in material terms that they are forced to enter into exploitative relations with older people. That seems bad from a relational point of view even if young people know that the day will come when they are the exploiters (cp. Chapter 6.4).

lives view, since at t both parties know that they are taking turns looking after one another.[12]

To motivate the complete-lives view, consider David Miller's (1998; cp. Chapter 1.3) ideal of relational equality. Miller thinks that the ideal of equality is not simply a distributive ideal – rather, it is an ideal regarding a way of relating to one another. With some qualifications, Miller, inspired by Michael Walzer (1983), thinks that such an ideal is compatible with inequality across different spheres of justice. You and I can relate as equals, because while I do much better than you do in one sphere – e.g. I earn much more than you do – you do much better than I do in other spheres – e.g. in terms of the academic quality of your work you do much better than I do and, accordingly, esteem-wise you are much better off than I am. Moreover, we are unable to convert superiority in one sphere into superiority in another. As Walzer puts it: there is no dominant good, say, equivalent to money, in the sense that if you have superior amounts of money, you are able to convert those advantages into a whole range of other advantages in other spheres, e.g. superior political influence (Anderson, 2008b: 264, 266).

Suppose you go along with Miller's notion of relating as equals and his view that this ideal is compatible with *synchronic* inequalities between individuals across different spheres. Could you then deny that relating as equals is also compatible with *diachronic* inequalities? After all, like the synchronic inequalities that Miller deems just, diachronic inequalities do not have the same individuals coming out on top at any given time (/in any sphere of justice) and advantage in one diachronic sphere is non-convertible into advantages in another diachronic sphere, as it were.[13]

To answer this question, we can ask why Miller could be right that dispersed synchronic inequality across spheres is compatible with people

---

[12] It might be suggested that this is only an issue that pertains to telic forms of relational egalitarianism, where it is a matter of interpreting the value of relating as equals, and that the same question does not arise in relation to deontic relational equality, which says, 'Do not at any given moment dominate, exploit, oppress etc'. (cp. Bidadanure, 2016: 246, 255; Chapter 6.5). I agree, of course, that if this is what deontic relational egalitarianism says, then there is no such issue. However, this is just one version of deontic relational egalitarianism and another version is the complete-lives version of the relevant norms: 'Do not, when considering how you and the other person relate to one another over your complete lives, dominate, exploit, oppress etc'.

[13] There is a complication here relative to my case of Adrian and Beatrice. Walzer's synchronic, across-sphere inequalities obtain between the same individuals, whereas diachronic, across-age inequalities do not obtain between the same individuals. The people who present-day young people will be inferior to once they grow old will be different people from those whom they are presently superior to. However, this seems sufficient to avoid any form of social hierarchy – at least, this is so if people are sufficiently aware of how places will change over time (cp. Baker, 2015: 78).

relating as equals. Presumably, one important reason is that one's self-conception is affected by the awareness that, while one might excel within one particular sphere, there is a whole range of other spheres where one does (much) less well than those individuals whom one outshines in the particular sphere in which one excels. Presumably, one reason why people are aware of other spheres than those in which they do well is that people are, as it were, situated more or less simultaneously in all spheres of justice.

If this is so, then something similar is likely to be true of Adrian and Beatrice and perhaps even true of age-based inequalities more generally. For instance, young people who interact with old people might have available to them thoughts similar to the thoughts of people who interact with others in spheres where they do particularly well, e.g. 'True, I am in much better health than old Mike, who needs our help. However, once I get to be as old as he is now (if I do), then I will probably be no better off than he is now and I will then need younger people to help me'. Similarly, old Mike can think back on his athletic prowess as a young person. Hence, to the extent the indicated mechanism is the one that renders inequalities across spheres compatible with the ideal of regarding and, partly because of that, relating as equals, an analogous mechanism should make the ideal compatible with diachronic age-based health inequalities.

Admittedly, the extent to which this is the case depends on the degree to which people actually have thoughts along the lines illustrated.[14] If they do not, they might see old people as inferior on account of their failing mental capacities (among many other things), even if, in some sense, they know that someday they themselves will be in a similar predicament. However, the same is true of inequalities across spheres. If all you and I really care about, or at least focus on, is academic achievement, we might not relate as equals – recall that to relate as equals, we also have to regard one another as equals (Chapter 3.3) – even though I do better than you do money-wise.

There is a lot to be said for the complete-lives view. Take the case of parents and under-age children. In one sense – though perhaps not the sense which is central to the scope of the ideal of relational equality in relation to age – they do not relate as equals, e.g. parents make decisions on behalf of their children in the child's best interest (and are so permitted by

---

[14] There might be other mechanisms which render synchronic inequality across spheres compatible with relational egalitarianism. The one that I have discussed here strikes me as the most plausible one.

the state), even if these decisions are against their children's will. Similar relations between citizens would be condemned by any relational egalitarianism. Why is the relation between children and parents not problematic?[15] Arguably, one explanation appeals to the fact that, initially, each of us was a child in someone's care such that, from a whole-lives perspective, our having had others acting paternalistically on our behalf in our childhood (if we were lucky) involves no objectionable relational inequality. If this explanation works in the case of children, might it not also work in the case of other age-based inequalities?

Whichever is the more plausible of the two views, it is interesting that while Anderson and Scheffler do not explicitly address the issue of justice between age groups, their accounts of the ideal of relational equality seem to have different implications with regard to the two versions of relational equality that I have distinguished between in this section.

Consider first Anderson's harshness objection (Chapter 2.3). Recall that according to Anderson, egalitarian justice requires that the state acts to ensure that all citizens, whatever their past choices, can participate as equals in society. In the case invoked by her harshness objection, this implies providing the motorcyclist with medical care despite his risky choice. If we extend this line of reasoning to old people, the state should act to ensure that elderly people can participate as equals in society. More generally, it appears that Anderson rejects lifetime relational egalitarianism and favours time-relative relational egalitarianism (cp. O'Neill, 2008: 149).

One troubling implication of this is that, other things being equal, people who live long lives, which at the end involve extended periods of seriously reduced health interfering with their ability to participate fully in society on an equal standing – 'equal-status monsters', we may call them (uncharitably) – have a claim to almost all of a society's resources, e.g. at the expense of worse-off people who live quite short lives though in good health at any point in time during their lives.[16] From the point of any

[15] Some might be tempted to respond to this question that the ideal of relational equality only pertains to relations between adults. However, this view is deficient. First, it gives rise to a new and no less challenging question: Why does the scope of relational equality not extend, partially at least, to children, given the gradualist nature of the distinction between children and adults? Second, it seems incredible that the relational ideal has nothing to say about the relation between children and parents per se, e.g. that it is indifferent, setting aside indirect effects on the social relations between adults, to the choice between authoritarian and non-authoritarian family structures (cp. Schapiro, 1999).

[16] Anderson might bite the bullet at this point and concede that this is an implication of her view, denying that it amounts to an objection. I do not find this bullet-biting any more attractive than the comparable utilitarian bullet-biting in response to an objection appealing to utility monsters. A response which is more plausible, to my mind, appeals to values other than justice to explain why not almost all of society's resources should be spent on equal-status monsters.

whole-lives distributive egalitarian view this is a serious mistake, since the former group of people are better off.

Consider next Scheffler's position. As we saw in Chapter 2.6, the egalitarian deliberative constraint is crucial to his account of what it is to relate as equals. Scheffler (2015: 28–9) contends that satisfying the constraint is compatible with reaching decisions that do not leave the parties who relate as equals equally well off. Indeed, he thinks that it is unlikely that participants in egalitarian personal relationships will 'attempt to satisfy the [deliberative] constraint through the self-conscious application of a fixed distributive formula', though the constraint will 'exert pressure in the direction of egalitarian distribution' (Scheffler, 2015: 33, 34). In relation to age, the deliberative constraint implies that each member's interests count equally.[17] This of course leaves open how exactly we should flesh out the equal concern for all members' interests. More specifically, there is nothing in the present formulation that rules out even large inequalities between age groups (Scheffler, 2015: 40). Suppose that the best we can do to promote everyone's interests *ex ante* is to make sure that young people are much better off than old people. If a community decides to spend most of its resources on young people in ways that might flout Anderson's sufficiency requirement in the case of old people, whose capabilities are very costly to enhance, this would seem entirely compatible with Scheffler's deliberative constraint. After all, Scheffler (2015: 26) notes that 'the egalitarian deliberative constraint is best understood diachronically rather than synchronically', and this renders the deliberative constraint immune to the equal-status monsters objection. Hence, unlike Anderson's position, Scheffler's appears compatible with complete-lives relational egalitarianism. This provides indirect support for – or, at least, illustrates – my claim that relational egalitarians might take different views on inequalities between age groups and that on some of these views, (even very significant) age-related inequalities are compatible with the ideal of relational egalitarianism.

In sum: relational equality can be interpreted differently when it comes to age. It can either take a complete-lives or a time-relative form. I have suggested that this distinction is quite parallel to what we see in the discussion of distributive equality and that the most plausible version of relational egalitarianism involves both a complete lifetime and a time-relative perspective.

---

[17] 'Interests' might be understood either from a whole-life perspective or a time-relative perspective.

5.4   Site

In this section, I turn to another issue in relation to the specification of the relational ideal that is parallel to an issue that arises in relation to any full specification of distributive ideals of justice in general and luck egalitarianism in particular. This issue is the issue of the site of principles of justice, i.e. the issue of what sort of entity they apply to (Cohen, 2008; Tan, 2014: 1).

Because one can sort entities in infinitely many ways, there are infinitely many ways in which one can approach the question of the site of justice. There are three distinctions that have been salient in the debate and which are particularly interesting. First, there is a distinction between the view that justice applies to individual actions and the view that it applies to sets of actions of a certain kind. Second, there is a distinction between the view that principles refer to non-normative items such as individual actions or patterns of individual actions and the view that they refer to normative (or norm-constitutive) items like rules, laws, constitutions etc. Third, there is the distinction between the view that justice applies to individual agents (or entities suitably related to individual agents), e.g. individual citizens (or individual human beings) and their actions, and the view that it applies to collective agents, e.g. states (or the UN) and their actions.

One influential view combines the first taxa in the three distinctions and holds that principles of justice apply to the actions of individuals and, thus, that in principle people in the course of their daily lives on countless occasions either conform with or act in violation of the requirements of egalitarian justice. Call this the *individualist approach*.

Another influential view combines the second taxa in the three distinctions and holds that principles of justice apply to institutional structures, where, in the standard case, this is understood to comprise the basic laws of a state regulating sets of actions. Call this the *institutionalist approach* (cp. Tan, 2014: 1).

Those who have defended the individualist approach have done so arguing that principles of justice apply to individual actions as well as to institutional structure: principles of distributive justice 'apply to the choices that people make within the legally coercive structures to which, so everyone would agree, principles of justice (also) apply' (Cohen, 2008: 116). No one has defended the view that principles of justice do not apply to institutional structures. Hence, the central question in relation to site is whether principles of justice apply to individual actions in the course of people's daily lives *in addition to* institutional structures (Tan, 2014: 20, 53).

Accordingly, by 'an individualist approach' I will mean a view according to which the site of justice includes individual actions as well as institutional structures.

In this section, I defend the individualist approach. I start with a brief sketch of the discussion of the site of distributive justice. I then argue that the reasons that are standardly offered in defence of the institutionalist view – e.g. the overdemandingness objection; the publicity constraint and the epistemic difficulty of knowing whether one complies with the requirements of justice; and the alleged intrusivess of a notion of justice that extends beyond the basic structure – do not motivate an individualist approach when it comes to relational equality. If anything, these reasons would appear to motivate a strongly individualist approach in the case of relational justice. I conclude by taking a look at how Anderson and Scheffler have addressed the issue of site. My overall line of argument is that the site of relational justice is best construed as pluralist, i.e. as one that extends beyond institutions to individual agents and their actions in their daily lives.

The issue of site has not been discussed extensively in relation to luck egalitarian principles. Rather, the focus has been on Rawls' difference principle, which in at least one of its versions holds that inequalities are just only to the extent that they are necessary to make the worst off as well off as possible.[18] Because Rawls took an institutionalist approach to justice, he did not take the difference principle so construed to imply that, in their daily lives, individuals are required by justice to take into account whether their actions, e.g. their insistence on incentives for using their, say, extraordinary talents in ways that are beneficial to the worst off, render inequalities necessary for promoting the situation of the worst off (Chapter 4.5). Perhaps Rawls, and Rawlsians in general, embrace some very limited individualist approach, since they could accept that individuals have a political obligation of justice to vote for and, perhaps in other ways too, support parties that, through the state, would promote justice, including the realization of the difference principle (Rawls, 1999: 99; Scheffler, 2006: 103; Tan, 2014: 28, 30, 40).[19] However, from a Rawlsian perspective, individuals in their daily lives, e.g. as consumers, as employees or as family

---

[18] On Scheffler's view, Rawls' difference principle does not require that the worst off are made as well off as possible, but that any inequality serves to make them as well off as possible. Hence, one way in which one could realize the difference principle without a Cohenian egalitarian ethos would be simply to eliminate inequality (Scheffler, 2006: 116–17).

[19] According to Tan, 'genuinely personal choices' are 'not directed at institutions' (Tan, 2014: 41).

members, are not required, as a matter of justice, to act with the aim of realizing the difference principle.[20]

As I have already noted, along with G. A. Cohen's articulation of his own luck egalitarian theory of justice, he developed a critique of the Rawlsian incentive argument for inequality based on an individualist approach to egalitarian justice (Chapter 4.5).[21] As Cohen saw it, it would be an odd view that, on the one hand (and simplifying a bit), holds that citizens are required as a matter of justice to vote for parties that, say, through taxation policies work for making the worst-off as well off as possible, and, on the other hand, holds that once out of the voting booth it is permissible for citizens to seek to maximize their amount of primary good even if by doing so – together with others who act in similar ways – they will knowingly make the worst-off worse off than they would have been had talented people abstained from the relevant self-seeking behaviour as economic agents. According to Cohen, this picture involves a certain kind of absurd psychological schism. It also sits uneasily with, for instance, Rawls' description of a well-ordered society as one in which people express their fraternal feelings and refrain from using morally arbitrary advantage like inborn talents as bargaining chips in a quest for personal enrichment (Cohen, 2008: 123). To support his individualist approach he appeals to the feminist slogan 'The personal is political' (Cohen, 2008: 116), noting that unjust forms of sexism and racism can persist in the course of people's daily lives, even if the basic structure of society is cleansed of the two forms of injustice. In view of this, an institutionalist approach looks impoverished, since a sexist and racist society does look more unjust than one without racism and sexism even if the relevant two societies are equally non-sexist and non-racist when it comes to the basic structures of society.

Whatever is the right approach to distributive principles, there is a similar issue in relation to relational justice. In his critique of recipient-oriented theories of justice, i.e. theories according to which 'individual shares are of ultimate concern' (Schemmel, 2012a: 127), Schemmel posits the importance to justice of how social institutions, notably the state, treat

---

[20] This complicates the debate. Some institutionalists say that principles of justice do apply to individuals as well, but that they apply primarily to institutions (cp. Scheffler, 2006). Others say that principles of justice apply to both individuals and institutions, but that the principles that apply to individuals and institutions are different (cp. Tan, 2014; Schemmel, 2012a). The former debate is quite tricky, because it is hard to distinguish the primary from the secondary topic.

[21] Strictly speaking, Cohen's fundamental site of justice is distributions and accordingly, the basic structure and people's choices within it are only 'secondarily' sites of justice (Cohen, 2008: 126).

individuals. More specifically, he thinks that the attitudes expressed by social institutions in their dealings with citizens (or for that matter non-citizens) is of primary concern from the point of view of justice.[22] While not discussing the distinction in depth, Schemmel distinguishes between liberal and radical relational egalitarians: 'A liberal egalitarian view will insist that standards of appropriateness for individual attitudes are different from those for institutions: it will not subject individuals to as stringently egalitarian demands as institutions, make space for prioritizing individual relationships, and permit inegalitarian personal attitudes in so far as they do not endanger egalitarian institutions. As opposed to that, radical egalitarian views may recognize that institutional settings raise special issues, but will demand that people display similarly stringent egalitarian concern in their private lives' (Schemmel, 2012a: 137).[23]

One issue deserves special attention. In the quote from Schemmel, the message is conveyed that the insistence of radical egalitarians on people displaying 'similarly stringent egalitarian concern in their private lives' implies that in a radical egalitarian society there is no 'space for prioritizing individual relationships'. However, it is unclear that this is what radical egalitarians are committed to. They might well say that what it is to relate as equals depends on the nature of one's relations – at least, relations of a certain kind, e.g. not the sort of relations of which feudal hierarchy consists – such that it is compatible with the most stringent egalitarian position that I express more concern for my children than for other citizens. Relating as equals is different from distributive equality in this regard, since what it means to bring about distributive equality is not context sensitive in the same way.

I will now consider three of the reasons that are standardly given for why the scope of distributive justice is somehow restricted in the way implied by

---

[22] Schemmel thinks that different attitudes can be ranked from more (e.g. hostility) to less disrespect-ful (e.g. mere neglect) and that acts, institutions etc. that express more disrespectful attitudes are more unjust than acts that express less disrespectful attitudes: 'In each such case, social hierarchies are instantiated or made possible by such implicit judgements of worth, and this is what the relational egalitarian primarily objects to' (Schemmel, 2012a: 134; Chapter 3.7).

[23] Schemmel seems to allow what is surely right, that distributions can have a certain unjust expressive content. Suppose that a state could remedy gross inequalities but fails to do so. In that case, from a Dworkinian perspective the state fails to express 'equal concern and respect' and the distribution which is a result of state inaction can be said to express the state's lack of equal concern and respect. Similarly, Pogge, to whom Schemmel appeals (2012a: 138), thinks that an unequal distribution which is racially biased is worse because of its expressive content than an equally unequal distribu-tion which is not racially biased. The upshot of this is that the expressivist view of justice not only applies to actions or the social relations which these involve, but might also apply to distributions, in which case friends of the expressivist view might have a foot in both the relational and the luck egalitarian camps.

the institutionalist approach. First, one argument appeals to the over-demandingness of the individualist approach (cp. Tan, 2014: 19–49). Schemmel makes an argument of this sort: 'in order to avoid such over-demandingness, a liberal conception of justice has to limit its concern with distributive inequalities in some principled manner. Limiting concern with natural inequality seems one good way of doing that, since it achieves the desired aim while at the same time fulfilling the intuitive requirement that recourse to such a demandingness restriction is not available if a society has itself caused a morally relevant inequality: if I am causally responsible for your disadvantage, I cannot claim that compensating you would be over-demanding' (Schemmel, 2012a: 131; cp. Tan, 2014: 21; Nagel, 1991: 18; Scheffler, 2006: 106–10).[24]

Whatever the force of the overdemandingness objection – I am sceptical of its force in general and of Schemmel's version, which seems to portray as optional the way in which a conception of justice avoids overdemanding-ness, in particular – it is unclear that the requirement of relating to others is overdemanding, at least in standard contexts – or at any rate overly demanding compared to a situation in which only institutions were under an obligation to relate to individuals as equals.[25] For instance, the requirement to regard one another as equals seems close to costless – indeed, if it is good for us to think of ourselves in this way, it might even be costly for us not to comply with the requirement (see Chapters 6.2 and 6.3). Similarly, to the extent that the requirements of relational justice take an expressive form, as Anderson and Schemmel seem to hold, in general it will be quite cost-free for individuals to comply with the requirements of relational justice.

Perhaps in some cases, where people have been brought up in strongly hierarchical societies and find it abominable to express equal concern and respect for others whom they regard as inferior, complying with the demands of expressive justice will be costly. However, at most this shows something about the requirements of relational justice under non-ideal

---

[24] The overdemandingness objection comes in different versions. In some versions, it consists of the assertion that compliance with all putative moral demands is overly costly. In other versions, it consists of the assertion *pace* unreasonably demanding moral theories that 'individuals can live their day-to-day life relieved of the burden of asking at every instance whether a given personal transaction or decision is consistent with the requirements of social justice' (Tan, 2014: 24–5). On the latter version, the demandingness is not located in what justice demands, but in constantly inquiring what social justice demands. The requirement of relating as equals might not be very demanding, but asking whether one complies with it at every instance could be very demanding.

[25] An example of a non-standard context is one in which I am threatened at gunpoint not to relate to someone as an equal.

circumstances and does not speak to what relational justice requires under ideal circumstances. Also, depending on how demandingness is cashed out, the most natural response to the present point is to curb the demands of justice, e.g. by adopting an agent-centred prerogative, rather than to restrict the site of justice.[26]

There is an additional reason why relating to others as equals should not be taken to be overly demanding when understood as a requirement that applies to individuals in their daily lives. Consider the difference between deeming all paintings by French impressionists valuable and actually valuing all of them, e.g. because I have not expended the time required to get to a point where I value each of these paintings in all cases. It might be held that I do not thereby – i.e. because some of the paintings I deem equally valuable, aesthetically speaking, leave me cold, as it were – manifest any flawed aesthetic appreciation. Perhaps we should draw a similar distinction between deeming someone to be equally valuable and actually valuing this person equally. It might be, for instance, that I value members of my family as equals, and that I deem us and members of other families equally valuable, e.g. families I am not personally acquainted with, and yet do not value members of other families as much as I value members of my own family. If we understand what it is to relate to others as equals in this way, we can explain why the requirement to relate to others as individuals does not imply some kind of thoroughgoing overdemanding impartiality in the way in which one deals with family, friends and any other person whom one interacts with.[27]

I now turn to the second reason that is commonly offered in defence of the institutionalist view. In a different context Andrew Williams defends the standard Rawlsian view of incentives-based inequalities. He notes that for Rawls, an institution is 'a public system of rules, which defines offices and positions with their rights and duties, powers and immunities, and the like. These rules specify certain forms of action as permissible, others as forbidden; and they provide for certain penalties and defences, and so on, when violations occur' (Williams, 1998: 233; Rawls, 1999: 55). A system of

---

[26] Tan mentions this possibility but dismisses it on the grounds that it merely 'restates the very problem that the institutional approach is meant to solve' (Tan, 2014: 31). This is too quick. Admittedly, merely to endorse agent-centred prerogatives leaves open the question of how it should be specified, but the question of the right specification of the agent-centred prerogative is surely not a restatement of the problem of how one should regulate and order 'the different compartments of a moral agent's life', i.e. justice and personal pursuits (Tan, 2014: 33–4).

[27] It requires second-order impartiality in that, if we give priority to friends and family over others, we cannot resent or resist that others do the same to us when we fall in the last category relative to them (cp. Tan, 2014: 73–5).

rules is public if, and only if, 'individuals are able to attain common knowledge of the rules' (1) general applicability, (2) their particular requirements, and (3) the extent to which individuals conform with those requirements' (Williams, 1998: 233; cp. Rawls, 1993: 266–8). While the difference principle, on its standard Rawlsian interpretation, satisfies the publicity constraint so construed, Cohen's version does not. The rules involved in an egalitarian ethos of the sort Cohen envisages are 'so informationally demanding that individuals are incapable of mutually verifying the status of their conduct' – in other words, those rules fail to conform with (3) (Williams, 1998: 234). Moreover, it is almost impossible for an individual to know whether a given decision harms or benefits the worst off, so an egalitarian ethos enjoining talented people to benefit the worst off as much as possible also violates (2).[28]

Elsewhere I have expressed doubts about whether publicity really is a constraint on principles of justice and whether a Cohenian ethos fails to satisfy it (Lippert-Rasmussen, 2008). However, my present point is that, at least on some standard understandings of what it is to relate to others as equals, the requirement to relate as equals satisfies (2) and (3). That is, instances of blatant racism or sexism clearly are incompatible with the requirement to relate as equals (cp. Tan, 2014: 65–6). The crucial difference between the difference principle – and, more generally, distributive views – and the relational ideal here is that whether my act promotes the position of the worst off (or, more generally, promotes a favoured distributive pattern) depends on what others do, whereas whether I relate to another as an equal does not – at least not to any comparable degree. Since, generally, it is impossible for an individual to know what all others will do, it is, often, impossible for them to know whether they promote the situation of the worst off. This is not saying that there are no cases, e.g. cases involving implicit bias or microaggressions, where it is unclear whether one satisfies the requirements of the relational ideal (Chapter 3.5). The existence of such difficult cases is implied by virtually any norm and in any case their existence does not form a publicity-based reason for denying that relational equality applies in those instances of daily interactions where its requirements are clear.[29] In part for that reason,

---

[28] One might suggest that, in most cases, it is extremely likely that any individual action will make no difference to the overall badness of inequality. Hence, if we are act egalitarians, we are morally free to do what we like, in which case it is quite easy to know that our conduct conforms to egalitarian justice. Obviously, Cohen cannot press this reply to Williams' publicity objection.

[29] For instance, it is certainly difficult to know which basic structure of society makes the worst off as well off as possible and, thus, to tell if Rawls' difference principle is satisfied.

it is also easier for people to know whether (3) is satisfied. In any case, the main motivation for including (3) in the publicity requirement is that people want to be assured that they are not being suckers while others free ride (cp. Cohen, 2008: 147–8). However, it is far from clear that relating to others as equals involves a similar issue. For instance, if we benefit from relating to others as equals (cp. Chapters 6.2 and 6.3), one is not a sucker just because one relates to others as equals while one's peers do not.[30] Hence, the standard publicity objection, whether or not it defeats individualist approaches to distributive ideals, does not undermine an individualist approach to the relational ideal.

Schemmel proposes a third reason against an individualist approach or, as he calls it, a radical egalitarian approach – intrusiveness – in the course of describing three ways in which relational egalitarianism can be developed. On this radical view, 'individuals should display attitudes of benevolence and fraternity (or sorority) towards each other both in public and private life, and institutions should express equivalent collective attitudes' (Schemmel, 2012a: 142). He finds this view troublesome because 'we may find it unduly intrusive for institutions exercising collective power to act in the name of fraternity, or some similar value' (Schemmel, 2012a: 142).

It is, however, difficult to see how the concern to avoid undue intrusiveness motivates a rejection of the individualist approach. First, according to Schemmel, what we might find unduly intrusive is that institutions that exercise collective power express attitudes regarding our personal choices. But, assuming that there are no similar concerns with how individual agents express their attitudes, this concern would motivate a purely individualist approach rather than an institutionalist one. Second, in any case it is difficult to see why a friend of the individualist approach should insist that the state express benevolence and fraternity rather than simply the equality of all citizens (or beyond). Admittedly, one might hold the view that this is a *good* that a relational egalitarian state should produce, but I do not see why a state that does not but which expresses equal concern and respect for citizens should be condemned from the point of view of relational equality (Chapter 3.6). Third, the mere expressing of an attitude towards someone is not intrusive – at least not in

---

[30] There might be a different rationale for (3) – that how widespread compliance with the relational ideal is affects how costly it is to comply with it, e.g. presumably it can be quite costly for non-sexist men to relate to women as equals in Saudi Arabia today. However, if this is the underlying rationale for (3), then what is required is not knowledge of how widespread compliance is in general, but knowledge of how widespread compliance is among those with whom one interacts. I suspect that such knowledge is much easier to come by than knowledge of general compliance.

the way that some find very objectionable, e.g. it need not involve scruti-
nizing or assessing any of their inner lives. I infer that Schemmel's concerns
about intrusiveness do not motivate a rejection of the individualist
approach.

Before concluding, I will briefly review Anderson and Scheffer's positions to show that, in effect, they take different positions on the site issue.
Starting with Anderson, her approach is institutionalist in its emphasis.
Take her description of the 'most fundamental test any egalitarian theory
must meet', to wit, that its principles express 'equal respect and concern for
all citizens' (Anderson, 1999: 289). The emphasis on *citizens* is best
explained by the view that the sole site of egalitarian justice is the state.
If the site includes individuals and their interactions with other individuals
in general, as Scheffler holds, why not say that the most fundamental test is
whether the principles of a putatively egalitarian theory of justice express
'equal respect and concern for all *persons*'? Also, her central illustrations of
how luck egalitarianism expresses disrespect towards citizens involve the
state disrespectfully communicating the grounds for which it compensates
victims of bad brute luck, e.g. that they are untalented, unattractive etc.
While she thinks that 'citizens make claims on one another' (Anderson,
1999: 289), the agent who is supposed to comply with those demands is
citizens acting together, i.e. the state.[31]

In other places, however, Anderson subscribes to the view that the site of
distributive justice extends to individuals: 'Relational egalitarians identify
justice with a virtue of agents (including institutions). It is a disposition to
treat individuals in accordance with principles that express, embody, and
sustain relations of social equality. Distributions of socially allocated goods
are just if they are the result of everyone acting in accord with such
principles' (Anderson, 2010a: 2, 22).[32] The fact that she writes 'including
institutions' suggests that she thinks that justice is also a virtue of individual agents, and accordingly that the site of justice extends to them.[33]

Turning now to Scheffler, he submits that equality is 'a moral ideal
governing the relations in which people stand to one another . . . It claims

---

[31] In her discussion of whether individuals are entitled to compensation due to 'defects in appearance',
she seems to assume that the question is whether there is 'an obligation for society' to pay for it
(Anderson, 1999: 309). More generally, she assumes that the (sole?) aim of justice is to supply
'principles for collective willing' (Anderson, 1999: 310).

[32] Confusingly, Anderson (2012a: 44) contends that '[j]udgments of virtue are made from a third-
person perspective of an observer and judge'.

[33] It is a further claim that the site of justice extends to the actions of individual agents on a day-to-day
basis. Tan, for instance, would acknowledge that individuals sometimes make institutional choices,
e.g. cast a vote in an election, and in those cases their choice is regulated by principles of justice.

that human relations must be conducted on the basis of an assumption that everyone's life is equally important, and that all members of a society have equal standing' (Scheffler, 2003a: 21–2).[34] As we have seen, he then distinguishes between equality construed as a moral, a social and a political ideal, respectively. Construed as a moral ideal 'it asserts that all people are of equal worth and that there are some claims that people are entitled to make on one another simply by virtue of their status as persons' (Scheffler, 2003a: 22). This is hard to square with a purely institutionalist view. How could it be the case that individuals interacting with one another outside any institutional context cannot either conform or fail to conform to the relational ideal construed as a moral ideal? What seems clear is that equality, as Scheffler understands the ideal, applies very broadly – recall that his paradigm example of an egalitarian relation is that which obtains between spouses – and that he makes no exceptions such that, say, interactions between persons taking place outside any institutional context are not regulated by relational equality. What is also clear is that he thinks that what it is to relate to one another as an equal varies from context to context, e.g. what it is for citizens to relate to one another as equals is different from what it is to relate as equals when people are not co-citizens.[35]

In sum: as with the distributive ideal we can distinguish between individualist and merely institutionalist relational theories of justice. I have argued that the former version is the more plausible one. The concerns that some theorists think motivate an institutionalist approach to distributions do not really apply to relations; the reasons offered in favour of this approach seem dubious; and, finally, it is hard to understand why one should relate as an equal to some people whom one relates to and not to others, especially in light of the fact that what it involves to relate to someone as an equal varies from context to context, where context includes the sort of social relations one has to the person in question. While Anderson and Scheffler seem to think that the site of their

---

[34] The first claim seems unrestricted, while the second claim is restricted in the sense that it is only about how members of the same society should relate to one another.

[35] In a response to Cohen's individualist approach, Scheffler defends Rawls' view, arguing that Cohen fails to show that the basic structure is not the primary subject of justice. However, Scheffler's own relational ideal implies that the site of justice extends beyond the basic structure. Clearly, he thinks that the relational ideal applies to interpersonal relations in general. However, he also distinguishes between equality as a moral and a political ideal and perhaps he wants to say that distributive justice only pertains to equality as a political ideal. If so, that leaves open whether there is any substantial disagreement site-wise between Cohen and Scheffler in the sense that those requirements pertaining to the actions of individuals in the course of their daily lives that, e.g. Cohen would describe as requirements of distributive justice are requirements that, from a Schefflerian perspective, could be seen as deriving from equality as a moral ideal.

relational ideal extends beyond institutions, Anderson also holds that the issue of institutions (or basic structure) is the primary site of justice.

5.5   Scope

The question of the scope of principles of egalitarian justice concerns the proper set of agents among whom principles of justice apply (Tan, 2014: 1). The question of scope is different from the question of site. The latter concerns who or what is that which should conform to egalitarian justice, whereas the former concerns those to whom justice is owed. Site concerns the givers of justice and scope concerns takers of justice, as it were.

Traditionally, principles of egalitarian justice have been defended as principles whose scope is defined by state borders. Hence, traditionally if you defend distributive equality, you mean distributive equality between citizens who belong to the same state and not distributive equality between people who are citizens of different states (cp. Dworkin, 2000; Nagel, 2005). Obviously, this is hugely significant, since interstate inequality tends to be even more massive than intrastate inequalities. The dominance of statist views on the scope of distributive justice might have changed, however, over the last two decades, which have been characterized by an increased focus on global justice (cp. Caney, 2005; Fabre, 2007; Miller, 2012; Rawls, 2001a; Risse, 2015).

Interestingly, many who have written on global justice have assumed that some version of the distributive ideal provides the correct answer to the question of global justice, though, of course, they differ on what sort of distribution they think global justice mandates. Few, if any, efforts have been spent on developing a relational account of global justice. As a striking result of this, at a time at which many friends of the distributive ideal have declared that they are cosmopolitans, few have discussed, let alone endorsed, cosmopolitan relational egalitarianism (but see Nath, 2011, 2015; Norman, 1998: 49).[36]

Some might suggest that this fact reflects that people who are citizens of different states do not relate to one another in any sufficiently substantive way – e.g. citizens of different states do not take part in the same

---

[36] O'Neill (2008: 136–7) adopts an intermediate position between statism and cosmopolitanism grounded in his view about what makes inequality bad. Note also that, in the global literature, 'relational' is sometimes used to refer to the view that distributive justice obtains only between individuals who are subjected to (and authors of) the same (coercive) institutional framework. I use 'relational' in a broader sense such that it could involve non-coercive, non-institutional social relations.

cooperative venture for mutual benefit between free and equal individuals – for their relations to fall under the scope of the relational ideal. In an age of globalization, this may not seem very persuasive, and it is likely that many pairs of individuals who are not co-citizens have thicker social relations to one another than a good deal of pairs of citizens from their respective countries.[37] At any rate, restricting the scope of the relational ideal in this way ignores the prior and important question of whom we should be socially related to in the first place, whether or not we are socially related presently.

Returning to Anderson and Scheffler, it is striking that the focus in their discussion of the relational ideal fits the statist framework best. Starting with Anderson, she embraces a non-cosmopolitan version of relational egalitarianism: 'In liberal democratic versions of social-contract theory, the fundamental aim of the state is to secure the liberty of its members. Since the democratic state is nothing more than citizens acting collectively, it follows that the fundamental obligation of citizens to one another is to secure the social conditions of everyone's freedom . . . [Democratic egalitarianism] claims that the social condition of living a free life is that one stand in relations of equality with others' (Anderson, 1999: 314–15).[38]

While Anderson develops her ideal of democratic equality from within a statist perspective, she also explicitly acknowledges the need to transcend this perspective. For instance, she seems to suggest that the globalization of the economy means that 'we are all implicated in an international division of labour subject to assessment from an egalitarian point of view' (Anderson, 1999: 321n78), though, for reasons of space, she does not expand on what this implies regarding global justice. This is a pity, since, as I will now explain, some of her remarks made in the course of disparaging the 'atomistic' view of human production suggest that the sort of

---

[37] As Schemmel (2012b: 12) puts it: '[T]he empirical claim that institutional arrangements triggering concern of social justice exist, as a matter of fact, only within the boundaries of established nation-states . . . has attracted much criticism also from the side of theorists of justice who accept the fundamental claim that justice is about fair cooperation: they have pointed to the pervasive and coordinated nature of global social and economic interaction'. Schemmel, however, accepts that between individuals who are not placed within 'common institutional arrangements', 'no concern of social justice is triggered' (Schemmel, 2012b: 12; cp. Nath, 2015: 188–92). Part of Scheffler's account of the value of relating as equals – that it makes one's life better to relate to others as equals because it prevents certain illusory self-conceptions (Chapter 6.2) – sits uneasily with a restriction of the scope of relational equality to people who live within the same institutional framework. Presumably, the relevant illusions can be fostered by hierarchical relations even to people with whom one does not share an institutional framework.

[38] By 'others' she means 'all other citizens'.

egalitarian view she favours has radical implications in relation to global distribution.

In the course of her discussion of justice within a state, she appeals to Cohen's principle of an interpersonal test (cp. Chapter 4.5) and suggests that when we apply it to citizens engaged in a cooperative venture, we can infer a number of conclusions. For instance, we can infer that citizens 'are not to be deprived of basic capabilities on account of where they live' (Anderson, 1999: 323) and that 'no role in the productive system shall be assigned such inadequate benefits that, given the risks and requirements of the job, people could be deprived of the social conditions of their freedom because they have fulfilled its requirements' (Anderson, 1999: 325). Given that the global economy forms one large cooperative venture, these remarks suggest that Anderson's democratic equality, when applied globally, requires the implementation of a minimum wage at a high level globally, since any failure to do so could not, as Anderson sees it, pass the interpersonal test. Whether she would embrace these implications, I do not know. However, they seem a natural extension from her views on the interpersonal test, justice between citizens engaged in a cooperative venture, and her brief remarks on globalization.

Turning now to Scheffler, as we have already seen, his relational ideal is multilayered (Chapter 2.6). He contrasts the distributive ideal of equality with the way in which the ideal of equality 'is more commonly understood . . . a moral ideal governing the relations in which people stand to one another' (Scheffler, 2003a: 21):

> As a moral ideal, it asserts that all people are of equal worth and that there are some claims that people are entitled to make on one another simply by virtue of their status as persons. As a social ideal, it holds that a human society must be conceived of as a cooperative arrangement among equals, each of whom enjoys the same social standing. As a political ideal, it highlights the claims that citizens are entitled to make on one another by virtue of their status as citizens, without any need for a moralized accounting of the details of their particular circumstances. (Scheffler, 2003a: 22; cp. Scheffler, 2003a: 23n42)

Crucially, this multidimensional account suggests that what, say, equality as a moral ideal requires can be different from what equality as a political ideal requires, e.g. the claims one can make simply by virtue of one's status as a person can differ from the claims one can make by virtue of one's status as a citizen. Also, while Scheffler does not elaborate on this, in principle, one of the demands that one can make simply by virtue of one's status as a person is to be socially and politically related to others – perhaps particular others. If not, then the ideal of equality is silent on the important question of whom we should be socially related to and only speaks to how our social relations should look given that they already obtain. As already suggested, this is an important lacuna in an account of justice – a particularly important one in an age of mass migration.

Finally, the notion of equality that Scheffler describes is one that goes much beyond formal equality. Take his description of relational equality as a political ideal and consider a state in which all citizens can make certain claims on one another provided that the details of their particular circumstances – circumstances which are such that establishing them would involve a 'need for a moralized accounting' – are of a particular kind. This would not satisfy relational equality as a political ideal, even though there is a sense in which all citizens are treated equally. This casts light on how, for Scheffler, the relational ideal is not autonomous – its content derives in part from values other than equality, *in casu* respect and/or privacy (cp. Scheffler, 2015).

My main aim here is to point to the fact that Scheffler's ideal of relational equality has broader scope than Anderson's in that, as a moral ideal and, thus, as an ideal *sans phrase*, its scope extends to relations between individuals who do not share any institutional framework. However, what relational equality requires depends on how people are related, and in this sense Scheffler's relational ideal has an important anti-cosmopolitan aspect as well.[39] Those aspects are what Scheffler has in mind when, for instance, he notes that 'people who are committed to the social and political ideal of equality may end up supporting a system that tolerates either more or less inequality of income and wealth than luck egalitarianism does' (Scheffler, 2003a: 24), where it is clear from the context that the inequality he refers to here is inequality between different members of something like a state.

In sum: just as there is a question of the scope of distributive principles, there is a similar question about the scope of relational principles of justice. It is natural to assume that the latter has a narrower scope than the former in that the latter scope can extend no further than actual (or possible) social

---

[39] Scheffler believes that 'special circumstances may at times give rise to special rights', so even as a social and political ideal relational equality does not imply that we should always relate in identical ways to others. It might be replied that the mere fact that the requirements of relational equality as a moral ideal differ from the requirements of relational equality as a social and political ideal implies nothing about whether the latter requirements are more stringent. However, if they are not, in one important respect they would be redundant. In another way, however, they would not, since they would have important implications for who is obligated to satisfy one's claims.

relations, whereas the scope of distributive principles might extend beyond that. That being said, it seems that, presently, social relations are such that it is difficult to see why national borders should define the scope of relational principles of justice. Despite this, arguably, relational egalitarianism has been developed mostly from a state-focused perspective. In part this is due to the fact that its articulation has been tied to the Rawlsian idea of a cooperative scheme between free and equal individuals:

> '[D]emocratic reciprocity holds that citizens may support and impose on each other only those economic, social and political institutional arrangements that all can reasonably accept. Because a social arrangement that allows for excessive social and economic inequalities between citizens will not be one that all can reasonably accept, democratic reciprocity must require . . . the regulation of such inequalities among citizens via a distributive principle'. (Tan, 2008: 666)[40]

Suppose we take a cosmopolitan view of the requirements of relational justice. Is that view not impossibly demanding? Again, it should be borne in mind here that what it is to relate to one another as an equal varies from context to context, e.g. what it is for citizens to relate to one another as equals is different from what it is to relate as equals when the people involved are not co-citizens. To support this idea recall that in Chapter 3 I argued that relating as equals involves treating and regarding one another as equals. The regarding part is one that can be satisfied in a way that is not, as such, demanding. So perhaps we can be cosmopolitan relational egalitarians and still believe that what our ideal requires differs depending on whether we are co-citizens or not. In this respect, the relational ideal is very different from the distributive ideal, since it is harder to see that it makes sense to say that whether or not two people are equally well off depends on whether they are co-citizens or not.

Not only might contextualist cosmopolitanism fit many of our intuitions best; it seems odd to deny that the relational ideal has the widest possible scope. Consider:

(1)   All persons are one another's moral equals.
(2)   All persons, irrespective of citizenship, are socially related to one another.

---

[40] As Schemmel puts it: the focus of democratic equality is 'on what we may justifiably do to each other through our collective institutional arrangements, on how arrangements that we may justifiably impose on each other must be structured. More specifically, DR [democratic reciprocity] focuses on arrangements of social cooperation, and seeks to answer the question when, on which terms, such arrangements are to be regarded as fair' (Schemmel, 2012b: 9).

(3) If (1) and (2), then, irrespective of citizenship, all persons should relate to one another as equals.
(4) Thus, irrespective of citizenship, all persons should relate to one another as equals.

Assuming that (4) implies that relational egalitarianism has universal scope, it seems that for relational egalitarians not to be cosmopolitans, they would have to deny one or more of the three other premises of this argument. Some people argue that not all human beings are persons and fewer people argue that it is unclear whether at the end of the day all persons are moral equals (Arneson, 1999a; McMahan, 2002). That being said, the former claim does not challenge (1) and while the latter claim does challenge (1), it does not do so in any specific anti-cosmopolitan sense, e.g. if moral status is a scalar thing and supervenes on the degree to which one is rational, that would not mean that we have any more reason to ascribe non-instrumental significance to state borders than if we embraced (1).

(2) might be easier to challenge, since there are many pairs of persons who are not co-citizens and who are not socially related to one another. One might respond that the same is the case when it comes to pairs of citizens, e.g. I have never interacted with more than a tiny percentage of my co-citizens. The counterreply might be that we can be indirectly socially related, even if we are not directly socially related, e.g. we can be so because we are subject to the same legally enforced rules. This seems fine, but then we might reply that people who are not co-citizens could be indirectly socially related in the same sense and be subjected to the same rules, e.g. international conventions that their countries have signed. Hence, while (2) can be challenged, it would be difficult to challenge it in a way that motivates a statist, as opposed to a cosmopolitan, scope.[41]

---

[41] Schemmel (2012b: 13) suggests that global institutions 'may not give rise to comprehensive egalitarian claims on the part of individuals to equality in a currency of justice like resources, insofar as the domain of the institution in question may be non-comprehensive (in the case of the WTO: only international trade and the benefits and burdens it creates, not the economic development of its member states as a whole). So it might still be the case that cooperation within states creates the most comprehensive egalitarian requirements, if participation in state-based cooperation continues to govern most parts of most individuals' lives'. Three replies: first, presumably, there could be and maybe actually are libertarian states that 'govern' fewer 'parts of most individuals' lives' than some super-state institutions, e.g. the EU. Hence, Schemmel's point does not motivate a statist scope. Second, suppose that a group of individuals form a set of institutions that govern some part of their lives. Might relational egalitarians not think that they should extend the reach of their institutions? For instance, might they not think that in light of the fact that economic conditions affect social conditions, if a group of individuals lives under an institution that governs their economic conditions, they ought to extend the reach of their shared institution to social conditions?

Consider finally (3). To challenge that premise one would have to claim that the fact that two persons are one another's moral equals and are socially related to one another is not a sufficient condition for their being required to relate as equals. Broadly speaking, there are two things relational egalitarians could say here. They could say that there are additional, non-relational facts, e.g. that these relations are embedded in a shared institutional framework, or, more demandingly and Rawls-style, that they are so and the bearers share a public culture of democratic values that must obtain for the relevant relation to fall under the scope of relational equality. Or, alternatively, they might say that not just any social relation suffices for moral equals being required to relate as equals – only social relations of particular kind, e.g. social relations that are sufficiently significant give rise to the relevant objection.

It is hard to see what the candidate non-relational fact could be, but I do not have any argument for why no such candidate exists. I also have doubts about the qualified social relations view.[42] I think people are required to relate as equals even if their social relations are thin and short-lived, provided that they are moral equals; e.g. I do not see why one is not required to avoid hermeneutical injustice against one's equals when one is only thinly socially related to those persons (cp. Chapter 3.2).

In sum: just as distributive egalitarians must determine whether the scope of equality extends beyond the state, so must relational egalitarians. While relational egalitarians like Anderson and Scheffler have both tended to emphasize non-cosmopolitan aspects of relational equality, both also suggest possible cosmopolitan extensions of their relational ideal, though for different reasons. Anderson does so because the relevant institutional framework which triggers the demands of relational equality in a globalized economy extends much beyond state borders. Scheffler does so because relational equality as a moral ideal governs how people should relate to one another also independently of any shared social and political framework. Thus, given that one adopts a Schefflerian version of the relational moral ideal, it is difficult to see how one could avoid accepting a cosmopolitan scope. Admittedly, my arguments do not amount to a decisive defence of

---

Third, is it clear that the fewer aspects of people's lives that are governed by shared institutions, the less comprehensive egalitarian claims these give rise to?

[42] If you take the view that relating as an equal is valuable for persons, or that it is impersonally valuable, then unless you qualify that view – e.g. by saying that it is valuable to relate as equals provided that one's relations satisfy certain other conditions such that, standardly, citizens and non-citizens are not socially related in the right way – then it is unclear how the view about the value of relating as equals could support a non-cosmopolitan view.

cosmopolitan relational egalitarianism, but at least they show what relational egalitarians must argue if they want to defend a non-cosmopolitan version. Also, I have pointed to the need for relational egalitarians to address the question of under what circumstances we ought to have the sort of relations to other individuals to which the relational ideal applies. To my knowledge, no relational egalitarian has addressed this issue so far.

5.6   Conclusion

In this chapter, I have looked at four issues which any full specification of the relational ideal must address: intergenerational justice, justice between age groups, the site of justice, and the scope of justice. One important aim of this chapter is to show that these issues of specification are strikingly similar to issues faced by friends of distributive justice. Another important aim is to articulate the most plausible version of the relational ideal. On that note, I have defended the following views: that relational justice involves both a time-relative and whole-lives perspective; that the site of relational justice plausibly extends beyond institutions to the actions of individuals in the course of their daily lives (and, if anything, does so much more plausibly than in the case of any distributive ideal); and that relational equality is best seen as a cosmopolitan idea, albeit one which, at a first-order level, allows for partiality. Finally, I have argued that the issue of intergenerational justice points to the limits of the relational ideal. Because we are not relevantly socially related to (past and) future generations, and because there is such a thing as intergenerational justice – I did not defend this claim, but it is widely accepted – the relational ideal must at least be supplemented with some form of distributive ideal. This provides some background motivation for the ecumenical project that I shall pursue in Chapter 7. But first I must turn to the rationale for relational equality.

CHAPTER 6

Justification of and by the Ideal

6.1 Introduction

Most agree that a society in which individuals relate as equals is valuable. Some see this value as instrumental, while others see it as non-instrumental. Those who subscribe to the former view might hold that it is important that we relate as equals because the alternative results in frustration, anguish etc., presumably especially on the part of those who are related to as less than equals. Those who take the latter view hold that relating as equals is valuable – only or also – independently of its causal effects, e.g. because it is valuable in itself, or because it is part of a greater whole which is valuable in itself.

Relational egalitarians have rightly pointed out that luck egalitarians have expended too little effort in defending luck egalitarianism. They have not had much to say about what makes equality valuable and have tended to presuppose an audience of distributive egalitarians, to whom no such justification is dialectically necessary (cp. Arneson, 1989; Cohen, 2011: 3). Instead, they have focused on exploring what sort of distributive equality is valuable given that some of sort of distributive equality is valuable. In doing so, they have ignored the more basic question about whether distributive equality is valuable and why. They have, as Anderson puts it, failed to explain what the point of distributive equality is. Some might think that, in a similar way, relational egalitarians have failed to explain, or at least said too little about, what the point of relational equality is (Tomlin, 2015). My goal in this chapter is to explore the question of what makes relating as equals valuable or morally required. Ultimately, the answer to this question depends on the account of what it is to relate as equals offered in Chapter 3. For instance, any account of what makes relational equality valuable must accommodate the fact that relating as equals has moral, social and epistemic as well as aesthetic dimensions. Any such account must also acknowledge the fact that relating as equals has two components: treating and regarding one another as equals.

Section 6.2 discusses the view that relational equality is instrumentally valuable. I believe that relational equality is indeed instrumentally valuable. However, even if so, this is less interesting in the present context. If the concern for relational equality is purely instrumental, then the disagreement between luck and relational egalitarians is shallow in the sense that assuming, as some studies suggest, that distributive equality too is instrumentally good, relational egalitarians will have to say that relational and distributive equality are justified for the same reason. Hence, Sections 6.3 and 6.4 explore two alternative views: that relational equality is constitutive of the good for persons and that it is impersonally good. Section 6.5 addresses a different relational view: that, in view of the fact that persons are each other's moral equals, relating as equals is morally required whether or not doing so is valuable. On this view, relational equality is a deontic norm, which is not simply reducible to or derivable from the claim that relating as equals is a valuable state of affairs. Section 6.6 takes one step back and assesses the claim – often made or suggested by relational egalitarians – that in exploring the value of equality, the concerns of so-called real-life egalitarians have a privileged epistemic status relative to the concerns of political philosophers of an egalitarian bent and relative to real-life non-egalitarians.

My main contention in this chapter is that relational egalitarians have suggested quite different accounts of what justifies relational equality and that, while they have been more attentive to the question of the value of relational equality than luck egalitarians have been to the question of distributive equality, they have not had as much to say in response to that question as one should reasonably expect. I argue that the most plausible view says that relating as equals reflects a deontic requirement rooted in the fact that we are one another's moral equals. In Chapter 7 I will propose a grounding of relational (and luck) egalitarianism in fairness.[1]

6.2   Instrumentally Valuable

Let us first consider the instrumental view of relational equality. On this view, relational equality is valuable because of its positive causal effects, e.g. solidarity (Nagel, 1979: 106). To say that something 'merely' has instrumental

---

[1] Fairness and moral equality are connected in the following way: If X and Y are moral equals, it is unfair that they are differently situated absent justifying facts about their differential exercise of responsibility. However, if they are moral unequals, it may not be unfair that they are differently situated even absent justifying facts about their differential exercise of responsibility (Chapter 7.6).

effect may sound slightly derogatory, but it is not (cp. Mason, 2015: 141–2). The fact that I live in an atmosphere which contains roughly 20 per cent oxygen has merely instrumental value for me: if an atmosphere of that kind were not causally necessary for life I would not see it as valuable in any way. Still, it is extremely valuable for us that we live in such an atmosphere. Ultimately, we might suspect that most valuable things are only instrumentally valuable, especially if we hold a highly abstract and monistic view of value, e.g. that only pleasurable mental states are valuable.

On a purely instrumental view of the relational ideal, if we could avoid the negative effects of hierarchical relations, treating one another as equals would have no value at all (cf. Arneson 2010, 32–44). Few relational egalitarians take this view. That being said, some relational egalitarians certainly hold that relational equality is instrumentally valuable in part at least. For instance, Samuel Scheffler believes that relating as equals (or living in a society where people relate to one another as such) is 'good both intrinsically and instrumentally' (Scheffler, 2005: 19). One of the ways in which the latter is the case is that hierarchy creates 'patterns of deference and privilege' that 'exert a stifling effect on human freedom and inhibit the possibilities of human exchange . . . [Patterns of deference and privilege] distort people's attitudes towards themselves, undermining the self-respect of some and encouraging the insidious sense of superiority in others' (Scheffler, 2005: 19).[2]

I am inclined to believe Scheffler is right about this. However, I also believe that there are limits to how much support relational egalitarians can derive from this claim. First, while, like Scheffler, I find it quite plausible that since, generally, hierarchy distorts human relations and people's self-conceptions in all sorts of ways (which, let us assume *arguendo*, we all think are disvaluable), causal relations often turn out to be surprisingly different from, and much more complex than, one would have expected. Hence, to provide a serious argument for the instrumental value of relational equality, one would have to be much more attentive to the relevant social science literature than relational egalitarians are on the causal effects of hierarchy on human relations and psyche.[3]

---

[2] Similarly, I am unsure why relating as equals cannot involve developing a 'sense of solidarity and of participation in a shared fate' that relies on 'unsustainable myths or forms of false consciousness' (Scheffler, 2005: 19) (or for that matter relating as equals relying on no unsustainable myths or false consciousness). Scheffler does not explain why egalitarian relations are not, or at least less, susceptible to such illusory forms of consciousness.

[3] I do not say this in a spirit of criticism – it is perfectly legitimate in a philosophy journal article (or book, I hasten to add) which merely sketches the contours of a view to rely on empirical hypotheses of the sort Scheffler and other relational egalitarians rely on.

Moreover, one would also have to be more specific about the relevant non-instrumentally valuable effects that relational equality brings about. Take the 'insidious sense of superiority in others', which Scheffler takes to be a concomitant of hierarchy.[4] Is such an insidious sense non-instrumentally bad for the person who judges herself to be superior or is it (only) instrumentally bad in that the view is mistaken and that the relevant mistake will often lead the holder of that belief to act in ways which turn out to have very bad consequences for the person in question?

Second, even if relational egalitarians provided solid evidence for ways in which relational equality is instrumentally valuable, this at most justifies them in making a very weak claim on behalf of relational equality, i.e. that it is instrumentally good in some respects. But presumably this claim is much weaker than the claim that relational egalitarians really want to assert – namely, that relational equality is better *all things considered* than hierarchy – and in any case a rather uninteresting claim: presumably, very many things that are thoroughly bad, all things considered, do have some good effects. To justify this more ambitious claim, relational egalitarians must show that once we take into account not only the ways in which relational equality is instrumentally good, but also the ways in which it is instrumentally bad, if any such ways there are, as well as the ways in which relational inequality (assuming this is to be the only alternative) is instrumentally as well as non-instrumentally good and bad, the overall balance comes out in favour of relational equality. Note also that when we compare relating as equals with relating as unequals, there are ways of relating as unequals which are are only slightly different from relating as equals (Chapter 2.6). Hence, if these are the ways of relating that are being compared to relating as equals, it would be surprising if these are instrumentally *much* worse for us, though this may depend on the relevant value in relation to which relating as equals is said to be instrumentally valuable. For instance, small deviations from relating as equals might result in great losses of solidarity, but only the small stifling of human freedom.

Despite these complications, again I am inclined to think with Scheffler and others that social equality is all things considered better than social hierarchy (but see Arneson, 2010: 41–2). However, if you look for an argument to this effect in the relational egalitarian literature that I have surveyed here, you will look in vain. For instance, you will not find any

---

[4] One might suspect that for many knowing that they enjoy a superior distributive position in itself involves a similar insidious sense of superiority and, thus, that awareness of one's superior distribution position involves the same instrumental disvalue as being at the top of a social hierarchy.

response to the retort from friends of hierarchy that relating as equals involves the opposite dangers, e.g. that 'truthful relations among people' and 'genuine self-understanding' might be harder to achieve if people are firmly committed to relating as equals, because it prevents us from relating to people who are truly excellent in the way we should and prevents us from fully understanding the extent to which we fall short of such exemplars. Likewise, you will not find any arguments to the effect that, say, conformity is not an effect of relational equality and, thus, that individuality is best served by relational inequality.[5]

Third, suppose that relational egalitarians were to lift the burden of argument identified under the two previous points. Even then they would have failed to provide a satisfactory instrumental defence for the claim that the ideal of relational equality is superior to the ideal of distributive equality. One reason why is that nothing in the distributive ideal implies that relational equality – or for that matter any other (political) ideal, e.g. democracy, retribution, autonomy, anti-perfectionism – is not, all things considered, instrumentally valuable. Not only is the claim that relational equality is, all things considered, instrumentally valuable not incompatible with the distributive ideal; it is a claim which, in a sense, is in a different ballpark altogether than the claim which defines the distributive ideal, to wit, that a particular distribution is non-instrumentally valuable or required. Hence, if all that relational egalitarians want to assert is this, not only is what they are saying compatible with the ideal of distributive equality, but they are also simply addressing a different question from the one which friends of the distributive ideal address. If so, this leaves one wondering why relational egalitarians have given so much attention to perceived deficiencies of the ideal of distributive equality.

In sum: I have little doubt that relational equality is instrumentally valuable, though, for reasons indicated, its instrumental value might be small depending on the relevant form of unequal relations that form the baseline. However, relational egalitarians have done little to show that it is (they have mostly hinted at it) and even less to show that, all things considered, it is instrumentally valuable. And even if they did corroborate the latter claim, in doing so they would not be expressing any view which is not completely compatible with the distributive ideal, including luck egalitarianism. I conclude that it would be much more interesting if

---

[5] Such arguments are found for instance in classical defences of social hierarchy by Burke (1987 [1790]) and Plato (1983 [377–370 bc]).

relational equality were non-instrumentally valuable (too), so this is the question to which I turn now.

6.3 Non-Instrumentally Valuable for Persons

Broadly speaking, there are two ways in which relational egalitarians might argue that relational equality is non-instrumentally valuable (whether, in addition to that, instrumentally valuable or not): they might argue that it is non-instrumentally valuable for persons because what is valuable for persons is constituted by relating to others as equals, or they might argue that relational equality is impersonally valuable, i.e. it is non-instrumentally valuable whether or not it is non-instrumentally valuable for persons.[6] In this section, I explore the first possibility.

There are various views on what is non-instrumentally good for people. On one widely accepted taxonomical view, broadly speaking there are three different, main accounts of what makes people's lives good: mental-state accounts, preference-based accounts, and objective-list accounts (Parfit, 1984: 493–502). The first view submits that goodness for persons consists of their mental states being pleasurable (or good). The preference-based account submits that goodness for persons consist of their – actual or relevantly hypothetical – preferences being satisfied. The objective-list account holds that there are certain things that are good for people independently of their preferences or mental states.

If we are to argue that relational equality is non-instrumentally good for people, the most promising way of doing that is to defend an objective-list account of goodness for people. While it might be true that people's mental states are better, e.g. more pleasurable, if they relate as equals – the sense of humiliation one can suffer from being treated as less than an equal can be intensely unpleasant – it is also clear that, at best, it is contingently true that relational equality makes mental states more pleasurable. However, presumably relational egalitarians do not think that relational equality is valuable contingent only on people experiencing relating to others as equals as being pleasurable, in part because, as a matter of fact, it seems

---

[6] If relational egalitarians were to argue that goodness for persons simply consists of relating to others as equals, they would be making the claim that relational equality is non-instrumentally valuable for persons. However, I disregard this view, since, clearly, relational equality is not the whole of personal goodness. A person who relates to everyone as a perfect equal, but who suffers constant pains and who spends most of his life counting blades of grass on Port Meadow lives a worse life than one who relates to everyone as a perfect equal, suffers no pain and spends most of her life writing insightful philosophical treatises.

that some people derive pleasure from relating to others as superiors, and yet relational egalitarians do not think that relational equality is somehow not justifiable to such persons. Moreover, as I analysed relating as equals in Chapter 3, it has two components: treating and regarding as equals. Since, by and large, only the latter component pertains to people's mental states, only that part of relating as equals can be said to be non-instrumentally valuable in an account based on mental states.[7] Hence, in this account, a state of affairs in which no one relates as equals because, although everyone regards everyone else as equals, they fail to treat them as such might not be worse in the relevant respect than one in which everyone relates as equals. Hence, relating as equals has no non-instrumental value for us relative to the relevant baseline.

A problem similar to the one just discussed seems to be involved in attempting to ground relational equality in people's preferences. Obviously, many people do prefer to relate to others – at least to some others – as equals, and for them relating to others as equals is good on a preference-based account. However, some people prefer not to relate to others as equals and, presumably, relational egalitarians will want to say that their ideal applies to these people as well. If so, what is good for individuals cannot consist in actual preference satisfaction, assuming that the justification for relational equality lies in how it benefits people.

At this point, friends of a preference-based account could move to an account based not on people's actual preferences, but on hypothetical preferences instead. Those who favour this move would focus on the preferences that people would have if they were better informed and better able to process the information available to them. Presumably, there are people who prefer relating to others as superiors, who would instead prefer to relate as equals if they were better informed or more rational, e.g. if they did not have false beliefs about the possibility of having deep personal relations to someone whom one treats as an inferior. But there might also be people who prefer to relate as equals, but who would, if better informed, prefer to relate to others as superiors. Moreover, in any case relational egalitarians want to defend a claim which is much stronger than that: to wit, that no one who is suitably ideally informed and rational would prefer hierarchical to egalitarian relations. To show that this is so seems quite difficult, unless of course to be relevantly informed includes being

---

[7] I say 'by and large' because on the communicative notion of expressing, treating someone as an equal involves a certain communicative intention.

informed about what is objectively valuable for persons. This takes us to the objective-list theory in a way which seems to make preferences epiphenomenal.

Assuming that we endorse an objective-list account of well-being, on what grounds could relational egalitarians claim that relational equality is good for people? There are various ways in which they might support the claim that relational equality is part of what is objectively good for people. For instance, they might say that deep personal relations are constitutive of living well. Hence, if two persons live identical lives except for the fact that one person enjoys deep personal relations and the other person does not, the former person lives a better life. Relational egalitarians might then add that deep personal relations can – not as a matter of causality, but as a matter of the nature of deep personal relations – obtain only between persons who relate as equals (cp. Mill, 1988 [1869]: 26). Or they might say that – again as a matter of the nature of deep personal relations – egalitarian personal relations are somehow deeper and, thus, better for people than inegalitarian ones, all other things being equal (Griffin, 1986: 56–92; Tomlin, 2015: 164). Or they might simply say that 'it is bad for people if they are servile or too deferential, even if this does not frustrate their desires or affect their experienced well-being' (Parfit, 2000: 86; Rawls, 2001b: 131; O'Neill, 2008: 123).

Another line of argument relational egalitarians might offer is this: living well is living in truth. Since people are moral equals, they live in truth only if they live as moral equals and in ways which are fitting for moral equals. Hence, a slave owner who is being treated as a superior lives in untruth and, thus, lives in a way which is worse for him than if he lived together with his slaves – who would then not be his slaves – as an equal.[8]

A third line of argument is that freedom and autonomy are objectively valuable: 'To be subject to another's command threatens one's interests, as those in command are liable to serve themselves at the expense of their subordinates . . . Such a condition of subjection to the arbitrary wills of others is objectionable in itself, and has further objectionable consequences' (Anderson, 2008a: 145–6; cp. O'Neill, 2008: 130n30; Tomlin, 2015: 13n46).[9] Since, by definition, relational equality implies not being

---

[8] Some relational egalitarians express themselves in such a way that they seem to hold the view that relating as equals is better than relating as an inferior, but not necessarily better than relating as a superior. For instance, Scanlon writes: 'it is an evil for people to be treated as inferior, or made to feel inferior' (Scanlon, 2000: 204; Tomlin, 2015: 12).

[9] Cp. 'servitude, except when it brutalizes, though corrupting to both, is less so to the slaves than to the slave-masters. It is wholesomer for the moral nature to be restrained, even by arbitrary power, than to

subject to others' (arbitrary) commands, relational equality is good for people.

No doubt there are other items of an account of objective value for persons which are tied, by their very nature, to relating to others as equals. And, of course, relating to others as equals, or at least to some significant others, might in itself be held to be a constituent of a good life. The main advantage for relational egalitarians of focusing on an objective-list account is that it implies that relational equality is valuable, whether or not people find pleasure in relating to others as equals and whether or not they prefer relating to others as equals.

Whichever way relational egalitarians argue that relational equality is constitutive of the personal good, they must answer the following questions: Does a person's life go better the greater the number of people to whom he or she relates as an equal? Does a person's life go worse the greater the number of people to whom he or she relates as an unequal? If the answers to these two questions are affirmative, it seems we should encourage people to maximize the number of people with whom they relate as equals. Call this view the *maximizing view*.

The maximizing view has some unattractive implications. Suppose you have ten friends, all of whom you relate to as equals, and I have twenty. If everything else is equal – e.g. the amount of time we spend with friends – it does not seem to me that, for that reason, I have a better life than you have.

A view which avoids this counterintuitive implication is one according to which, once one relates to a certain threshold number of people as equals – perhaps people with whom one is otherwise significantly related – then whether or not one relates to more people as equals is neither good nor bad for one. Call this the *threshold view*.

There is some plausibility to the threshold view. However, it is also clear that it does not serve the typical argumentative purposes of relational egalitarians well. Suppose we live in a society in which it is true of everyone that they enjoy a threshold level of egalitarian relations to a significant number of others. Suppose that politically speaking the relevant society is a hierarchical one. Given the threshold view and the relevant assumption about everyone enjoying a threshold level of egalitarian social relations, we would not make people's lives better by turning this hierarchical society into an egalitarian one. Yet this is what relational egalitarians would favour. Hence, they cannot justify relational equality by appeal to its value for

---

be allowed to exercise arbitrary power without restraint' (Mill, 1988 [1869]: 82; cp. Anderson, 2012a: 50).

persons – at least not when the latter is construed along the lines of the threshold view.

At this point some might accept the critical points that I have made so far about the maximizing and the threshold views, but argue that I have been barking up the wrong tree, since both views are obviously inadequate as accounts of how relational equality is non-instrumentally good for us.[10] Both views assume that the value of egalitarian social relations is a uni-dimensional thing in that they go into the same pot whether they are personal relations, the sort of social relations we have to others qua members of civil society, political relations, or simply the sort of social relations one might have to another simply qua a human being with whom one interacts. However, one might think that each type of social relation is independently constituent of a person's good. Hence, we might suggest for instance:

> For any type of relevant social relation and for any person, if a person enjoys social relations to a sufficient number of people and if these relations are suitably egalitarian, then that person's life is better.

On this view – call it the *spheres of relational equality view* – if a person does not enjoy political relations to anyone else (and assuming that political relations are a relevant kind of social relation), it would make that person's life better to start relating to others in a political and egalitarian way. So to live the best life possible it is not enough, say, to enjoy a large number of egalitarian personal relations – one must also enjoy egalitarian social relations of other kinds. Also, the spheres view has the advantage that one might say that the relevant threshold number of persons to whom one can relate such that relating as an equal to an additional number of people does not make one's life go better varies – even in nature, i.e. in terms of whether it is an absolute number of people or a ratio or something else – from one sphere of relations to another. So perhaps when it comes to friendship, once one relates as an equal to ten friends, relating as an equal to a greater number of friends does not make one's life better, whereas when it comes to citizenship, once one relates to a million co-citizens as an equal, e.g. through the relevant political institutions, one's life can still be improved by relating to more people as an equal provided that there are more co-citizens than one million.

---

[10] Alternatively, some might suggest that while the positive value of relating as equals reaches a certain level after which further egalitarian relations do not result in more prudential value, there is no such threshold for the negative value of inegalitarian social relations. Still, an objection of the sort I raised against the maximizing view seems to apply to the present asymmetric view as well.

While the spheres view might avoid some of the problems of the maximizing and the threshold accounts of the personal value of relational equality, it is beginning to look amazingly complex and quite unlike other values that we think are non-instrumentally good for people. Moreover, it is unclear that it might not need to be refined further. Might, for instance, cosmopolitan relational egalitarians who want to ground relational equality in its non-instrumental personal value not have to claim that it does actually benefit people if they were to have egalitarian political relations to all people? Hence, at this point one might start to wonder whether it would not be more promising for relational egalitarians to ground their ideal in some other way.

There are at least three other problems with an account of the value of relational equality based on its being constitutive of what is good for persons that add force to this worry. First, the claim that relational equality is valuable because relational equality is non-instrumentally good for people renders the disagreement between distributive and relational egalitarians shallow in a sense related to the one which we encountered in the previous section as well: luck egalitarians can care about relational equality in the same way that relational egalitarians do. They too can accept an account of the personal good according to which relating to others as equals is constitutively good. They will simply add that, setting aside concerns about responsibility, fairness requires that people live equally good lives. Or to put this in more general terms: luck egalitarianism is a distributive principle. The claim that relational equality is constitutive of the personal good is entirely neutral not only with regard to what the correct distributive principle is, but also with regard to whether egalitarian justice is to be cashed out in terms of a distributive principle or in some other way, as relational egalitarians claim. Accordingly, one cannot ground a concern for relational equality simply in a concern for the personal good – not even if relating to others as equals constitutes the personal good all on its own. This points in the direction of the second problem.

Saying that relational equality is constitutive of the personal good is not to say that people should relate as equals.[11] Indeed, for all that has been said so far, someone who embraces the present view should concede that in many cases we should *not* relate to others as equals. For presumably even if relating to others as equals is constitutive of the personal good, it is not the

---

[11] Moreover, there might be relations which are such that the personal good is partly constituted by not relating as equals, e.g. perhaps good relations between parents and children are better for the parties involved if they are inegalitarian.

only constitutive good, e.g. if I am in physical pain throughout my entire life and you are not, my life is worse than yours, even if we both relate to an equal number of people in an equally relationally egalitarian way. Perhaps this is so even if to some degree some of your friends relate to you as inferiors or superiors. In short: at most, relating to others as equals is one among several factors that constitute a good life. Hence, to make people's lives as good as possible – assuming that we have such a duty – perhaps sometimes we should render them better off in terms of these other constitutive factors at the expense of the degree to which they relate to others as equals. Admittedly, I have not shown that we should make people's lives as good as possible. However, that is not the present point. The present point is that even if we agree that the good life is constituted in part by relating to others as equals, much more needs to be said about why that implies that we ought, morally speaking, to relate as equals. Perhaps such a story could be provided. But presently it has not been told and, in view of my previous points in this section, it faces some serious obstacles.

The third problem is to explain in what sense of relating as equals it is non-instrumentally good for persons to so relate. For instance, in Chapter 3.2 I argued that one dimension is the empirical dimension. However, it seems very unlikely that it is non-instrumentally good for us to relate as equals – whether this claim pertains to the regarding or the treating component – empirically or socially speaking (assuming, realistically, that often and as a matter of fact we are not empirical or social equals).[12] Similarly, in Chapter 3.3 I introduced the communicative notion of 'treating as', which implies that X treats Y as an equal if X's treatment of Y is intended to communicate the message that Y is X's equal. While the communicative aspect of social relations might be central to the concerns of relational egalitarians, I doubt it makes any non-instrumental difference to goodness for people, e.g. I do not think that two persons who are identical in all respects other than that one of them often communicates or is the recipient of communications of messages of equality, while the other is not, live lives that are unequally good. A similar point pertains to the expressive and the presuppositional notions of 'treating as'.[13]

In sum: the conclusion to draw from the present section is somewhat analogous to the one I drew in the previous section. I am open to the idea that relational equality is indeed non-instrumentally valuable to people.

---

[12] This is not to deny that some ways of not relating as social and empirical equals might undermine our relating as equals in other dimensions.

[13] For the record, I believe that the motivational notion of 'treating as' is the most plausible candidate for a notion of 'treating as' that is non-instrumentally good for individuals.

However, I also pointed out that an account of that personal value which has a chance of fitting relational egalitarian purposes has to be quite complex. Finally, I offered three reasons for why even a suitably complex view faces some serious challenges: namely, that any view of what is non-instrumentally good for people is neutral on what egalitarian justice requires; that, in any case, it might not be best overall for people to relate as equals; and, finally, that it is unclear which notion of relating as equals is the bearer of non-instrumental value for people.

6.4 Impersonally Valuable

In view of the arguments in the two previous sections, relational egalitarians might submit that, whether or not relational equality is instrumentally valuable and whether or not relational equality is non-instrumentally good for people, relational equality is non-instrumentally, impersonally good (cp. Nagel, 1979: 108; cp. Scheffler, 2005: 21; Fourie, 2012: 119ff). Martin O'Neill appears to subscribe to this view: 'the Non-intrinsic egalitarian can allow that certain kinds of egalitarian relations have a value that is not reducible to the effects on individual welfare that those social relations may have' (O'Neill, 2008: 141–2).[14]

On this view, the world is a better place if, say, friends and family members relate as equals, if employers and employees relate as equals, if citizens relate as equals, and – assuming that we are cosmopolitans – that all human beings relate as equals, even if none of these egalitarian relations benefit those who are involved in them, or anyone else for that matter. No doubt we might say that it is very likely that egalitarian relations are massively beneficial for individuals – at least, compared to *very* unequal social relations. However, on the present view the value of relational equality is not contingent on relational equality being good for individuals, and in a way that is a good thing. Consider the slave society which I introduced in Chapter 1. Presumably, relational egalitarians will prefer – in one respect at least – an egalitarian society to this slave-based society even if, amazingly, the latter is instrumentally preferable and even better for the people living in that society. The impersonal value of relating as equals is a potential basis for such a claim.

Saying that relating as equals has impersonal value implies that something can have value even if it is good for no one. Some reject that anything

---

[14] Non-intrinsic egalitarianism is the egalitarian position favoured by O'Neill. It falls, he contends, under neither Parfit's telic nor deontic concepts of egalitarianism.

can have value if it is not valuable (in any way) for someone. Call this the *person-affecting requirement* (Temkin, 1993: 256–8). This is not so much an argument as a label for a position which one must reject if one holds that it has impersonal value to relate as equals. In fact, rejecting the person-affecting requirement is a position that one holds if one holds any of a number of fairly common views about value. For instance, if one subscribes to a retributivist view, one believes that retribution has impersonal value even if it is valuable to no one. If one believes that nature has value even setting aside its value for animals and human beings such that it would be bad if species diversity were reduced in a way not bad for any specimens, one rejects the person-affecting view of goodness. The more items one can mention that appear to have impersonal value, the less plausible the person-affecting view is.

One item which is often claimed to have impersonal value and which is particularly relevant in the present context is distributive equality. One way to bring out that distributive equality insofar as it has value must have impersonal value is to imagine a levelling-down situation. Suppose we must choose between everyone being at 100 or, alternatively, one half being at 150 and the other half at 149. The first and equal state of affairs is worse for everyone involved than the second and slightly unequal state of affairs. Indeed, it is likely that the former situation could be described in such a way that it is good for no one in any respect. Yet distributive egalitarians seem committed to claim that the equal state of affairs is in one respect better than the unequal state of affairs in which everyone is better off. If so, equality must have impersonal value and, of course, if there are no impersonal values, it is, as friends of the levelling-down objection infer, a mistake to believe that distributive equality is non-instrumentally valuable.

Some relational egalitarians find the levelling-down objection forceful. Anderson (2010a: 20–1), for instance, endorses a version of the levelling-down objection to distributive equality, according to which justice cannot require a 'gratuitous waste of a good . . . for the sole purpose of ensuring that no one has more than others'.[15] However, if it is impersonally valuable that people relate as equals, relational egalitarians cannot press the objection against distributive egalitarians. While it could be the case that distributive equality has no impersonal value, whereas the fact that people relate as equals has impersonal value, that requires an argument which does not rest on the person-affecting principle. This reflects the fact that, unlike

---

[15] Admittedly, the levelling-down objection is normally seen as an objection to telic egalitarianism and here Anderson is concerned with what justice requires.

the claim that relational equality is good for people, the claim that relational equality has impersonal value is of the same sort as, albeit consistent with, the claim that distributive equality is impersonally valuable.[16]

To assess the contention that relational equality has impersonal value, we must address some of the same questions that we looked at in the previous section in order to learn more about the exact shape of that value. Is it, for instance, impersonally better the greater the number of people who relate to one another of equals, or is there some threshold such that once a sufficient number of egalitarian relations exist, it does not make the world better that additional egalitarian relations are formed? If we take the maximizing view, it would follow that by adding new people who relate to others as equals, we make the world better from the point of view of relational equality.[17] While I do not know of anyone who has explored population ethics from this point of view, I suspect that once we ascribe impersonal value to relational equality, population ethics becomes an interesting test case for relational equality.[18]

Impersonal relational egalitarians will also have to say something about whether people who are treated as less than equals are wronged. Given that X is not wronged simply because Y fails to promote something of impersonal value which somehow implicates X, it seems that such an explanation is not easy to give, which is a problem to the extent that we think that victims being related to as less than equals are being wronged. Admittedly, impersonally inclined relational egalitarians might simply insist that relational inequality is impersonally wrong, but add that it does not wrong anyone in particular – most relevantly, it does not wrong those who are treated as less than equals. While this is a possible move, I suppose that

---

[16] O'Neill believes that the levelling down objection is weak. He thinks equality which is good for no one in any respect might be better than inequality, because the former state of affairs involves the 'eradication of servility, domination and exploitation' (O'Neill, 2008: 142, 146) – states of affairs which, according to O'Neill, are (also) impersonally bad. Accordingly, O'Neill does not think that the value of equality is mysterious because of its impersonal nature, but because of its specifically arithmetical nature (O'Neill, 2008: 148; for my reply to the argument, see Chapter 2.5).

[17] Suppose relational equality has no positive impersonal value. It is just the case that relational inequality has negative impersonal value (cp. Persson, 2001: 31). Hence, a world without people is exactly as good as a world with people, all of whom relate as equals. On this view, we do not make the world a better place by adding more people and, accordingly, the present implication is avoided. However, the negative value view has the possibly equally unattractive implication that a world with no people is better than a world with billions of people, all of whom relate to one another as 'almost equals'.

[18] I also suspect that many of the same problems, e.g. the mere addition paradox (Parfit, 1984: 419–41), that face e.g. a distributive egalitarian principle will face relational equality in its present version as well.

most believe that relating as unequals is wrong in large part because it wrongs those who are treated as less than equals.[19]

Friends of the impersonal view will also have to address the question of whether non-egalitarian relations – generally or in the case of some particular social relations – have impersonal value. The mere fact that egalitarian social relations have impersonal value does not imply that hierarchical relations cannot have impersonal value too. Moreover, just as it would be very implausible to claim that the only thing that has value for people is relational equality, it would be very implausible to claim that the only thing that has impersonal value is relational equality. A world of people who are constantly being tortured but relate as equals is worse than a world of people who live amazingly good lives and who do not quite relate as equals. Hence, pluralist relational egalitarians have to concede that sometimes it can be better, all things considered, to bring about a state of affairs in which people do not relate as equals.

Friends of the impersonal value account also have to face an issue which friends of the personal value account avoid depending on the scope of relational equality.[20] Suppose that the scope of relational equality is not universal, i.e. at least for some social relations it is not impersonally valuable that all individuals relate to one another (cp. Chapter 5.5). Rather, it is impersonally valuable that subsets of people who are socially related to one another in certain ways relate as equals. By way of illustration: it is not impersonally valuable that all human beings relate politically as equals. Rather, it is impersonally valuable that all Swedes relate politically as equals, impersonally valuable that all Finns relate politically as equals, and so on and so forth. Moreover, it is more valuable, impersonally speaking, that a greater number of subsets of people who are socially related to one another in the relevant way relate as equals than that a lower number of subsets of people do so. Thus, a world in which only the Swedes relate as equals is worse than a world in which it is true of citizens of any nation that they relate to other members of their nation as equals. Presumably, people can and do have preferences about how a certain impersonal value is realized even if, *ex hypothesi*, this does not, directly at least, affect the quality of their own lives. Swedes might prefer that they relate as equals, and Finns that they do etc. Hence, on the assumption that the satisfaction of people's impersonal preferences matters from the point of view of

---

[19] This remark is in tension with the essentially impersonal account of the wrongness of discrimination that I give in (Lippert-Rasmussen, 2013a: 165–83).

[20] Tomlin (2015: 24) finds it puzzling how the value of relationships – e.g. the egalitarian relationship in which citizens stand to one another – can be 'found outside our lives'.

justice, the present view about the impersonal value of relational equality might well give rise to an issue of distributive justice. Suppose I – a gifted statesman leading a powerful nation – can either make it the case that Swedes relate perfectly as equals and Finns fail abysmally to do so, or alternatively make it the case that Swedes and Finns are quite close and equally so to relating as equals. If distributive justice requires that I realize the second option – something I find quite plausible – it follows that the claim that relational equality is impersonally valuable is not a way of avoiding distributive issues. Rather, it is to make a claim which is not only consistent with a concern for distributive justice, but which might well give rise to a new set of questions in distributive justice (cp. Tomlin, 2015: 24).

In sum: while it better serves the argumentative aims of relational egalitarians to claim that relational equality has impersonal value than to claim that it is good for people, it is far from clear that this will actually be a satisfactory position for relational egalitarians to take. For one thing, it does not follow in any very direct way that people ought to relate as equals. Moreover, ascribing impersonal value to relational equality is not only consistent with, but might actually give rise to new issues in, distributive justice, in which case relational equality cannot be seen as an alternative to the distributive ideal, which is how relational egalitarians tend to think of their view.

6.5 Not (Primarily) Valuable, but Required

In the three previous sections, I looked at a number of suggestions about how relational equality is grounded in the value of egalitarian social relations. In view of the fact that none of the attempts looked particularly promising, perhaps the right response is to say that relational equality is not grounded in value – at least not in any straightforward way. Rather, the ideal of relational equality should be understood as a claim about how we ought to relate to one another. As a matter of fact, we are one another's moral equals and in relating as equals we honour that fact, and this is what grounds the ideal of relational equality. Embracing this view – deontic relational egalitarianism – might make it easier to see how relational egalitarians can answer the challenge to explain why they are not simply addressing a question which is different from the one distributive egalitarians are asking, e.g. what makes someone's life good (cp. Section 6.3)? The requirement that if people are co-citizens, say, they should relate as equals seems to be a requirement of egalitarian justice, i.e. one that, unlike the claim that relating as equals is good for us, is in the same ballpark as the luck egalitarian claim that it is unjust, and therefore bad, if some people are worse off than others through no responsibility of their own.

Christian Schemmel is a relational egalitarian who is committed to deontic relational egalitarianism:

> Relational egalitarianism . . . is a view about social justice; its aim is to specify rights and duties that individuals have as members of society, and which normally override other social values . . . The objection to [inegalitarian] relationships is not merely that they are, in some sense, bad for people, but that they constitute unjust treatment: domination involves subjection to the arbitrary exercise of power on the part of somebody else; marginalization involves an unjust denial of opportunities to participate in basic social and political institutions. (Schemmel, 2011: 366; cp. Schemmel, 2015)

Anderson also appears to subscribe to a version of deontic relational egalitarianism: 'Egalitarians base claims to social and political equality on the fact of universal moral equality . . . egalitarians seek a social order in which persons stand in relations of equality' (Anderson, 1999: 313).[21]

Before exploring this proposal I want to draw attention to a similar and quite influential distinction that Derek Parfit makes with regard to distributive equality. Parfit distinguishes between two forms of distributive egalitarianism: telic and deontic. Telic egalitarianism is a view about value. It claims that it is in itself bad if some people are worse off than others (Parfit, 1998: 4). Deontic egalitarians do not think that it is in itself 'bad if some people are worse off than others' (Parfit, 1998: 6). While it is often unjust, according to deontic egalitarians, that some people are worse off than others, '[their] objection is not really to the inequality itself. What is unjust, and therefore bad, is not strictly the state of affairs, but the way in which it was produced' (Parfit, 2000: 90). More specifically, deontic egalitarians think that 'we should aim for equality, not to make the outcome better, but for some other moral reason. We may believe, for example, that people have rights to equal shares' (Parfit, 2000: 84). Or, one might add, we might believe that we, or the state, have a duty to treat one another, or, in the case of the state, its citizens, with equal concern and that doing so implies aiming for distributive equality. In short, telic egalitarians believe equality is valuable, deontic egalitarians believe that there is a moral requirement to aim at distributive equality.

[21] Tomlin (2015: 18) suggests that Scanlon's contractualist approach involves a similar view of relational equality as a matter of how we relate as equals.

The point I want to make here is that we can draw a similar distinction between telic and deontic relational egalitarians: the former think relational equality is valuable, while the latter think it is morally required. The fact that a similar distinction can be drawn between telic and deontic forms of relational egalitarianism is significant for a number of reasons. First, it shows that the distance between distributive and relational egalitarianism is smaller than many would have thought. Second, it alerts us to the possibility that some objections to the distributive ideal that relational egalitarians canvass are sometimes best understood as objections to telic forms of egalitarianism rather than as objections to distributive egalitarianism. In the two previous sections, I explored versions of telic relational egalitarianism. In the present section, I scrutinize deontic relational equality.

As I noted earlier in this chapter, relational egalitarians have rightly taken luck egalitarians to task for their failure to say much about why we should favour distributive equality in the first place. Suppose we are deontic relational egalitarians. Are we not then susceptible to a similar critical point, i.e. that we contend that there is a norm of justice that we ought to relate as equals and that there is little, if anything, that we even *can* say that grounds this claim?

I think relational egalitarians are in a better position than this challenge implies. First, deontic egalitarians need not claim that the requirement to relate to others as equals is fundamental. For instance, they might say that it is derived from a requirement of respecting others and the claim that part of what it is to respect others (who are one's equal) is to relate to them as equals. Or they might argue, as I will do in Chapter 7, that relational equality is rooted in fairness. If so, relational equality is grounded in a deeper value. Admittedly, one might ask how that value is grounded and it may be that the fairness principle is fundamental in the sense that it is not in turn grounded in some more basic norm. This is simply in the nature of grounding of values: at some point we get to a value that is not in itself grounded in another and deeper value. This is no different whether we are telic distributive egalitarians or deontic relational egalitarians.

The fact that some normative principle is fundamental in that it is not grounded in a more basic normative requirement does not show – and this is the second point relational egalitarians can make – that we cannot be justified in accepting that principle. Perhaps we can intuit the principle itself or we can say that it coheres well with a number of other principles and justifies a number of moral judgements about particular cases which we find very plausible. The latter coherentist justification is one which most theorists subscribe to in political philosophy. It implies that we can be justified in – and say a lot of things in justification for – accepting even fundamental (non-epistemically speaking) principles.

Should we accept deontic relational egalitarianism? I am inclined to think that we should. Treating people as unequals is unfair to them. However, much depends on the exact nature of the pertinent deontic relational norm that we endorse. First, at least after a point, the stronger it is – i.e. the greater the loss in terms of values like welfare that we are required to endure in order to comply with the norm – the less plausible it is. Second, the more specific we make the norm, e.g. if we make claims such as treating people as equals implies the 'one person, one vote' principle, the less plausible deontic relational egalitarianism is.[22] Third, the norm of treating as equals is more plausible to the extent that its specification depends on the nature of the relation between the relevant individuals, e.g. that the norms are such that relating as equals involves different things depending on whether one relates simply as human beings or as partners with children.

Suppose that we are justified in accepting some form of deontic relational egalitarianism. Because deontic relational egalitarianism is in the same ballpark as luck egalitarianism, one might ask whether distributive egalitarianism would then be superfluous. I believe not. There would still be questions which may be about egalitarian justice and which nevertheless are questions which deontic relational equality does not speak to.[23] Suppose we believe that as a powerful nation we can bring about either that members of one nation relate perfectly to one another as equals, or that members of five different nations show significant improvements – from the point of view of deontic relational justice – in how citizens relate, though their relations will still not satisfy the ideal of deontic relational justice perfectly. At least possibly, deontic relational egalitarianism does not tell us what to do in this matter and even if it does, there is the question about whether such an answer is ultimately grounded in a prior view about what constitutes a fair distribution. Nothing in deontic relational egalitarianism rules out that questions such as these involve distributive principles.

---

[22] People who are young and will be around for a long time have a stronger interest in the outcome of political decisions than people who are old and can expect to be around for a shorter period of time. Treating people differently on the basis of how weighty their interests are is a better way of specifying the norm of relating as equals. Hence, it seems voting power should be differentiated on the basis of expected lifetime, such that younger people have more votes than older people, since they have a greater stake in the political decisions made now than those with only a few years left to live.

[23] Such questions include questions relating to intergenerational justice or justice to animals (Chapter 5.2).

Hence, even what I take to be the most promising form of relational egalitarianism does not imply that there is no such thing as distributive justice.

In sum: deontic relational egalitarianism might seem the form of relational egalitarianism that comes closest to what is intuitively attractive about relational egalitarianism and, moreover, might be the form that comes closest to being a competitor to the ideal of distributive equality. However, even so-construed relational egalitarianism leaves space for the distributive ideal.

6.6   Aims of Real-Life Egalitarians and the Value of Equality

Before concluding I would like to engage in a slightly digressive metareflection on how we should think about the value of equality. In their critique of the distributive ideal of equality and luck egalitarianism in particular, relational egalitarians have appealed to the history of the egalitarian movements – 'real-life egalitarians', as those who take part in such movements are called – arguing that, unlike luck egalitarian theorists, real-life egalitarians are concerned with the nature of egalitarian social relations – 'racism, sexism, nationalism, caste, class and eugenics' (Anderson, 1999: 312; cp. Anderson, 2012a: 40, 53) – rather than with distributive equality. Schemmel makes a similar observation: 'This expressive interpretation of the relational objection fits well with the claims of past and present egalitarian movements, such as movements for the equality of women, of homosexuals and of ethnic minorities. Such movements generally demand treatment that affirms their equal moral status' (Schemmel, 2012a: 134). The wider upshot of this observation is that this putative discrepancy between the concerns of real-life egalitarians and luck egalitarians casts doubt on the ideal of distributive equality (Anderson, 1999; 2012a, 40; Scheffler, 2015: 22; Wolff, 2010: 336–40; Young, 1990: 15).[24] So far in this chapter, we have discussed the value of relational equality without any attention to the views of real-life egalitarians. If relational egalitarians' critique of how luck egalitarians have failed to accommodate the concerns of real-life egalitarians is warranted, one might suspect that the approach that I have adopted in this chapter is misconceived.

In assessing this critique of how luck egalitarians have failed to accommodate the views of real-life egalitarians, there are two rather different

---

[24] Perhaps some relational egalitarians only mention the divergence and do not want to put any argumentative weight on it. If so, I do not address their views in the present section.

questions we should ask. First, is relational egalitarians' description of the concerns of real-life egalitarians true? Much here hangs on how we distinguish real-life from non-real-life egalitarians. If, for instance, we count labour unions and socialist and social democratic parties as real-life egalitarian movements, at least in a European context it would be false to say that such movements have been unconcerned with distributive issues unless these impinge on the possibility of people relating as equals.[25] Similarly, do animal liberationists count as real-life egalitarians? If so, clearly at least some real-life egalitarians are strongly concerned with issues other than social relations. If not, what should one think of the fact that many animal liberationists understand their views as a natural anti-speciest extension of how egalitarians have rejected other isms like racism and sexism? There is a very real danger here that any identification of who counts as real-life egalitarians depends to a very large degree on how one prior to that identification understands the ideal of equality and, thus, that there is a vicious circularity involved in appealing to facts about what real-life egalitarians are concerned with in order to support one's understanding of the ideal of equality.

Suppose, however, that real-life egalitarians have not been concerned with distributive inequality per se. Would that show – and this is my second question – that egalitarian justice is not about distributions as such? One reason that, at most, this is a quite weak reason to think so is that, presumably, real-life egalitarians are primarily concerned with bringing about (what they see as) desirable changes. In doing so, they have to balance a number of different concerns.[26] One important concern, of course, is the question of which injustices are gravest. However, another important concern is feasibility: some of the most feasible changes involve only minor injustice and in the case of some of the gravest injustices it might be unfeasible – at least for the time being – to eliminate or even reduce them, in which case it makes more sense to focus on the former if

[25] Somewhat ironically, some relational egalitarians mention Marx's critique of the Gotha programme as a forerunner of contemporary relational egalitarianism (Chapter 1.3). But that critique was a critique of the programme of the Social Democratic Worker's Party of Germany – a real-life egalitarian movement, if any ever existed – written by a theoretically inclined critic in the reading rooms of the British Museum.

[26] Admittedly, Anderson and Scheffler might simply make the weak claim that this is one (weak) reason to think that luck egalitarianism is misguided that real-life egalitarians are unconcerned with distributions per se, where this is not taken to imply that this is a stronger reason than that apparently many non-real-life egalitarians are concerned with distributions per se. However, if that is the claim they want to make, they are not very clear about the extremely limited role they think it plays in the overall argumentative landscape.

the aim is to make a change for the better. A third important consideration concerns values other than egalitarian justice. Suppose certain reforms would be great in terms of egalitarian justice, but would clash with other values that egalitarians deem weighty. If so, that would be a significant reason not to focus on those reforms, even if they are strongly desirable from the point of view of egalitarian justice. The latter two concerns mean that we have reason to believe that, at least in this respect, the concerns of real-life egalitarians are a less reliable guide to the nature of egalitarian justice than the concerns of political philosophers, who are under no pressure to take feasibility and competing values into account when articulating their views about egalitarian justice. Further, there seem to be perfectly sound justificatory reasons why theorists and practitioners/activists who are committed to exactly the same values nevertheless have very different focuses.

There is another question one might ask. The emphasis on the concerns of real-life egalitarians suggests that we can disregard the indifferences and antipathies of real-life non- or anti-egalitarians. However, why should we attach greater weight to the sympathies of real-life egalitarians than to the antipathies etc. of real-life non- or anti-egalitarians? After all, non- and anti-egalitarians have ideas about the contours of the ideal they are indifferent to or reject, and they have counterfactual intuitions about what form of equality – e.g. equality of welfare or equality of resources – is valuable, assuming, falsely in their view, that equality is valuable. Relational egalitarians simply ignore such views.

To justify this neglect, relational egalitarians might say there are obvious reasons why real-life anti-egalitarians are disposed to distort the ideal which they oppose, e.g. it is often easier to shoot down a caricature than the real thing. However, the reverse tendency to distort is a reason to be sceptical about the accuracy of the ideal of equality as real-life egalitarians portray it. After all, they too have a sell to make. In the absence of any argument for asymmetric scepticism on this matter, perhaps the right conclusion to draw is that insofar as a philosophical account of egalitarian justice should pass muster vis-à-vis the concerns of real-life people, as it were, it should be attentive to the concerns of egalitarians and anti-egalitarians alike.[27]

[27] Alternatively, relational egalitarians might say that what they are really in the business of doing is reconstructing the concerns of real-life egalitarians. However, on this construal they are not contributing to the field of political philosophy as opposed to the history of political ideas.

In sum: it is not clear that real-life egalitarians are not concerned with distributions per se. And even if it were, it is not clear why that would be a strong reason to reject the distributive ideal.

6.7   Conclusion

In this chapter I have asked why relational equality is valuable. I have argued that it is probably valuable in a number of ways; that relational egalitarians offer or suggest different answers to this question; and that some of these answers will not serve the typical argumentative aims of relational egalitarians, e.g. to sketch a position which represents a critical alternative to the distributive ideal of equality, well. For instance, while relating as equals might well be good for us, that in itself is compatible with the distributive ideal of equality: indeed, it seems natural to think that enjoying relating as equals calls for some account of how we should distribute this good or, to put it in a less active form, which distribution of this good is the most desirable one. I have argued that while equality might have impersonal value, there are considerable issues surrounding how to flesh out this idea and that, in any case, it does not fit very well with the idea that people who are being treated as inferior are wronged and are in a different position from someone who can simply complain to someone else that they make the world a worse place. This leaves us with deontic relational egalitarianism. I suggested that in some version or other – bear in mind the many different versions of relating as equals that I distinguished between in Chapter 3 – it might well be justified. I have also suggested that such a justification need not consist in deriving it from a more basic normative principle which we are justified in accepting. However, I did not go as far as to argue that we are more justified in accepting it if we cannot ground it in such a way, and in the next chapter I shall argue that it, like some version of a distributive ideal, can be grounded in fairness.

PART III

Relational and Distributive Equality

CHAPTER 7

Pluralist Egalitarianism

7.1 Introduction

In previous chapters, I argued that while relational egalitarianism captures some important aspects of egalitarian justice, Anderson's and Scheffler's objections fail to refute luck egalitarianism and for that matter fail to show that egalitarian justice has no distributive component. I also argued in Chapter 5 that relational egalitarians face some issues about how to specify their theory which are quite similar to those faced by luck egalitarians. And in Chapters 5 and 6 I argued that, on many understandings of relational equality, the relational ideal leaves open the possibility that a full account of egalitarian justice must also involve distributive concerns. At this point, one might wonder whether one could not simply adopt a dualist account of egalitarian justice which combines luck and relational egalitarian justice, e.g. one which says that egalitarian justice obtains if, and only if, people's distributive positions reflect nothing other than the comparative exercise of responsibility and people relate as equals unless their not doing so reflects their differential exercise of responsibility.

Such a pluralizing response is similar to moves in different argumentative contexts made by egalitarians. For instance, telic egalitarianism implies that, in one respect, a world in which everyone suffers equally is better than one in which everyone lives terrific lives, although some slightly more so than others; if equality is the only value, the former is better than the latter, all things considered. This is implausible and, accordingly, telic egalitarians had better be pluralists and endorse other values, such as welfare (Parfit, 1998; 2000). Similarly, advocates of egalitarian justice are unlikely to claim that it is a complete account of justice or, alternatively, they might reason that egalitarians qua egalitarians value more than justice, i.e. they value people relating as equals. For instance, most would accept that retributive justice is captured by a different set of concerns than those captured by egalitarian justice. Hence, most advocates of egalitarian justice are not just pluralists about value in general – they are pluralists about justice. Accordingly, it should come as no surprise if egalitarians are pluralists about egalitarian justice.

One reason one might find this move unattractive is that luck and relational egalitarianism are (or should be defined so as to be) logically incompatible (Section 7.2). I take up this suggestion noting, *inter alia*, that, as I have defined the two positions, they are consistent with one another. Section 7.3 responds to a different suggestion by Elizabeth Anderson: to wit, that the two views, considered as first-order principles of justice, whether consistent or not, are rooted in different and incompatible ideas about moral justification; that is, in second- and third-person views of moral justification, respectively. On the former view, who justifies which claims to whom makes a difference to the force of the justification, whereas on the latter, third-person view, such context variation makes no difference to justification. Drawing on the work of Cohen (2008) and Darwall (2006), I argue that the two accounts are not rooted in different conceptions of moral justification. Section 7.4 scrutinizes an ambitious take on the disagreement: that, really, relational egalitarianism can be reduced to a particular and unusual form of luck egalitarianism, one according to which, say, everyone should have equal amounts of social standing. I argue, first, that formally speaking the two views are different and, second, that at least Scheffler's deliberative constraint is irreducible in this way. In relation to the second claim, I argue in Section 7.5 that this is partly because Scheffler's dispositional egalitarianism is different from luck egalitarianism as well as relational egalitarianism. Section 7.6 builds on this analysis and proposes an ecumenical account of luck egalitarian justice, which accommodates all three forms of egalitarianism. I explore now whether this ecumenical ideal can be grounded in fairness. That this is an attractive position is the main claim that I defend in this chapter.

7.2   Consistency

In Chapters 1.1 and 1.2 I defined luck and (outcome) relational egalitarianism as follows:

> *Luck egalitarianism*: It is just only if everyone's distributive shares reflect nothing other than their comparative exercise of responsibility.
> *Outcome relational egalitarianism*: A situation is just only if everyone relates to one another as equals.

The two views are compatible as they stand. However, relational egalitarians will typically add:

> *The incompatibility claim*: Everyone relates to one another as equals only if it is not the case that everyone's distributive shares reflect nothing other than their comparative exercise of responsibility.

Given the incompatibility claim, luck and relational egalitarianism are incompatible in the sense that you cannot realize both.

There are, however, at least two things to realize about the incompatibility claim. First, as I noted in Chapter 1.2, it is unclear why the ideal of relating as equals implies that people's distributive positions should be insensitive to their exercise of choice and responsibility (cp. Fourie et al., 2015: 105). Clearly, unlike Dworkin, Anderson and Scheffler think that, at least in some cases, relating as equals requires that people's distributive positions display some insensitivity to choice and responsibility. However, this incompatibility does not derive simply from a statement of relational egalitarianism, but from a particular substantive interpretation of what it is to relate as equals which is embodied in the incompatibility claim. Moreover, as I argued in Chapter 1, that issue is not an issue that separates luck egalitarianism from relational egalitarianism, but one that separates luckist from non-luckist versions of relational egalitarianism.

Second, the incompatibility claim cannot plausibly be construed as an analytical truth. There is nothing logically impossible about a situation in which people's distributive positions reflect nothing but their exercise of choice and responsibility *and* in which they relate as equals (even if this is construed in a responsibility-insensitive way). Suppose, for instance, that everyone is equally well off; everyone has more than the relevant sufficiency threshold; and everyone exercises their choice and responsibility in similar ways. Here people might both relate as equals and satisfy luck egalitarianism. Hence, luck egalitarianism and relational egalitarianism are compatible, in the sense that they can be co-realized. Moreover, since luck egalitarianism only states a necessary condition for justice, it does not even rule out that there are additional conditions for justice such as the condition expressed by outcome relational egalitarianism. This means that we could try to combine the two views without inconsistency in pretty much the same way that some might try to combine concerns for freedom and equality in a complex account of justice.

At this point, some might concede that, given my definitions of luck and relational egalitarianism, all this does indeed follow, but this simply shows that one should define them differently such that the two views *are* incompatible by design, as it were. One could do that by adding a negative component to each definition stating the negation of the other view. Alternatively, and more eloquently, one could revise the definitions such that they both state sufficient conditions of justice:

> *Luck egalitarianism*: It is just *if*, and only if, everyone's distributive shares reflect nothing other than their comparative exercise of responsibility.
> *Outcome relational egalitarianism*: A situation is just *if*, and only if, everyone relates to one another as equals.

On the assumption that it is possible that everyone's distributive shares reflect nothing other than her comparative exercise of responsibility even if not everyone relates to one another as equals, and vice versa, then the two views would be incompatible (even if sometimes co-realizable).

In response to this complaint, I have two replies. First, exegetically speaking it would be in one way unfortunate to define luck egalitarianism in such a way that it rules out that there are other necessary conditions for justice than the perfect responsibility sensitivity of people's distributive shares, since, for reasons explained in Chapter 1, it is often stated in such a way that it does not rule that out (Lippert-Rasmussen, 2015a: 87–98; Miklosi, forthcoming: 6; Temkin, 1993: 13).[1] Specifically, if my arguments in Chapter 8 are correct, there are elements of relational egalitarianism present in the views of justice of at least one paradigm luck egalitarian, G. A. Cohen, and distributive components in the views of at least one paradigm relational egalitarian, Elizabeth Anderson. Hence, we make better sense of their positions if we do not define luck and relational egalitarianism as being inconsistent.[2]

Second, systematically speaking, such a definition would not be fruitful, because what seems crucial to both positions are their positive accounts of what justice requires, not their negative claims about nothing else being necessary for justice. In any case, if we include these negative parts as essential to luck egalitarianism and relational egalitarianism, we can then simply rephrase the question which is the focus of this chapter to one about

---

[1] Anderson characterizes the luck egalitarian position as that 'inequality [in the distribution of non-relational goods] is unjust' if 'it is caused by morally arbitrary factors' (Anderson, 2010a: 2). The relational egalitarian position is that 'inequality [in the distribution of non-relational goods] is unjust' if 'it reflects, embodies or causes inequality of authority, status or standing' (Anderson, 2010a: 2). Both positions state sufficient conditions of unjust inequality and, thus, are compatible.

[2] Admittedly, there are other luck egalitarians of whom something like this is untrue. Arneson, for instance, seems to think that unequal social relations are unjust if, and only if, they result in unjust inequality of welfare etc. (Arneson, 2000: 341–2). Still, even he seems to have doubts about a purely distributive account of the wrongness (or injustice) of discrimination (Arneson, 2006).

whether the positive parts of the definitions of luck and relational egalitarianism are compatible.

In sum: as I have defined luck and relational egalitarianism, they are different but logically compatible. One could define them differently such that they are logically incompatible, e.g. by including in the definition of each of them a negation of the other position. However, this would seem exegetically inappropriate, first, for reasons which will be described in greater detail in Chapter 8, and, second, for the reason just expounded: it is not theoretically fruitful.

7.3 An Underlying Disagreement about Justification?

In the previous section I argued that luck and relational egalitarianism are logically compatible. Hence, as far as consistency goes, nothing prevents one from combining them into an overall account of egalitarian justice. Even if this point is conceded, some might resist such a move on the grounds proposed by Elizabeth Anderson: to wit, that there is a deep disagreement underlying secondary disputes between luck and relational egalitarians, such as the debate over the distribuendum of justice. This deep disagreement concerns:

> the standpoint from which principles of justice are justified. Luck egalitarians follow a *third-person* conception of justification. In a third-person justification, someone presents a body of normative and factual premises as grounds for a policy conclusion. If the argument is valid and the premises are true, then the conclusion is justified.[3] The identity of the person making the argument and the identity of her context are irrelevant to the justification. By contrast, most relational egalitarians follow a *second-person* or *interpersonal* conception of justification. This follows from their contractualism . . . In a second-person justification, a claim of justice is essentially expressible as a demand that a person makes on an agent whom the speaker holds accountable. Justification is a matter of vindicating claims on others' conduct. Vindication involves demonstrating that the claims are addressed to those properly held substantively responsible for the conduct in question, by persons entitled to the moral authority or standing to hold them to account. (Anderson, 2010a: 2–3; cp. Anderson, 1999: 322)

Call this methodological issue the *justification disagreement*. If it adequately captures a deep disagreement between luck and relational egalitarians, the

---

[3] I ignore here that if the premises are not justified (even if true), a valid argument cannot confer justification on the conclusion.

Table 7.1 *Taxonomy of Different Conceptions of Justification*

	Context-insensitive	Context-sensitive
Conduct claim-independent	Pure third-person conception	Hybrid
Conduct claim-dependent	Hybrid	Pure second-person conception

conciliatory project of pluralist egalitarianism seems futile, since its two positions involve inconsistent views about what moral justification consists in.

Unfortunately, Anderson offers non-congruent characterizations of the two views of moral justification. Describing the third-person conception of justification, she writes: 'In a third-person justification, someone presents a body of normative and factual premises as grounds for a policy conclusion. If the argument is valid and the premises are true, then the conclusion is justified' (Anderson, 2010a: 2). From this it appears that it is insufficient, in terms of second-person justification, to justify a policy conclusion by presenting a valid argument for it invoking only true normative and factual premises. But rather than characterizing second-person justification this way, she ties it to 'vindicating claims on others' conduct' (Anderson, 2010a: 3). This involves two problems.

First, because there are two different distinctions involved, there are now four – not two, as Anderson thinks – conceptions of justification to consider. Call justifications that conform to Anderson's characterization of third-person justification 'context-insensitive' and those that do not 'context-sensitive'. Call justifications meeting Anderson's characterization of second-person justification 'conduct claim-dependent' and those that do not 'conduct claim-independent'. These two distinctions cross-cut, giving us four different kinds of justification, two of which are hybrids in that they combine Anderson's second- and third-person conceptions of justification as shown in Table 7.1 above.

Context-insensitive, conduct claim-dependent justification holds that a distribution of goods, say, is unjust only if the following two conditions are met: (1) the relevant distribution reflects the fact that some people do not comply with the demands others can reasonably make on their conduct, and (2) the fact that these demands are reasonable can be given a context-insensitive justification. On this view, which may well be the position of Dworkinian luck egalitarians, unavoidable and irremediable inequality is not unjust, because it fails to satisfy (1).

Context-sensitive, conduct claim-independent justification is the other hybrid. On this view, something might be unjust even if (1) the relevant object of injustice does not reflect the fact that some people do not comply with the demands others can reasonably make on their conduct, and (2) it can be given a context-insensitive justification. On this view, unavoidable, irremediable inequality may or may not be unjust. While it does not reflect the failure of some people to comply with the demands others can reasonably make on their conduct, it may be that it is incapable of being given a context-relative justification. This might be so if some people (reasonably) reject the view that natural inequalities are unjust. Given that they hold such a view, and given that one cannot justify a certain view by appealing to a principle that one (reasonably) rejects, they (as opposed to people who subscribe to no such principle) cannot justify, or demonstrate, to others the injustice of such inequalities. As Rawls (1999: 190) puts it: 'A person's right to complain is limited to violations of principles he acknowledges himself'. It is also arguable that one does not have authority, in Darwall's sense, to hold someone else to account for failing to comply with a principle one does not accept oneself (Darwall, 2006: 8).

The second problem which Anderson's characterization of the distinction between second- and third-person justification gives rise to is that in her arguments against luck egalitarianism Anderson nowhere offers an example of a justification that is context-sensitive. While she offers examples of justifications that might involve unreasonable demands, these fail from a third-person perspective as well, if they fail.

Take her discussion of Salieri's luck egalitarian complaint that Mozart has a greater natural musical talent than he has (Anderson, 2010a: 10). Anderson thinks that the complaint cannot be vindicated from a second-person point of view. However, she fails to show why any justification of the inequality between them would be context-sensitive. Instead, what she does is to assert that it 'is unreasonable to demand that people do things beyond human capacities' (Anderson, 2010a: 10). However, an argument for the conclusion that there is no injustice in Mozart's musical talents being greater than Salieri's appealing to this premise comes across no differently in a third-person context – say, Brahms uttering the argument to Tchaikovsky – from the way it comes across in a second-person context – say, Mozart uttering the same argument to Salieri and appealing to the presumed fact that it is beyond human capacity to prevent *his* musical talents being greater than Salieri's. The idea of context-relative justification is irrelevant to its assessment.[4] If it is sound, it can be employed by anyone to justify to anyone that the unequal distribution of natural musical talents across Salieri and Mozart is not unjust.[5] Hence, Anderson's core illustration of a complaint that might succeed from a third-person, but not from a second-person, point of view fails.

As we saw in Chapter 2.3, Anderson also employs the 'principle of interpersonal justification' to rebut certain principles – not arguments – that she ascribes to luck egalitarians (Anderson, 1999: 322–5). As with the Mozart–Salieri argument, none of these involve context-sensitivity of the kind apparently rendering the relevant principles justified when formulated in the second person but not in the third person, and vice versa. For instance, she contends that the view that firefighters who voluntarily engage in 'dangerous occupations' from which consumers benefit have no claim to assistance from consumers fails to be interpersonally justified: 'The principle "let us be served by occupations so inadequately compensated that those in them shall lack the means necessary to their freedom, given the risks and conditions of their work" cannot survive the test of interpersonal justification' (Anderson, 1999: 323). This principle might indeed be implausible, but it is as implausible in (pure) third-person form (i.e. 'let people in non-dangerous occupations be served by occupations so inadequately compensated that those in them shall lack the means necessary to their freedom, given the risks and conditions of their work') as it is in its second-person form.[6]

In light of these considerations, I will understand Anderson's notions of second- and third-person justification as follows:

---

[4] The general form of the relevant argument here is: 'If X being better off than Y is beyond our human capacity to change, it is unreasonable to require anyone to eliminate this inequality. If it is unreasonable to require anyone to eliminate an inequality, then it is not unjust. It is beyond human capacity to change X's being better off than Y. Hence, X's being better off than Y is not unjust'. This argument, so I claim, comes across no differently whether uttered by X (Mozart) or someone else (Tchaikovsky).

[5] Context variation plays an essential role in Cohen's critique of the incentive argument for inequality (cp. Chapter 4.5). On his view, an unequal distribution is unjust precisely because, while it can be justified in some contexts – e.g. where untalented people are justifying to other untalented people the need for incentives for talented people – it cannot in other argumentative contexts – e.g. where talented people are attempting to justify to untalented people the idea that talented people should be given incentives – despite its validity and the truth of the premises appealed to. The asymmetry arises because, so Cohen argues, it is the talented people who make it true that incentives are necessary for making the worst off as well off as possible; while non-talented people can see the incentive-seeking behaviour of talented people as something that must be taken as given when determining what justice requires, talented people themselves must regard this behaviour as something which they should abstain from in light of their embrace of the difference principle.

[6] I say 'pure' because Anderson's principle is not formulated as a pure second-person principle (which would require those in dangerous professions to be referred to as 'you').

According to a second-person conception of justification, if something is unjust, then necessarily some agent has failed to comply with claims on her conduct that others could reasonably make (Anderson, 2010a: 5; cp. Anderson, 2008b; 251–3). According to a third-person conception of justification this is not so.[7]

The question then becomes whether relational egalitarianism is committed to the second-person conception of justification in this sense, and luck egalitarians are committed to the third-person conception of justification in this sense. I think neither.

First, suppose there is such a thing as hierarchical social relations, which, however, do not involve any agent failing to comply with claims on her conduct that others could reasonably make. Such relations might exist, because even though people comply with all reasonable demands, together and unintentionally, they bring about objectionably inegalitarian social relations. Alternatively, it could be true – I am not saying that it is – that we are genetically hardwired to bow and scrape before the stunningly beautiful and intelligent. If that were so, it would be beyond human capacity not to bring about the objectionably inegalitarian social relations this involves and accordingly, in light of Anderson's own view, no one can reasonably require others not to bring them about. However, relational egalitarians might object to hierarchical social relations even in these two cases. Moreover, in objecting to artificial unintended or to 'natural' hierarchies, relational egalitarians would not be asserting anything inconsistent with our definition of relational egalitarianism. I conclude that relational egalitarianism is not tied to Anderson's conception of second-person justification.[8]

This leaves us with the question of whether luck egalitarianism is tied to her conception of third-person justification. Note, however, that given our

---

[7] Anderson writes both that the relational view is that equality (read: justice) is 'a kind of social relation between persons' (Anderson, 2010a: 1) and that justice itself consists in certain principles 'that regulate [agents'] conduct' such that if they conform to the principles their conduct is desirable in a certain way. However, both cannot be right. First, people might act in conformity with the relevant principles and yet create unjust unequal social relations inadvertently – say, because we are genetically hardwired to bow and scrape before stunningly beautiful or amazingly intelligent people. Second, people might violate the relevant principle and yet not create unjust unequal relations – say, because they infringe the relevant principles by seeking to subordinate each other, but are unsuccessful, such that equality of 'authority, status' and 'standing' prevails (Anderson, 2010a: 2).

[8] Similarly, the issue about the second- or third-person justification is orthogonal to whether equality concerns the 'distribution of non-relational goods' or a certain 'kind of social relation between persons – an equality of authority, status or standing' (Anderson, 2010a: 1; see Lippert-Rasmussen, 2015b).

conclusion in the previous paragraph it has already been established that both relational and luck egalitarians can embrace a third-person conception of justification. Hence, even if we conclude that luck egalitarians are indeed tied to Anderson's third-person conception as I have reconstructed it, we would still have shown that the two camps are not separated by the kind of deep disagreement which would render the ecumenical project that I will describe shortly impossible. Hence, in a sense I have already established what I need to establish to pursue the ecumenical ambitions of this chapter.

There are two reasons why Anderson thinks luck egalitarians are tied to a third-person conception of justification: first, that they see levelling down as good in one respect and, second, that they subscribe to the notion of natural inequalities. The former reason is not particularly strong. Within the family of second-person conceptions of justification, various accounts of the claims we can reasonably make on one another's conduct are on offer. On a Scanlonian account we cannot reasonably make claims on each other on the basis of impersonal reasons (Scanlon, 1998: 218–23). However, Scanlon also thinks that one can make a demand on another on the basis of an 'interest', but it is unclear why one cannot have an interest deriving from valuing some state of affairs considered impersonally valuable, such as equality (cp. Scanlon, 1998: 222). In any case, Anderson's preferred account of second-person justification is Darwall's (2006). On his account (Darwall, 2006: 28), if there is, say, an obligation to protect 'cultural treasures' independently of the way this would promote the 'needs and interests of free and rational individuals' – something which he does not take a stand on – then such protection is something 'free and rational individuals have the authority to demand of one another'. Clearly, then, Darwall thinks the very idea of second-person reasons is compatible with having reasons to promote what is impersonally valuable and, while this is not his example, distributive equality is one candidate.

The second reason why Anderson thinks luck egalitarians are committed to a conception of third-person justification is that they think that there is such a thing as purely natural, unjust inequality. Such inequality would have obtained regardless of what any human being did. Very few, if any, inequalities between two people are likely to be purely natural inequalities, since, had some of their ancestors not conceived when they did, this pair of individuals would not even have existed, and as a result the inequality would not have obtained. Very many inequalities with perfectly natural-looking causes (e.g. those arising from difference in musical talent between Mozart and Salieri) are not, or do not give rise to, purely natural inequalities in the present sense. As Anderson notes, Mozart could have crippled his musical talents and, accordingly, her conception of second-person justification does not on its own rule out that the relevant inequality between Mozart and Salieri was unjust. However, even if Anderson's core example fails in this respect, the key point remains that luck egalitarians would condemn pure natural inequalities as unjust if they existed. Such condemnation cannot be justified on the conception of second-person justification and, hence, one can infer that they are, as Anderson says, committed to a third-person conception of justification. While this might have no practical relevance since very few inequalities are likely not to be inequalities which reflect that someone, somewhere, and at some point in time, failed to comply with demands others could reasonably make on this person, this difference might nevertheless be thought to be highly theoretically significant.

I have three replies to this point. First, I repeat my remark that preceded my treatment of purely natural, unjust inequalities: to wit, that there is nothing in relational egalitarianism as such that prevents it from being combined with a conception of third-person justification. Hence, it is possible to develop an ecumenical egalitarian theory based on a conception of third-person justification that incorporates elements from both luck and relational egalitarianism.

Second, even if we disregard the previous point, which is my main response, some people might subscribe to a deontic version of luck egalitarianism:

> *Deontic luck egalitarianism*: It is just only if everyone's distributive shares reflect nothing other than her comparative exercise of responsibility, provided such non-reflection results from some agent failing to comply with claims on her conduct that others could reasonably make.[9]

On this view, there is no such thing as purely natural, unjust inequality. Also, the view might be combined with a view on what claims on others' conduct agents can reasonably make such that the view does not condone levelling down. Still, the view is clearly a luck egalitarian view and not a relational view. It follows that the distinction between conceptions of second- and third-person justification is not at the root of the disagreement between luck

---

[9] Ronald Dworkin, who is normally seen as a paradigmatic luck egalitarian, believes that distributive inequality is unjust only when it reflects failure on the part of the state to treat its citizens with equal concern and respect. If there are no social relations, there are no states. Accordingly, his view does not apply to purely natural inequalities obtaining in situations without social relations.

egalitarianism in a slightly broader sense than I have adopted, on the one hand, and relational egalitarianism, on the other hand.[10]

Third, Anderson assumes that either one embraces a conception of third-person justification or one embraces a conception of second-person justification, but not both, and as I have reconstructed her distinction the two positions really are mutually exclusive. However, one could embrace what, in spirit at least, amounts to an ecumenical conception of justification. One could say, for instance, that in the case of purely natural states of affairs, these can be unjust, but that in the case of all other states of affairs, if these are unjust, then this must be wholly or in part because someone has failed to comply with demands that others could reasonably make on this person.

This concludes my reasons for asserting the main point of this section: that luck and relational egalitarianism are not incompatible because they are rooted in different and incompatible ideas about justification (they are not). However, one more preliminary issue – the reductionist challenge to relational egalitarianism – needs to be dealt with before I turn to an elaboration of an ecumenical version of egalitarianism.

7.4   Reduction

According to the reductionist challenge, whenever people do not relate as equals, there is some good that is unequally distributed, and whatever is unjust about the former can be expressed in terms of a claim about what is unjust about the latter.[11] If so, relational egalitarianism is reduced to a subspecies of distributive egalitarianism, which focuses on a particular kind of *equalisanda* – those goods that derive from, or are constituted by, the existence of certain social relations. If the reductionist challenge is vindicated, then it would be self-contradictory to include a negation of the distributive ideal in the definition of relational egalitarianism (cp. Section 7.3). Note also that, for reasons that were brought out in the previous section's discussion of purely natural inequalities, there is no comparable reductionist challenge to luck egalitarianism, since luck egalitarianism applies even in situations with no social relations (Arneson, 1999b: 226).

To support the reductionist challenge, consider a two-person case where X and Y relate to one another. We can then define a certain

---

[10] On this view, one would have to reject what we can call foundational luck egalitarianism, i.e. the view that what makes a distribution unjust is that it does not reflect people's differential exercise of responsibility (cp. Chapter 8.2).

[11] In this and the following two sections I draw on work published in Lippert-Rasmussen (2017).

good – the good of social standing (cp. Miller, 1995: 206) – as a good which X would have more of than Y insofar as X relates to Y as Y's superior; less of insofar as Y relates to X as X's superior; and equal amounts of insofar as they relate as equals. We can then add that distributive equality is perfectly satisfied if it is true of all pairs of people in a certain society that the relevant two individuals have equal amounts of social standing.[12] Essentially, this move transforms a concern for the egalitarian nature of social relations into a concern for the distribution of a certain good, i.e. social standing. If generalizable, *any* concern for social relations can be transformed into a concern for the distribution of a certain good.[13]

In an early response to the reductionist challenge, David Miller argued that equality of status obtains:

> when each member of society regards him- or herself as fundamentally the equal of all others, and is regarded by others as fundamentally their equal. It should be obvious that status in this sense is not a good that can be directly distributed equally. There is nothing one can hand out to individual people in the way that one can hand out titles to income or property. Nor does it seem likely that there will some other good Y, the appropriate distribution of which will lead to equality of status. (Miller, 1995: 199)

In Miller's view, equality of welfare is a distributive ideal of equality despite the fact that welfare, e.g. in the sense of preference satisfaction,

---

[12] Friends of the egalitarian distributive ideal are not committed to there being precise and elaborate measures of the amount of unjust inequality. The view I sketch here is very simple and incomplete, but this does not mean that it is not a version of the ideal of distributive equality.

[13] Interestingly, Anderson (2012a: 41) concedes that such a move is possible. She retorts, however, that there is nothing 'more to' enjoying enjoying equal amounts of social standing etc. 'than standing in certain symmetrical relations with others. By contrast, within the distributive conception of equality, the good to be distributed equally – resources, welfare, capabilities and so on – is such that the amount one has is typically logically independent of the amount of good that the others in the comparison class independently have and also often logically independent of that person's social relations to the others in the comparison class' (Anderson, 2012a: 41). This reply, at least when employed as an objection to the reductionist move I make, strikes me as unpersuasive. First, because of her own qualifications – 'typically' and 'often' – she cannot claim to point to a necessary difference between the distributive and the relational ideals. Second, the restriction in the range of goods friends of the distributive ideal can consider relevant to justice – only goods where the amount of it that one possesses is independent of the amount of it others possess – is not a restriction any friend of the distributive ideal subscribe to as far as I am aware. Third, and as an aside, the requirement of 'logical' independence is in any case an extremely strong requirement. Of many typical positional goods such as honour or prestigious degrees, which presumably are among the kinds of goods Anderson has in mind here, it is not true that how much a certain person has of that good is logically dependent on what others have. Finally, on the analysis proposed in this section the view Anderson describes is concerned with a non-social relation: to wit, '__ and __ have equal amounts of __', where the relevant currency of that relation is social goods. Hence, in a formal (though I agree with Anderson not a substantive) sense, the described view is distinct from a social relational egalitarian view.

cannot be 'directly distributed'. Hence, his argument for not regarding equality of status to be a distributive ideal depends entirely on whatever arguments can be built upon the last claim in the quoted passage; yet such arguments are implausible. First, there is no empirical asymmetry between equality of status and equality of welfare. Just as there is no good such that a certain distribution thereof will imply an equal distribution of social standing, there is no good which is such that a suitable distribution thereof results in equality of welfare. Moreover, Miller mentions ways in which very unequal distributions of certain goods, e.g. money, are likely to lead to *in*equality of status (Miller, 1998: 34). This implies that less unequal distributions of money are likely to lead to less inequality of status.

Second, an ideal could be distributive even if there is no good which we can distribute in such a way that the ideal is realized, e.g. equality of welfare if our access to the minds of others is indirect and imperfect at best.[14] Miller's reasoning presupposes that whether an ideal counts as distributive depends on what we are able to do, and not on the intrinsic nature of the ideal.

Third, even if whether an ideal is distributive depends on what we are able to achieve, Miller's implicit requirement is too strong. Instead, we might suggest that an ideal is distributive if there is some good which is such that some distributions thereof are likely to result in less inequality (of status) than are other distributions.

Scheffler is another relational egalitarian who has responded to the reductionist challenge, which he puts (in somewhat different terms) as follows:

> [I]t may seem that the relational view, if fully spelled out, must itself take a distributive form. For suppose that the members of society are committed to the ideal of a society of equals and are determined to structure their relations in accordance with that ideal. How could they go about doing this? The answer, it may seem, is that they would take care to ensure that certain important goods, such as status, power or opportunity, were distributed equally within the society. That is what it would mean for them to achieve a society of equals. But if that is correct, then the relational view is not really

---

[14] There is *a* sense of 'distribution' on which only material things that can be handed out physically and directly can be distributed (cp. Young, 1990: 8–9; but see Gheaus, 2016: 3; Lippert-Rasmussen, 2018 b). This is not the sense of 'distribution' that welfarist, or for that matter most resourcist, luck egalitarians care about. Typically, resourcist egalitarians care about the distribution of unredistributable internal resources.

an alternative to the distributive view but rather a version of it. (Scheffler, 2015: 22)

If the reductionist challenge is sound, then relational egalitarians cannot succeed in challenging distributive egalitarianism per se, since their view is simply a version thereof. This is not to say that luck and relational egalitarian theorists do not disagree, or that the former are right on those issues about which they disagree. It is to say that their disagreement falls within the scope of the much-discussed distributive 'equality of what?' question. This result is interesting, even if it is not prejudicial to how all of the disagreements between luck and relational egalitarians should be resolved.[15]

There is, however, a way in which one can resist the reductionist challenge. To explain it, I need to take a closer look at relations between individuals. Some relations between individuals are not social, e.g.:[16]

    __ is taller than __
    __ has more hedonistic pleasure in her life than __
    __ lives longer than __

Since relational egalitarians are concerned with the egalitarian character of *social* relations, presumably they are not concerned with the nature of these other types of relations as such. Examples of social relations are, e.g.:

    __ has authority over __
    __ oppresses __
    __ defers to __

Relational egalitarians are concerned with the nature of *social* relations. They want these relations to have a suitably egalitarian character (cp. Chapter 1.2). Some relations may be trickier to categorize as social or non-social than the samples above, e.g.:

    __ is wealthier than __

---

[15] This is not to say that this point is irrelevant to these disagreements. For instance, if the reductionist challenge is vindicated, there is pressure on relational egalitarians to explain why the distribution of goods other than the good of social standing, say, is irrelevant to justice.

[16] For X and Y to be in a certain social relation, it has to be the case (but is not sufficient) that they interact with one another or that X interacts with Z who, at an overlapping time interval, again interacts with Y, and so on and so forth (cp. Chapter 5.2). Even if this is quite an undemanding condition – e.g. it can be satisfied by people who are chain-connected through a series of partly overlapping pairs of interacting persons – it might still be true of two persons not so related that one is taller than the other, etc.

Table 7.2 *Possible Objects of Egalitarian Concern*

	Social goods	Non-social goods
Social relations	X has a superior rank to Y	n/a
Non-social relations	X has more wealth than Y	X is taller than Y

On the one hand, this seems not to be a social relation, since X and Y might never interact with one another, so 'being wealthier than' is not a feature of *their* social relations *to each other*. We can imagine that X is an Inca king in the Americas prior to Columbus and Y is a peasant in medieval Europe. On the other hand, it is impossible for X to be wealthier than Y without there being certain social relations between X and other individuals in X's society, on the one hand, and social relations between Y and other individuals in Y's society, the difference between which constitutes X's greater wealth and Y's lesser wealth.[17] What we should say in response to these two conflicting observations is that the relevant relation is a non-social relation; yet, unlike 'is taller than', it is a relation that exists between persons in virtue of their possession of a good – wealth – which is inherently social in nature.[18] In other words, there is a distinction between, on the one hand, the distinction between social and non-social relations and, on the other hand, the distinction between relations between individuals by virtue of their possession of social goods, and relations between individuals by virtue of their possession of non-social goods (see Table 7.2 above).

Nothing prevents distributive egalitarians from being concerned with the distribution of inherently social goods, i.e. what goes on in the lower left-hand box. However, the real issue, one might argue, is the nature of the relations with which luck egalitarians and relational egalitarians are

---

[17] Cp. Cohen's (2011: 182) view that a 'sum of money is *tantamount* to (≠ is) a license to perform a disjunction of a conjunction of actions'.

[18] Cp. Cordelli (2015: 86–110). Like me, Cordelli believes that some of the concerns of relational egalitarians can be accommodated within a distributive paradigm given a suitably broad notion of the relevant distribuendum, i.e. one that includes what she calls 'relational goods': 'goods that are distinctively produced through and available within relationships or that are themselves constitutive of certain relationships', where by 'distinctively' she means that 'the good cannot generally be produced or accessed outside of [ongoing and coordinated interactions between two and more persons through which some goods are produced and exchanged], at least not without changing the quality of the good' (Cordelli, 2015: 90; cp. Stemplowska, 2011: 116). However, something can count as a relational good in Cordelli's sense and not as a social good in my sense, because her use of 'generally' indicates that it is not a necessary features of an instance of a relational good that it involves the existence of certain social relations.

concerned, and here the claim is that the relation which friends of the distributive view are concerned with is not a *social* relation. That three-place relation:

'__ and __ have equal amounts of __'

is not as such a social relation, though it pertains to social, as well as non-social, goods.[19] This difference seems to suffice as a basis for rejecting the reductionist challenge, since relational egalitarians are interested in the nature of social relations, not in the abstract, triadic non-social relation of '__ and __ have equal amounts of __', whether applied to social or non-social goods.

This rebuttal of the reductionist challenge, however, establishes nothing of substance. It merely establishes a formal difference between the distributive and the relational view. However, for any social relation there is a pair of a corresponding non-social relation and social good such that the relevant corresponding distributive egalitarian and social egalitarian views will condemn or endorse exactly the same situations. Take, for instance, one of Anderson's (1999: 318; cp. Chapter 2.3) favourite examples of an injustice which she thinks luck egalitarians cannot accommodate because of their focus on the distribution of goods: namely that of gays and lesbians who, unlike heterosexuals, do not enjoy the 'ability to appear in public without shame, and not being ascribed outcast status'. This injustice no doubt involves a particular set of social relations. However, it can also be characterized as a matter of an unequal distribution across homosexuals and heterosexuals of the relevant presentational ability which Anderson mentions. This ability is a good in the sense that it is desirable to have it and undesirable not to have it. Also, although you cannot distribute that good in the way you can distribute money or land, like welfare it is a good that one can have more or less of. Indeed, that this state of affairs – to wit, that the relevant inequality in terms of presentational abilities obtains – obtains seems to be Anderson's central complaint about the situation. Moreover, the relevant objectionable social relations could not exist in the absence of an unequal distribution of the relevant presentational skills, just as this inequality could not exist in the absence of the relevant homophobically shaped social relations. Hence, at least in the case of one of Anderson's paradigm examples of an injustice, we can naturally translate it into an injustice in terms of the distribution of a certain good.

---

[19] Cp. Cohen's (2011: 3) remark in the quote from Scheffler Chapter 2.2 that 'there is something which justice requires people to have equal amounts of'.

Take next the relation of '__ exploits __', which may seem more resistant to a similar analysis. This is a social relation which has an objectionable inegalitarian form according to relational egalitarians (cp. Cohen, 2011: 5; Norman, 1998: 44). This is the first view – the relational egalitarian view. However, we can stipulatively introduce a certain good – call it 'exploitation standing' – such that, *ceteris paribus*, if, in a simple two-person case, X exploits Y and Y does not exploit X, then X has more of the good of exploitation standing than Y does. We can also extend the notion to cover cases where X is exploited by a greater number of people than Z is exploited by; cases where they are exploited by the same number of people but to unequal degrees; cases where X exploits Y in a major way and Y exploits X in a minor way, e.g. introducing exploitation standing relative to different dimensions; and to cases where X exploits some people at the same time as X gets exploited by others, etc.[20] We might then say that the relation we are interested in is the abstract triadic relation '__ and __ have equal amounts of __' (a relation which, due to its abstract nature, is not a *social* relation) where the particular value of the third relatum, '__', that we happen to be concerned with is the social good of exploitation standing. This is the second view: the distributive egalitarian view.

The difference between these two views appears merely formal: at least, the two views overlap, extensionally speaking. This suggests that while the reductionist challenge can be answered, formally speaking – there is an analytical distinction to be drawn between the two kinds of views – the nature of this distinction is such that it is morally irrelevant. More generally, substantively speaking any relational egalitarian view is equivalent to a certain form of distributive egalitarianism pertaining to a social good defined on the basis of the relevant social relation.[21] Admittedly, the fact that, in substance, relational egalitarianism is identical to a form of distributive egalitarianism does not show that, in substance, it is identical to distributive *luck* egalitarianism – after all, outcome and luck egalitarians disagree. However, this does not weaken the force of the reductionist challenge, which is directed at the goods versus relations aspect.

[20] While 'exploitation standing' is a term of art, it is natural to say, for instance, that members of one group are exploited more than members of another group, e.g. a group of people who exploit but do not get exploited themselves (cp. Wolff, 1998: 107 on 'respect-standing').

[21] The present way of drawing the distinction between relational and distributive egalitarianism rests heavily on a distinction between relations that are social and relations that are not. Above I simply relied on paradigm cases that fall in either of the two categories. For present purposes all I need to rely on is the claim that some relations between persons are social and others are not without having to submit any claims about the nature of these relations.

Some might concede that the distinction between an inequality in a social relation and an inequality in a non-social relation pertaining to the relevant corresponding social good is morally irrelevant, but deny that this casts light on the nature of relational egalitarianism on the following grounds. What, at a fundamental level, relational egalitarians object to is not that people do not relate as equals overall. They object to any unequal social relation between individuals independent of whether it is counterbalanced by an unequal, reverse-direction social relation. Relational egalitarians subscribe to a deontological view proscribing relating to others as unequals, and that view is not extensionally equivalent to any view to the effect that individuals should have equal amounts of a certain kind of social good.[22] Certain actions are unjust because incompatible with the spirit of an egalitarian relation, and, thus, impermissible. Such a view, the response goes, cannot be captured by the view that there is a certain good which everyone should have equal amounts of (cp. Schemmel, 2012a: 140; Chapters 4.5 and 6.5).

In response to this challenge, I concede the truth of the previous sentence, but deny its significance. First, the distinction of significance here is the deontological/non-deontological distinction, not the relations/distributions distinction. One way of seeing this is to remind oneself of a comparable deontological luck egalitarian norm: 'Do not act in ways that will result in someone being worse off than others through no responsibility of their own'. This view, too, is not extensionally equivalent to a certain view enjoining that everyone has equal amounts of some good, whether social or not. Second, the non-extensionally equivalent relational view is implausible, since counterbalanced unequal social relations are less bad, from the point of view of relational equality, than non-counterbalanced unequal social relations, when all else is equal. Third, most relational egalitarians *are* concerned with inequality of overall social standing, not with the inegalitarian nature of each and every social relation. David Miller, for instance, submits that relational equality does not require that 'people should be equal in power, prestige or wealth . . . What matters is how such

---

[22] A different challenge – the Walzerian challenge – says that relational egalitarians do not just think that, from an overall perspective, social relations should be egalitarian. Rather, or in addition to that, they think that there are different spheres of justice and that within each of these spheres people should relate as equals (cp. Chapter 5.3). This challenge, however, brings up a different distinction from the one that is at stake here. In principle, luck egalitarians could embrace the idea of different spheres of justice and contend that within each no one should be worse off in terms of the relevant good specific for that sphere through no responsibility of her own.

differences are regarded, and in particular whether they serve to construct a social hierarchy in which A can unequivocally be ranked as B's superior' (Miller, 1998: 31; cp. Anderson, 1999: 312; Scheffler, 2003a: 36; 2003b: 206).[23] My claim is that such a concern for the absence of hierarchical social relations is extensionally equivalent to a concern that people have equal amounts of whatever goods hierarchical social relations essentially involve, and that whatever non-extensional difference might exist between these two views is morally irrelevant.[24]

I do not claim, in general, that there can be no morally relevant differences between extensionally equivalent views. Rather, I argue by way of a counter-challenge here. That is, I challenge anyone to explain the morally relevant difference between rejecting hierarchical social relations in the way that Miller and others do, and an unequal distribution of whatever good hierarchical social relations consist of.

Finally, I find it difficult to conceive of the possibility that someone is superior to someone else in terms of their social relations, yet there is no good in virtue of which the former is better off than the latter. There is a difference between having a position in a web of social relations which is superior to that of others, and simply having a position which is different from that of others. The best way to account for that distinction appeals to some good that the former implies inequality of – the one in the superior position has more of that good than someone in an inferior position – and which the latter does not. The Secretary of State has a superior position in the Department of State compared to an intern. This is due to the fact that she has more of the good that we normally call authority than the latter has. The fact that some people are 'above' or 'below' others implies an ordering, which in turn suffices for the notion of distribution being applicable.

---

[23] In his critique of Dworkin's bureaucratic ideal of equality, Scheffler observes that Dworkin's ideal of distributive equality of resources 'does not require or even permit an equal distribution of power' (Scheffler, 2003a: 36–7).

[24] Accordingly, if, on the grounds that there is a deontological relational egalitarian constraint against exploiting anyone, someone objects to a non-hierarchical situation where X exploits Y, Y exploits Z, and Z exploits X in a way that leaves the three persons involved equally well off in terms of any possible equalisandum, the scope of my substantive reductionism does not extend to this view. Nor does its scope extend to a similar view regarding acts whose objective meaning is that some individuals have an inferior status (cp. Anderson & Pildes, 2000; Hellman, 2008; Schemmel, 2012a). In the latter case, I doubt, however, that the view is best construed as a form of relational egalitarianism. After all, one can act in ways the objective meaning of which is that a certain group of people with whom the agent has no social relations has an inferior status, e.g. a state refuses to accept responsibility for a tragically 'successful' genocide (= no present descendants of the group subjected to genocide with whom the state interacts socially) it committed almost a century ago (cp. Chapter 3.7).

I tentatively conclude that, in a substantive sense, the reductionist challenge is vindicated. While the reductionist challenge can be answered in a formal sense, substantively speaking the relational egalitarian position is reducible to a particular form of luck egalitarian position.

7.5 Dispositional Egalitarianism

In response to my cautious endorsement of the reductionist challenge in the previous section, some might suggest that we can do better, and that relational egalitarianism cannot be substantively reduced to a view about distribution. Return to Scheffler's egalitarian deliberative constraint, which I expounded in Chapter 2.6 (Scheffler, 2015: 25). As we saw, Scheffler (2015: 28–9) submits that the deliberative constraint is compatible with reaching decisions that do not leave the parties who relate as equals equally well off and, indeed, that parties that comply with it are unlikely to use any fixed distributive formula such as luck egalitarianism. Conversely, even if a strict distributive formula of equality were satisfied, the ideal of relating as equals might not be if one or more of the parties to the relationship fail to comply with the deliberative constraint. This connects with a more general point that he makes: to wit, that equality, as he construes it, is 'a form of practice rather than a normative pattern of distribution' (Scheffler, 2015: 31).[25] Hence, we cannot, as I did in Section 7.4, define a certain good – social standing – as something that, all other things being equal, two people have equal amounts of if, and only if, they relate as equals, and as one that one person has more of than the other person to the extent that the former relates to the latter as superior and the latter relates to the former as inferior (cp. Lippert-Rasmussen, 2015a: 195–6). Doing so would leave out the 'deliberative and practical dimensions' of relational equality (Scheffler, 2015: 31). More generally, there is a deep and genuine difference between distributive and relational views of equality.

Scheffler's attempt to rebut the reductionist challenge fails for two reasons. The first reason is that, however it is intended by Scheffler, the deliberative constraint is not best seen as a constraint on the nature of social relations.[26] Admittedly, given his description thereof, Scheffler's

---

[25] This passage suggests a fourth way – a practice-focused view – of construing the ideal of equality, one which I do not discuss in this book.

[26] Rawls (1999: 76) writes: 'Many different kinds of things are said to be just and unjust: not only laws, institutions and social systems, but also particular actions of many kinds including decisions, judgements and imputations. We also call the attitudes and dispositions of persons, and persons

deliberative constraints can reasonably be understood to pertain, in part at least, to social relations. However, when so interpreted it is less plausible than when interpreted to pertain to dispositions independent of social relations. Consider the following two questions: first, can the constraint (on its most plausible construal) be *satisfied* in the absence of social relations; and, second, can it be *violated* in the absence of social relations? If the answer to both questions is 'yes', this vindicates my present claim.

It is natural to think that the form of the constraint is a conditional, where the antecedent says that X and Y are socially related and the consequent then states what features this relationship must have to be an egalitarian one. If so, the antecedent is false if X and Y have no social relationship, and, thus, the constraint is trivially satisfied in the absence of social relations.

An additional and more substantive point is that even if X and Y are not socially related, we might still think that it is valuable if they are disposed in the way that the deliberative constraint requires.[27] Suppose that X and Y both live alone on deserted islands. One day Y's autobiography and a computer with Internet access wash ashore on X's island. A similar thing happens on Y's island. They read about each other and set out to chat with one another through Facebook, starting, so they think, to form all sorts of social conventions and to coordinate plans, though both of them are disposed to violate the deliberative constraint. Both believe that they interact with one another, but in fact they both interact with a sophisticated communications robot. Hence, they believe that they have social relations to one another, but in fact they are as solitary as they always were (cp. Chapter 5.2). My contention is that, disposition-wise, this is no less objectionable than an otherwise comparable situation in which they do chat with one another on Facebook and, thus, do succeed in forming social relations. Accordingly, if so, on its most plausible version (which then is not the conditional-style interpretation suggested in the previous paragraph), the deliberative constraint can be violated even in the absence of social relations.

It might be replied that there is no egalitarian reason to care about people's dispositions in the absence of their having social relations and that this shows that the constraint cannot be violated in the absence of social

---

themselves, just or unjust'. I am suggesting that the site of Scheffler's deliberative constraints is dispositions. Rawls' observation raises the question of whether there is any connection between the different subjects of justice. My ecumenical version of egalitarian justice supposes that there is.

[27] We might either think that their having inegalitarian dispositions is disvaluable, or we might think (additionally) that their having egalitarian dispositions is valuable.

relations.[28] Hence, the constraint really *is* a constraint on the nature of social relations – for it to apply to a set of people, they must be socially related. If people are not socially related, the deliberative constraint is neither violated nor satisfied, analogous to how some would argue that if there is no King of France, then 'The King of France is bald' and its negation are neither true nor false. We can strengthen this interpretation by noting that, as Scheffler describes the constraint, the object of the relevant dispositions which we normally act on is what we do and decide, and that this might be understood to mean what we do and decide *together*. Surely, doing and deciding together is a way of relating to one another, and my two Robinson Crusoe-like characters do not act or decide anything together, even though they falsely believe that they do.

In response, note first that at least some of the features of egalitarian social relations that Scheffler thinks make them valuable can also be instantiated in my scenario of people who falsely believe they have social relations. For instance, according to Scheffler, hierarchical social relations 'distort people's attitudes towards themselves, undermining the self-respect of some and encouraging an insidious sense of superiority in others' (Scheffler, 2005: 19; cp. Chapter 6.2). These defects might arise in my social relations-free, Robinson Crusoe-like scenario. Thus, part of what makes Scheffler care about egalitarian relations makes it unmotivated, by Scheffler's own lights, to restrict the scope of the deliberative constraint to settings involving social relations.

Second, it is odd to present a constraint that pertains to people's dispositions as a constraint on social relations. True, people who are disposed in ways compatible with Scheffler's constraint are likely to have relations of a certain egalitarian kind just as it is unlikely, but not impossible, that they will form suitable egalitarian relations even in the complete absence of egalitarian dispositions. However, strictly speaking, the constraint constrains people's *dispositions*, not their relations, even if we assume its *scope* does not extend beyond situations where people are socially related. By way of analogy: a constraint saying that if people are socially related, they should have equal amounts of resources does not constrain people's social relations, even if it applies only when they are socially related, and it would be odd to appeal to this constraint in an account of how relational egalitarianism differs from the distributive ideal. By way of further support for this claim, consider having a peaceful relationship. It is much more likely that X and Y have such a relationship if they are

---

[28] My initial formal point supports this claim as well.

peacefully disposed, but it is conceptually possible for them to be non-peacefully related even if they are peacefully disposed, e.g. if they misunderstand each others' intentions, and it is possible that their relations are peaceful even if they are belligerent, e.g. if through sheer luck no occasion for conflict arises. The criteria for relations being peaceful do not include anything about the dispositions of the involved parties. Arguably, the same is true about having an egalitarian relationship. Having certain egalitarian dispositions is not part of what defines egalitarian relations, even if the latter is very unlikely to obtain in the absence of the former. Arguably, two hierarchically disposed people, who do in fact treat and believe they should treat each others' interests as equally significant whenever deciding what to do together, but who are actually otherwise disposed – had circumstances been slightly different, they would have related otherwise – should not conclude, once they learn about each others' dispositions, that, despite appearances, they do not relate as equals. Rather, they should infer that their egalitarian relationship is an extremely fragile one. I conclude that the deliberative constraint is not really a constraint on the nature of social relations.

However, I concede that Scheffler's constraint is not reducible to a form of distributive egalitarianism. In the attempt to show that the distributive and the relational views are distinct, Scheffler has in effect brought to our attention a third view, *dispositional egalitarianism*. This view is neither about distributions nor about social relations, but holds that justice is a matter of how individuals are disposed to act:[29]

> *Dispositional egalitarianism*: It is unjust if some people (who are suitably related) are not disposed to relate to others in a way that respects the deliberative constraint.[30]

Dispositional egalitarianism is different from, but also compatible with, both distributive and relational egalitarianism. While I think dispositional egalitarianism is interesting and captures part of what egalitarians are concerned with – concerns that might not be reducible to a concern for distributions or the nature of social relations, whether the latter is substantially reducible to the former or not – the existence of a third distinct

---

[29] This view has an honourable history and Hume's (2004 [1751]: 83–98) view that justice is a(n artificial) virtue strikes me as a potential (non-egalitarian) predecessor (cp. Cohen's (2008: 317–18) example of the 'remarkably just person' who would rather forgo an advantage than unjustly enjoy more than do others who are no less deserving). Anderson also makes some – to my mind, confusing – remarks to the effect that for relational egalitarians 'justice is fundamentally a virtue of agents' (Anderson, 2008a: 139, 143; Anderson, 2010a: 22; cp. Miklosi, forthcoming: 22).

[30] The 'suitably related' qualification reflects that Scheffler does not think that the deliberative constraint governs all social relations.

egalitarian view cannot show that relational egalitarianism is not reducible to a particular form of distributive egalitarianism.[31]

My second reason for thinking that Scheffler's response to the reductionist challenge is unsuccessful derives from the fact that we might define a luck egalitarian deliberative constraint which is different from, but relevantly similar to, Scheffler's deliberative constraint:

> *The luck egalitarian deliberative constraint*: If you and I have an egalitarian relationship, then I have a standing disposition to treat the concern that you are not worse off than I am, in terms of the satisfaction of our strong interests, for reasons not suitably reflecting our differential exercise of responsibility, as constraining our decisions and influencing what we do. You have a reciprocal disposition with regard to my interests. In addition, both of us normally act on these dispositions.

Scheffler might retort that while this constraint will often constrain agents in the same way as his own deliberative constraint does, it will sometimes constrain us differently; and when this happens we see – perhaps for reasons relating to how people can live in an egalitarian marriage without wanting to level down – that his deliberative constraint is more plausible than the luck egalitarian deliberative one. However, my present concern is not to discuss which of the two constraints is the more plausible one. Rather, it is this: The fact that there is a luck egalitarian deliberative constraint shows that the issue between luck and relational egalitarians – or, strictly speaking, dispositional egalitarians – is not whether the locus of egalitarian justice is distributions or dispositions. After all, luck egalitarians might have luck egalitarian views on both matters. Rather, the disagreement concerns which distributions, if any, and which dispositions, if any, justice requires.

I conclude that Scheffler's response to the reductionist challenge is unsuccessful, although in the course of responding to it he introduces a third form of egalitarianism, which is irreducible to both distributive and relational egalitarianism.

7.6 Pluralist Egalitarianism

In the previous section, I noted that dispositional egalitarianism is different from, though compatible with, distributive as well as relational

---

[31] In Chapter 8, I argue that an ideal of egalitarian social relations plays an important role in Cohen's thinking about equality. Something similar is true of dispositional egalitarianism. An important strain in Cohen's views on capitalism is that it exploits 'low-grade motives' – fear and greed – and that this makes it deficient. It would, as Cohen (2009: 50) sees it, be better if we could all act in the spirit of 'cooperation and unselfishness'.

egalitarianism. In light of the reductionist challenge, this suggests that one might simply take the ecumenical egalitarian view that injustice obtains if the following disjunction is true:

> *Ecumenical (luck) egalitarianism*: It is unjust if, avoidably, any of the following three conditions are satisfied: (1) some people are worse off than others (through no responsibility of their own); (2) some people do not relate to each other as equals (through no responsibility of their own); or (3) some people, who are suitably related, are not disposed to avoid some people being worse off than others (through no responsibility of their own) or to relate to others as equals (through no responsibility of their own).[32]

If you ignore the words within the parentheses, you get ecumenical egalitarianism. If you do not, you get ecumenical *luck* egalitarianism. In either case, the stated position captures core elements from all three egalitarian views that I have discussed. In setting this out, the hope is that philosophers will see these elements as possibly combinable, perhaps even coherent, and not simply as parts of different, incompatible theories of egalitarian justice. Admittedly, if the reductionist challenge is substantively vindicated in the way I have argued, then (2) is substantively contained in (1). However, stating (2) still has a presentational point. Moreover, some might reject my substantive vindication, but nevertheless see the attraction of the ecumenical view.

My ecumenical egalitarianism is not perfectly ecumenical. Unlike luck egalitarianism as defined Chapter 1.1, it does not imply that unavoidable inequalities are unjust.[33] Also, it does not capture the luck egalitarian concern for responsibility, and although it accommodates relational egalitarianism as I defined it, it is inconsistent with the incompatibility claim (Section 7.2). However, my cautious embrace of the reductionist challenge suggests that this component must be rejected anyway. Moreover, the view is ecumenical in terms of the locus of justice.

Ecumenical (luck) egalitarianism is perfectly consistent. Compared to any of the three views of which it is formed, it takes a broader view of the locus of

---

[32] I include 'avoidably', i.e. would not have obtained had some agent who had it in his power to act differently acted differently, because ecumenical (luck) egalitarianism is intended to be an account of justice understood as an account of what we owe one another (cp. Section 7.3). This, however, is consistent with the ecumenical luck egalitarian principle being grounded in a concern for fairness, as suggested in the next section (cp. Vallentyne, 2015: 49; Norman, 1998: 40). Note also that the issues pertaining to what exactly it means to relate as equals, which I set out in Chapter 3, apply to my ecumenical view as well as to standard relational egalitarian theories.

[33] My definitions of relational and dispositional egalitarianism *also* imply that unavoidably hierarchical relations are unjust and that unavoidably inegalitarian dispositions involve injustice. As we saw in Section 7.2, whether unavoidable things can be unjust is an issue that is orthogonal to the issue between luck and relational egalitarians. Moreover, it is not true of luck egalitarian theorists that they all object to unavoidable inequalities (cp. Dworkin, 2000: 105).

justice. According to ecumenical egalitarians, the locus of justice encompasses not just distributions, but also social relations (whether reducible to distributions of social goods or not) and people's dispositions (independent of whether each affects any of the other loci of justice). This means that ecumenical egalitarians might say that, for instance, a certain situation is just in terms of its distribution, but nevertheless imperfect justice-wise, since some individuals are not disposed to relate to others as equals or are not disposed to respect the luck egalitarian deliberative constraint.

Ecumenical egalitarianism is more complex than each of the three views upon which it draws. For instance, ecumenical egalitarians must say whether a slightly more unequal distribution which involves people relating as equals to a significantly higher degree is better in terms of egalitarian justice than one in which the distribution is less unequal, but people less often relate as equals. However, this sort of trade-off might have to be made anyway. Suppose egalitarian justice is fully captured by a concern for distributions being equal. However, there is also an independent moral concern that people relate as equals. If so, we would still have to weigh these two concerns against one another; it is just that, unlike in ecumenical egalitarianism, this weighing does not take place within egalitarian justice, but is one that pertains to the concern for egalitarian justice versus other concerns, all of which, presumably, might bear on moral permissibility.

Suppose we agree that ecumenical egalitarianism is an internally consistent position. Even so, it might still seem like an arbitrary concatenation of different views with no significant relation to one another. To respond to this challenge – call it the *arbitrariness challenge* – I suggest that ecumenical luck egalitarianism is rooted in the value of fairness:

> It is unfair if people are differently situated if the fact that they are differently situated does not reflect their differential exercise of responsibility. (cp. Otsuka, 2004: 151–2).[34]

Fairness so construed, and admittedly there are other ways to understand it (Hinton, 2001; Hooker, 2005; Rawls, 1999: 10–15), grounds the distributive luck egalitarian component (since having unequal amounts of the relevant equalisandum is a way of being differently situated) and the relational luck egalitarian component (since not being treated as an equal is a way of being

---

[34] Wolff (1998: 106) understands fairness as 'the demand that no one should be advantaged or disadvantaged by arbitrary factors'. If one couples this understanding with the view that the only non-arbitrary factor as a result of which people can be differently situated is by their differential exercise of responsibility, then one arrives at my notion of fairness.

differently situated) of the ecumenical view.[35] This view of fairness is why the relational component cannot be combined with, say, non-egalitarian distributive ideals such as sufficientarianism or prioritarianism.

To reach the dispositional luck egalitarian element, one could appeal to the *transmission principle*:

> If a certain state of affairs or a certain way of relating to one another is unfair, then, all else being equal, a person is unfair to the extent that she is not disposed to act under a constraint of neither bringing about such an unfair state of affairs nor relating to others in this way.[36]

To see the need for the 'other things being equal' qualification, suppose X and Y are partners in love. X treats Y in a sexist manner. X treating Y in that way is an unfair state of affairs. I could have prevented this. Yet the transmission principle does not imply – implausibly, you might think – that I am unfair, for it might be the case that not all else is equal (cp. Smith, 2007: 478). Either I have the authority to interfere in the way I could have interfered with the couple's relations or I do not. If the former, the transmission principle implies that I am less of a fair person for not interfering. Given that I had the authority to act in a way that would have prevented this state of affairs from obtaining and given that there was no moral justification for my not so acting, this implication strikes me as plausible. If the latter, then not all other things are equal and, accordingly, the transmission principle does not imply that I am unfair for not intervening.

The transmission principle seems plausible in itself. In what sense could a person not be unfair (or, at any rate, not fail to be fair) if she is in no way disposed to bring about a fair state of affairs? In assessing this claim, observe that one might be somewhat disposed not to bring about a certain unjust state of affairs and yet fail to prevent it from obtaining because of a stronger, countervailing disposition, e.g. a disposition to avoid unreasonably large costs. Moreover, there seem to be quite similar and equally plausible transmission principles, e.g. 'if a certain state of affairs is morally

---

[35] Hinton (2001: 79–80) thinks that domination and exploitation are unfair even 'if such relationships were to be grounded in voluntary acts on the part of those subject to them' and, thus, rejects the view proposed here. However, Hinton ties domination and exploitation to 'denying' people 'fair terms of access to the external world or else to the goods that are produced by working on it' (Hinton, 2001: 81), and this undermines his view that voluntary domination and exploitation are unfair, since these do not involve anyone being denied access to anything – dominatees and exploitees can simply say 'no', as it were, if their being dominated or exploited is truly voluntary.

[36] 'Bringing about' refers both to doing and allowing.

bad, then a person is morally bad to the extent she is not disposed to avoid bringing about such a state of affairs'.

If we care non-instrumentally about persons not being unfair and we care about fairness, then we care non-instrumentally about persons being disposed to neither countenance that some people are worse off than others through no responsibility of their own, nor that people do not relate to each other as equals through no responsibility of their own. *Ex hypothesi*, to care about this simply is *part of* what it is to care about fairness.

The transmission principle ties fairness of states of affairs (where that includes unfairness of relations) to fairness of persons. This strikes me as plausible. Suppose we think that luck egalitarianism captures what fairness requires distribution-wise, but, Hume-like, also think that a fair person is simply one who respects the laws and keeps her promises. In that case, we could not say that two persons who are equally law-abiding and promise-fulfilling are unequally fair, even if one knowingly causes, and the other one does not, inequalities for which the worse off are not responsible. But it would seem odd, say, for the two persons who share the pertinent view about fair distribution, and despite their knowledge of the way in which they differ, to regard each other as being equally fair persons.[37] Still, the transmission principle does not say that what *makes* a fair person a fair person is that she is disposed to act under a constraint of not bringing about unfair states of affairs – something many virtue ethicists would deny. The principle is consistent with the view that what makes it unjust that some people are worse off than others through no responsibility of their own is that such a state of affairs is one that unfair persons are disposed to bring about. Nor does the principle say that we have reasons to care about whether persons are fair.

No doubt, some who are attracted to ecumenical luck egalitarianism will not embrace the grounding in fairness that I have proposed. For instance, if one holds, as Anderson does, that the ideal of equality is grounded in some contractualist notion of fair cooperation, one might reject the broad notion of fairness of the view proposed here. My aim here is not to show that ecumenical luck egalitarianism grounded in the way I have just proposed is more attractive than any other form of egalitarianism. Nor is it my aim to defend ecumenical luck egalitarianism against other forms of ecumenical egalitarianism beyond whatever defence lies in the suggestion that it is rooted

---

[37] A similar argument applies to the view that fair relations between people are relations in which no one relates to others as unequals (through no responsibility of their own) and its connection to views about what it is to be a fair person.

in fairness. My aim is to show that there is a rationale for a luck egalitarian view which extends to all three sites of justice discussed in this piece.

7.7 Conclusion

In this chapter, I have defended the following views: luck, relational, and dispositional egalitarianism are logically compatible with one another; the former two are not separated by some deeper disagreement about the nature of justification; while relational egalitarianism cannot, formally speaking, be reduced to distributive equality, substantively speaking the concerns of relational equalitarians can be articulated within a distributive paradigm; along the same lines I have argued that, in effect, Scheffler has introduced a third form of egalitarianism, which is irreducible, formally as well as substantively, to distributive egalitarianism; and, finally, I have proposed a form of pluralist egalitarianism that combines crucial elements from all of the three forms of egalitarianism that I have discussed in this chapter. To condense the present chapter into one sentence: While luck and relational egalitarian *theories* are different, they are much less different than suggested in a number of relational egalitarian critiques and can in fact be combined into a form of pluralist egalitarianism. In the next chapter I shall argue that at least one central relational egalitarian *theorist* has in fact – inconsistently or not – incorporated distributive elements into her thinking, while relational elements play a crucial role in some luck egalitarians' accounts of justice.

CHAPTER 8

Often the Twain Meet

8.1 Introduction

In previous chapters, I argued that luck egalitarianism can accommodate many of the views held by relational egalitarians; that relational and luck egalitarianism, despite their differences, face a number of similar issues of specification, e.g. in relation to scope, site and time; that the criticisms that relational egalitarians direct against luck egalitarianism can be accommodated; that the two views are not rooted in incompatible ideas of moral justification and that versions of them might – together with dispositional egalitarianism – be rooted in a more basic idea of fairness. Should these points be correct, one would expect that egalitarians from the two camps hold views that are more congenial to those belonging to the other camp than the usual contraposition of the two views as antagonistic would lead one to expect. In this chapter, I vindicate this expectation.

On the one hand, we find important luck egalitarian elements in relational egalitarianism. Despite their rejection of any fundamental distributive concerns, we find both in Anderson and Scheffler suggestions to the effect that equality of opportunity is not just desirable as an instrument for promoting suitably egalitarian relations, but that it is either independently desirable or desirable as a constitutive part of the relational ideal (Section 8.2). If so, this implies that any critique of equality of opportunity is a critique of a constitutive element of relational equality, in which case the distance between the relational and the distributive views seems further reduced.

On the other hand, we also find that luck egalitarians have various commitments that are best explained with reference to the relational egalitarian ideal. For instance, Dworkin and Cohen deny that a person with frustrated snobbish tastes or offensive preferences is owed compensation, even if it is pure bad brute luck that the relevant person holds such tastes or preferences (Sections 8.3 and 8.4). This is a very significant deviation from the luck egalitarian impulse to shield people from the effects of bad brute luck (Lippert-Rasmussen, 2013b). In Sections 8.5 and 8.6, I scrutinize other significant intersections between luck and relational egalitarianism: Dworkin's requirement that the state expresses equal concern and respect for its citizens, and Cohen's notions of the interpersonal test and a justificatory community. As we have seen, both notions are explicitly employed by Anderson, not only to criticize luck egalitarianism, but even to distinguish it – by using notions defined and embraced by luck egalitarians – from relational egalitarianism (Chapters 2.3 and 7.2). Section 8.7 takes a look at Cohen's ideas about camping-trip socialism and the notion that community restricts the amount of inequality that egalitarians can embrace, even when the inequality in question satisfies the requirements of luck egalitarian equality of opportunity. I submit that both Cohen's idea of a justificatory community and his idea of camping-trip socialism embody important versions of the relational ideal.

Freud famously coined the phrase 'narcissism of small differences'. I would not go as far as to say that the debate between luck and relational egalitarianism falls under this heading. The two currents of egalitarian thinking do involve a number of very important substantive disagreements. But perhaps the phrase 'narcissism of exaggerated differences' is apt in view of the fact that the disagreement between luck and relational egalitarianism is often presented as some kind of academic boxing match involving a clear winner and a knocked-out loser. The main claim I want to defend in this chapter is that there are significant affinities between the positions of different luck and relational egalitarian *thinkers*. Using the distinction I have previously employed between theorist- and theory-focused critiques, I should emphasize that, unlike the previous chapter, the present chapter is theorist-focused (Chapter 2.3). Hence, it does not speak to the issue of how relational and luck egalitarianism per se relate. Still, in part because of how this observation might have the potential to transform the nature of the debate about egalitarian justice, the present theorist-focused point about similarities is worth making.

8.2 Anderson on Equality of Opportunity and/or Capability

As we have seen, Anderson rejects the view that egalitarian justice focuses on distributions as opposed to social relations (Chapters 2.2 and 2.3). However, we also saw that in her flagship formulation of the difference between equality of fortune and democratic equality, for reasons she does not dwell on, she leaves open the possibility that people subscribing to the latter ideal actually care non-instrumentally, albeit secondarily, about distribution. And in fact, drawing on Sen, Anderson contends that 'egalitarians should seek equality for all in the space of capabilities', where capabilities 'consist of the set of functionings she can achieve, given the personal, material and social resources available to her' (Anderson, 1999: 316).[1] The suggestion here seems not to be that an equal distribution of capabilities is *causally necessary* for democratic equality. Rather, the suggestion seems to be that part of what it *is* for citizens to relate as equals is for them to enjoy equal capabilities, i.e. that they can achieve the same set of democratically relevant functionings, given the personal, material and social resources available to them. This impression is strengthened by what Anderson writes elsewhere, e.g.:

> An original structural injustice – denial of fair opportunities for education – generates additional structural inequalities in opportunities for exercising full epistemic agency, which is an injustice to the speakers. This is analogous to the socioeconomic injustice of a group suffering from poor employment opportunities because it has been denied decent educational opportunities. (Anderson, 2012b: 169)

At this point one might start to wonder why this does not make Anderson someone who, despite her scathing critique of luck egalitarianism, subscribes both to relational and to distributive equality (or distributive sufficiency as suggested by the previous quote), i.e. someone who, despite her rather uncompromising official line, deep down embraces a pluralist egalitarian position – perhaps of the ecumenical sort I defended in the previous chapter.

In response to the suggestion that democratic equality is closer to luck egalitarianism than one might think, Anderson might, first, say – in fact, does say – that the capability approach does not just look at the 'distribution of resources and other divisible goods' (Anderson, 1999: 319).[2] This, however, does not distinguish her view from luck egalitarianism. Luck egalitarianism is completely neutral on what the relevant equalisandum is and some of the luck egalitarians that she criticizes are in complete agreement with her about the fact that justice is not all about 'distribution of

---

[1] Similarly, Scheffler (2003a: 22, 36–7) mentions 'equal distribution of power' as one component of what it is to relate as equals in a political community.

[2] She cannot say that on her view the only basis for favouring equality of opportunity is to promote egalitarian social relations, since the former is part of what the latter amounts to and arguably would seem to be a constitutive part of that ideal, the realization of which is desirable even if the other constitutive parts are not realized, e.g. if citizens enjoy equal opportunities but in other respects do not relate as equals.

resources and other divisible goods'. Arneson agrees because he thinks egalitarian justice is all about welfare, and Cohen agrees because he thinks equality is in part about welfare.

Second, Anderson might also point to the fact that responsibility plays a different role in her theory. That is, it plays some role because democratic equality does not require that people actually achieve that same level of functioning, but it does not play the same 'make or break' role as it does in luck egalitarianism, because one's capability-related entitlements are unaffected by how one exercises one's choice (Anderson, 1999: 317).

This point definitely has some significance. While I do not think it serves to distinguish her theory from possible variants of luck egalitarianism, it sets it aside from at least some of the actual luck egalitarian theories that she goes over in her article. However, it clearly does not set it aside from distributive ideals of equality in general. As noted on several previous occasions, what role responsibility plays in a theory of egalitarian justice is different from the distribution versus relations issue (Chapter 1.3).

Finally, Anderson might reply that, despite the 'equality for all' quote in the first paragraph in this section, her view is not that, for all capabilities or for a bundle of capabilities that include all conceivable capabilities, people are entitled to *equal* capabilities. Rather, people are entitled, negatively, to 'whatever capabilities are necessary to enable them to avoid or escape entanglement in oppressive relationships' and, positively, 'to the capabilities necessary for functioning as an equal citizen in a democratic state' (Anderson, 1999: 316). This view does not amount to an embrace of a distributive ideal of equality – one that only allows a certain circumscribed role for responsibility and that takes capabilities, rather than resources etc., as its equalisandum. This is so because, while it might be the case that equality of capabilities is what is necessary to avoid oppression and achieve equal democratic citizenship, in principle it could also be the case that an unequal distribution of capabilities is what is necessary for achieving the two relevant goals. But what this means is that, despite the above-mentioned quote, Anderson does not really subscribe to equality of capabilities as opposed to a distribution of capabilities necessary for relating as equals (cp. Chapter 2.4). One might conjecture that the reason why she nevertheless chooses to express herself as she does reflects that, despite her official line, she does find some form of distributive equality attractive. This impression is strengthened once we take a look at what she writes about equality of opportunity in relation to racial integration.

In sketching her favoured integrative model of racially-focused affirmative action, she notes that this model begins with the observation that '[d]e facto racial segregation unjustly impedes socioeconomic opportunities for disadvantaged groups, causes racial stigmatization and discrimination, and is inconsistent with a fully democratic society. To remedy these problems, we need to practice racial integration' (Anderson, 2010b: 148). Affirmative action for racial minorities should be seen 'as a means to racially integrate the main institutions of civil society' (Anderson, 2010b: 136). One might find the final 'and' in the previous Anderson quote surprising. One would have thought that according to a champion of democratic equality the reason why impeding socioeconomic opportunities for disadvantaged groups is objectionable *is* that this is incompatible with a fully democratic society. But the most natural reading of this passage is that Anderson sees this as a list of distinct problems and that the first two items on the list are problems independently of how they might contribute to the incomplete realization of democratic equality. In that case, she does have some non-derivative concern about distribution: to wit, the distribution of opportunities.[3]

While this may be the most natural reading of Anderson, there is also another possible reading. One could say that equality, and not just sufficiency, of opportunity is important. This is not because the distribution of opportunity is in itself important. Rather, equality of opportunity is important because whenever it obtains, people who are worse off and demand a justification from their co-citizens (set aside the issues of sufficiency and cosmopolitanism (Chapter 5.5), both of which I think can be factored in, though at the cost of making an already complex view even more complex) for their being worse off can be told by those who are better off that a reason for their being so is the fact that they too had equally good opportunities initially which they did not take advantage of.[4] It is important here that the justification they offer is correct in the sense that it appeals to a fact about equality of opportunity which obtains

[3] She might retort that her concern is not with equality of opportunities per se, merely that members of disadvantaged groups have the opportunity to join the elite, though not necessarily equally good opportunities as members from advantaged groups; and she might say that the only reason such a deficient distribution is unjust is that it prevents people from relating as equals. The former reply sits uneasily with Anderson's claim to articulate the concerns of real-life egalitarians, who tend to demand equal, not just sufficiently good, opportunities. Obviously – and for good reason, I think – the NAACP and feminists do not advocate merely sufficiently good opportunities for African-Americans and women.

[4] Rawls mentions something along this line in his defence of the difference principle. He says that in a well-ordered society '[T]hose better circumstanced are willing to have their greater advantages only under a scheme in which this works out for the benefit of the less unfortunate' (Rawls, 1999: 90). Hence, in such a society, better off people can *truly* offer as a reason to the worse off that their being better off is necessary for the latter not being worse off.

independently of whether or not the people offering justifications to each other *believe* that they enjoy equality of opportunity.

At this point, it is useful to introduce a distinction between two conceptions of what it is to relate to one another as equals and a distinction between two relational, and for that matter two distributive, ideals. Starting with the first distinction, there is a difference between the following:

> *Internalist conception of relating as equals*: Whether or not X and Y relate as equals is determined solely by facts about how they regard (or ought to, given the evidence available to them) one another and the way in which they relate to one another.
> *Externalist conception of relating as equals*: The internalist conception of relating as equals is false, e.g. whether X and Y relate as equals is at least in part determined by facts of which X and Y are unaware (and of which it is not the case that they ought to be aware, given the evidence available to them).

If we say that for men and women to relate as equals, they must as a matter of fact enjoy equality of opportunity, we endorse an externalist conception of what it is to relate as equals. Similar claims apply to relating as equals, on the one hand, and freedom from oppression, domination, exploitation etc., on the other. This brings me to the second distinction I mentioned above:

> *First-order (outcome) relational egalitarianism*: A situation is just only if everyone relates to one another as equals (i.e. the view I introduced Chapter 1.2).
> *Foundational (outcome) relational egalitarianism*: What makes a situation just is the fact that everyone relates as equals.

This distinction is analogous to the distinction between the following:

> *First-order equality of opportunity distributive egalitarianism*: A situation is just only if everyone has equal opportunities (Chapter 1.2).
> *Foundational equality of opportunity distributive egalitarianism*: What makes a situation just is the fact that everyone enjoys equal opportunities.

What I have suggested here is that Anderson subscribes to foundational relational egalitarianism and first-order distributive egalitarianism with regard to capabilities (as well as first-order relational egalitarianism, though this is not relevant here). On the proposed interpretation, what makes a situation just is that people relate as equals – more specifically, that people can justify to one another their respective distributive positions etc. Given the proposed view of justification, this implies a commitment to first-order equality of opportunity. Moreover, because what is required is not just that people *believe* they enjoy equality of opportunity, but that they *actually do* so, the implied notion of relating as equals is externalist. Perhaps this is Anderson's real view, though she never describes it in those terms.[5] Whether or not this is so, it clearly makes sense for relational egalitarianism to adopt this view if they do not want to jettison, as Anderson does not appear to want to do (in some passages at least), the ideal of equality of opportunity.[6] Further, it is an interpretation that might make sense of some of the unexplained qualifications in the long quote from Anderson in Chapter 2.2. And it is an interpretation the broader significance of which is that friends of a foundational relational ideal might embrace a first-order distributive ideal.

In sum: Anderson embraces some form of equality (or sufficiency) of opportunity and it can reasonably be seen as part of what it is for individuals to relate as equals, perhaps even on Anderson's account. If so, in a sense a certain distributive concern is constitutive of Andersonian relational equality. Moreover, in her writings on racial integration she seems to treat a concern for distribution of opportunity as a freestanding concern for justice. In any case, the distributive ideal plays a greater role in Anderson's egalitarianism than the one it is officially assigned.

8.3 Offensive Tastes

In this and the next four sections, I show how prominent luck egalitarian theorists in various ways subscribe to the relational ideal. In this section

---

[5] Perhaps it also captures well what Scheffler has in mind when he says that a distributive view should be embedded in some broader account of why equality matters. The broader account I propose here is a certain kind of justificatory community.

[6] Harry Brighouse and Adam Swift take a position which is of the relevant externalist kind: '. . . a society that permits unjustified or illegitimate inequalities between its members *just is* one whose members are not treating one another, relating to one another, as equals. The distributions themselves *express* inegalitarian relationships. To live with others in an unequal society on terms that cannot be justified to those who have less is not merely a distributive failure; it is also a failure of relationship' (Brighouse & Swift, 2014: 27; see also Moles & Parr, 2018: 12–13; Norman, 1998: 40, 44; Schuppert, 2015: 120). There are limits to which external facts about people's relations can matter to the relational ideal, e.g. non-social relations such as '__ is taller than __' cannot be a constitutive part of people enjoying egalitarian social relations. Nath subscribes to a partially internalist view of social equality when she contends that 'what relations of equality require in particular cases ought to be sensitive to the views of the participants of the given relationship' (Nath, 2015: 199n26). Note, finally, that of the two components of relating as equals that I distinguished between in Chapter 3, one of them is constitutionally internalist, i.e. regarding one another as equals. The other element – treating as equals – may, but need not be, depending on one's favoured analysis of 'treating as'. If, for instance, one adopts the communicative notion of 'treating as', one's idea of relating as equals is internalist, but it need not be if one adopts the normative notion of 'treating as'.

I discuss offensive tastes; expound and reject Cohen's reason for opposing luck egalitarian compensation for the frustration of offensive tastes; and suggest that Cohen's resistance makes sense on the assumption that he implicitly subscribes to the relational ideal of equality. Hence, if this is correct, there is some reason to think that Cohen's egalitarian views were actually influenced by the relational ideal.

Rawls famously introduced the notion of an offensive preference, i.e. a preference for discriminating against other people or a preference for 'subjecting others to a lesser liberty' as a means of enhancing one's own self-respect. The notion's argumentative relevance derives from the fact that to the extent that, say, the frustration of offensive preferences detracts from a person's welfare, equality of welfare implies that its bearer should be compensated for the frustration of her offensive preferences (or that others should have their welfare lowered to match the offensive taste welfare deficiency). Like Rawls, Dworkin and Cohen deem this implication of equality of welfare implausible and respond by denying that frustrated offensive preferences are relevant to distributive justice. On Cohen's view, which is the one I focus on here, the deeper rationale for this denial is that, by virtue of their very content, offensive tastes are anti-egalitarian (Cohen, 2011: 9; Rawls, 1999: 30–1).

To assess this rationale, we need to surface a methodological point about different types of objections to welfare egalitarianism. Cohen distinguishes between such objections which are (1) 'plainly not egalitarian', (2) 'argu-ably . . . egalitarian', and (3) 'problematic with regard to how they should be classified' (Cohen, 2011: 6). If we object to welfare egalitarianism on the grounds that to implement it, we need to violate people's privacy, we are offering an objection of type (1). Given pluralism, a type (1) objection does not show that equality of welfare is not really ideally just. All it shows is that sometimes realizing that ideal clashes with a concern for other values. If instead we object to welfare egalitarianism on the grounds that, due to their recklessness, some people are bad converters of resources into welfare and that welfare egalitarianism implausibly implies that they should be compensated, in Cohen's view our objection is an objection of type (2). Even given pluralism, a type (2) objection shows that welfare egalitarians have misconstrued equality. In Cohen's view, the right inference to draw from this objection appealing to culpably bad converters is not that egalitarian justice is indifferent to welfare, but that it demands equal access to welfare – something that culpably bad converters enjoy *ex ante* – rather than equal welfare outcomes.

It is unclear which criteria Cohen applies to classify the relevant objections. He appeals to two ideas: (1) that objections of type (2) rest on the thought that people do not 'get an equal amount of something that they should have an equal amount of'; and (2) that the relevant objectionable feature involves 'an exploitative distribution of burden' (Cohen, 2011: 7–8). Cohen (2011: 5) connects (2) with his view that the 'primary egalitarian impulse is to extinguish the influence on distribution of both exploitation and brute luck'.[7] However, applying neither of these two ideas shows that an offensive preference-based objection is a type (2) objection. First, including offensive (and, for that matter, snobbish) preferences in one's comparison of welfare across individuals is perfectly compatible with the idea that there is something – i.e. preference satisfaction or hedonic welfare – that everyone should 'have an equal amount of'. Second, the inclusion of such preferences need not involve any exploitation, where an exploiter exploits an exploitee when the former takes 'unfair advantage of' the latter, because there is no sense in which people who are compensated for welfare deficits deriving from frustrated offensive (or snobbish) preferences, with which they are stuck, *take* advantage of others (Cohen, 2011: 5) – they do not use others to be better off than they otherwise would have been.

Despite these two observations, Cohen treats the objection that welfare egalitarianism is committed to compensation for frustrated offensive preferences as an objection of type (2):[8]

> From the point of view of justice, such pleasures deserve condemnation, and the corresponding preferences have no claim to be satisfied, even if they would have to be satisfied for welfare of equality to prevail. I believe that this objection defeats welfarism, and, hence, equality of welfare. But the natural course for a welfare egalitarian to take in response to the offensive tastes criticism is to shift his favour to something like equality of *inoffensive* tastes. (Cohen, 2011: 10)

Here Cohen makes no distinction between offensive preferences that have been deliberately cultivated and those that have not. Welfare deficits deriving from involuntarily acquired offensive preferences are not unjust.

---

[7] From the present perspective it is independently interesting that Cohen mentions elimination of exploitation as an aim of egalitarian justice alongside the aim of eliminating the influence of (differential) bad luck. Exploitation is one of the relations that Anderson (cp. Chapter 2.4) criticizes luck egalitarians for having lost sight of and, admittedly, despite being *mentioned* by Cohen it plays no role in his ensuing fleshing out of the motivating impulse.

[8] Presumably, Cohen would say the same about people whose welfare deficit is the result of a frustrated, masochistic preference for being discriminated against or subjected to a lesser liberty (cp. the discussion of hypercritical blame in Chapter 4.4).

After all, whether or not offensive preferences clash with the ideal of equality does not depend on whether they have been deliberately developed or not.

Cohen is not right to classify the offensive tastes objection as a type (2) objection. There are two reasons why. First, offensive tastes do not, by virtue of their content, clash with the ideal of justice if Cohen's ideal of equality of access to advantage exhausts the demands of that ideal. Suppose someone has a preference that whites have more than blacks in terms of some good not covered by equal access to advantage – presumably this is possible, since that ideal was never supposed to apply to all goods, only those that matter at some fundamental level – and suppose that this preference is frustrated. On this assumption, the pertinent offensive taste is not a preference for some state of affairs which is not perfectly compatible with the ideal of equal access to advantage. Accordingly, Cohen cannot say that the preference is offensive, because, by virtue of its content, it offends against justice and, thus, seems to lack any principled reason for excluding it from the range of preferences which matter from the point of view of luck egalitarian justice.

Second, consider a case in which someone leads a life that is worse than that of others, welfare-wise, because, through no choice or fault of her own, she was kidnapped and brainwashed into having strong, offensive preferences, which, as it happens, are frustrated. Compare this with an otherwise comparable case where the victim acquires strong, expensive, but inoffensive tastes, again not satisfied. On Cohen's account, there is no injustice in the first person being worse off, but there is injustice in the second person being so. However, the contention is that, from a luck egalitarian perspective, there is no relevant distinction between these two cases. The two people do not differ in their exercise of responsibility and, thus, the impulse guiding luck egalitarianism suggests that they could not justly be unequally well off given that such an equality cannot be justified by a differential exercise of responsibility (Cohen, 2011: 121).[9] Making welfare deficiencies deriving from frustrated offensive preferences exceptional is theoretically unmotivated.

The person with offensive preferences might even object that, strictly speaking, her welfare deficiency does not derive from her having offensive tastes. Think of her brother, who has the same set of preferences as she has,

---

[9] Perhaps it is tacitly assumed that people with offensive preferences have some degree of indirect control over them. At any rate, this would lend (in the context, illicit) support to view that the frustration of (involuntary) offensive preferences is irrelevant from a luck egalitarian point of view.

except for the fact that he has very cheap tastes with regard to housing and food. Accordingly, he is as well off as people with non-offensive preferences and better off than his more unfortunate, but, say, equally racist sister. I suppose Cohen does not want to lower the level of welfare of the racist brother. If so, can his sister not complain on sound luck egalitarian grounds that she is unjustly worse off than her brother due to her not having compensatingly cheap, inoffensive tastes? Because I see little chance of Cohen providing a principled luck egalitarian response to this case and in view of the further arguments above, I conclude that Cohen has not provided a sound luck egalitarian rationale for dismissing compensation for frustrated offensive tastes.

This raises the question of whether such a rationale can be found in relational egalitarianism. Consider, first, the objection relational egalitarians might have to offensive tastes. It seems natural to assume that, at least in a range of central cases, if X discriminates against Y or if X subjects Y to a lesser liberty than Z on account of their membership of different socially salient groups, then X neither treats, nor regards, Y as an equal. On Anderson's account, in such cases X appears to act from principles that do not express equal respect and concern – e.g. X is not equally concerned with Y's and Z's freedom. On Scheffler's account, it seems equally clear that, in a range of paradigmatic cases, X does not treat Y's interests as being as important as X's, if X treats Y disadvantageously relative to Z because of their membership of different socially salient groups and X belongs to the same socially salient group as Z. A person who harbours offensive preferences is, *ipso facto*, unlikely to respect Scheffler's deliberative constraint. Moreover, Scheffler mentions the standing citizens have to make claims upon one another simply by virtue of being citizens and irrespective of the sorts of identity, such as ethnic or religious identity, that are normally the basis of discrimination. I conclude that, generally, relational egalitarians condemn offensive preferences.[10]

Can relational egalitarians explain why people should not be compensated for offensive preferences? In a sense they can, for Anderson and Scheffler are not concerned with the distribution of welfare per se.[11] They do not think people with frustrated offensive preferences should receive compensation for their resulting loss of welfare per se, since they do not

[10] This is not to suggest that in all possible cases, relational egalitarians will resist compensation for frustrated offensive preferences. However, I suspect in those cases that underpin the intuitive appeal of the offensive tastes objection, relational egalitarianism will condemn compensation.

[11] This is perhaps less clear in the case of Scheffler, since it all depends on how he fleshes out the notion of interests.

think that justice requires that people with frustrated preferences, whether offensive, non-offensive or even highly commendable, should receive compensation for their resulting loss of welfare per se. Both of them would probably add that compensating people for frustrated offensive tastes is disrespectful to those who are the target of the relevant offensive preferences and, thus, that not only is there no positive reason to compensate people with frustrated offensive preferences, there is a positive reason not to.

In sum: luck egalitarians like Cohen are unable to explain why people with frustrated offensive preferences should not receive compensation for their resulting welfare disadvantage. However, he does deny that people with frustrated offensive preferences should receive compensation. Relational egalitarianism does a better, albeit imperfect, job of justifying this claim. This is some, admittedly inconclusive, evidence of Cohen subscribing to a form of relational egalitarianism in the midst of his flagship exposition of his luck egalitarian views.

8.4   Snobbery

The previous section argued that there is no luck egalitarian case for denying compensation for frustrated offensive preferences and that Cohen's resistance against providing such compensation is better explained by an unacknowledged commitment to a sort of egalitarian relational view. I now turn to another putatively anti-egalitarian preference, i.e. snobbish preferences.

In his influential argument against welfare egalitarianism, Dworkin pictures Louis, who has deliberately cultivated expensive tastes for plovers' eggs and pre-phylloxera wine and is now worse off than others (Dworkin, 2000: 48–59). Welfare egalitarianism implies that Louis should get extra resources to compensate him for this welfare deficit. Dworkin thinks this shows welfare is not the metric of egalitarian justice.

According to Cohen, this misunderstands the significance of Louis' case. First, Cohen notes that in his description of the case, Dworkin foregrounds Louis' *deliberate* cultivation of his expensive tastes, despite the fact that Dworkin wants to say something about expensive tastes in general (cp. Arneson, 1989). Second, Cohen distinguishes between deliberately cultivating a preference that just *happens to be* expensive and deliberately cultivating a preference *because* it is expensive. Here 'because' means *for the reason that* (Cohen, 2011: 99). In the latter case alone an expensive taste is snobbish. Cohen thinks that welfare deficiency due to the former kind of accidentally expensive preferences, as opposed to snobbish preferences, might deserve compensation (Cohen, 2011: 95). Using terminology introduced in the previous section, we can say that Cohen believes that the snobbish tastes complaint to equality of welfare is a type (2) objection, i.e. one that does not derive from values other than equality.

The main question here is whether, on the basis of his luck egalitarianism, Cohen can deny that people are due compensation when their welfare deficit is due to involuntary, expensive, snobbish tastes. However, before addressing this question, I need to address two conceptual questions about how snobbish preferences, on the one hand, relate to offensive and expensive preferences, on the other hand. First, it might seem that snobbish preferences form a species of offensive preferences, since the former appears to clash with the value of equality because they reflect a desire to see oneself as superior to others. However, while snobbish preferences often take this form, it is unclear that they must. It is possible for someone to have a snobbish taste without being motivated by a desire for superiority. You might have a preference for expensive sports gear in part because of its being expensive, while in all other areas you have inexpensive preferences. You might not mind the fact that your tastes in these other areas are inexpensive, nor that others have satisfied their expensive, snobbish preferences. In this kind of case, your snobbish taste is not offensive – it certainly does not involve a desire to see others as socially or morally inferior (cp. Chapter 3.2; cp. Anderson, 2012a: 49) – whether a welfare deficit resulting from it should be compensated for or not.

Second, it might similarly seem that snobbish preferences are expensive preferences by definition. However, cheap, snobbish preferences are possible, as are expensive, humble ones. By 'humble preferences' I mean preferences for something on the grounds that it is cheaper than the relevant goods others prefer – the reverse preference of a snobbish preference, as it were. To see that snobbish preferences can be cheap, imagine someone who falsely believes beer to be expensive and cultivates a preference for beer on that basis. To ensure that this badly informed snob reaches the same level of welfare as others, we may need fewer resources than we require to ensure that a better-informed person without snobbish preferences reaches the same level of welfare as others. Accordingly, objections to compensation for frustrated snobbish preferences per se cannot appeal to the consideration that it is unjust to demand a greater share of resources than others on account of one's expensive preferences.[12] To see that there can be expensive, humble preferences, suppose Dworkin's Louis falsely believes that pre-phylloxera claret and plovers' eggs are cheaper than the beer and risotto preferred by others and that he cultivates his humble preferences because of this belief.

With these two clarifications in mind, let us now turn to the main question in this section – can Cohen refuse, as he does, compensation for frustrated snobbish preferences on luck egalitarian grounds? I believe not. First, it is implausible to hold that snobbish preferences are simply irrelevant from the point of view of luck egalitarian justice. Imagine a case where everyone holds snobbish preferences through no choice or fault of their own, and where they are unequally well off as a result of the fact that some people's snobbish preferences are satisfied and others' are not. This case is worse, from the point of view of luck egalitarian justice, than one in which everyone's snobbish preferences are satisfied or frustrated to an equal degree.

Second, Cohen puts a great deal of emphasis on the fact that bearers of non-snobbish, expensive preferences typically identify with the preference as such while regretting that the preference is expensive (Cohen, 2011: 92–6). This distinguishes them from people with snobbish, expensive preferences, and this is why the latter are less deserving, or not deserving at all, of compensation. However, a distinction similar to the one Cohen rightly presses – the distinction between regretting the preference and regretting that it happens to be expensive to satisfy it – applies to snobbish expensive preferences, i.e. there is a distinction between regretting that it happens to be expensive to satisfy one's preferences and regretting that one is in a social context in which it is valuable for one to satisfy snobbish preferences. Just as a bearer of a judgemental preference that happens to be expensive can 'regard it [the expensiveness of satisfying their preference] as a piece of bad luck for which they should be compensated, on pain of incoherently repudiating their own personality, on pain of confessing to a most bizarre alienation from themselves', so bearers of expensive, snobbish preferences can 'regard it as a piece of bad luck for which they should be compensated' that they find themselves in a context where the satisfaction of such preferences has value for them (Cohen, 2011: 93). *If* the former

---

[12] Given his multidimensional metric of egalitarian justice, Cohen might think snobs with cheap preferences are due some compensation for being under-resourced. However, given his refusal to accommodate snobbish preferences, he would presumably be committed to denying compensation on welfare deficit grounds.

shows, as Cohen believes, that the case for compensating expensive preferences is not defeated, so does the latter.[13]

Third, much of the same reasoning presented in Section 8.3 in relation to offensive preferences applies in the case of snobbish preferences as well. The satisfaction of snobbish preferences is compatible with everyone having equal access to advantage; and even if the content of these preferences is specified in such a way that their satisfaction really does prevent everyone from having equal access to advantage, it is unclear why this should be taken to imply that they should be disregarded. After all, it might simply be my bad luck that I am stuck with frustrated snobbish preferences. On the basis of this and the two previous arguments, I infer that from a luck egalitarian point of view there is no reason to deny compensation to someone who is worse off than others due to involuntary frustrated snobbish preferences.

But if Cohen's refusal to provide compensation for frustrated snobbish preferences cannot be grounded in some luck egalitarian rationale, could it be grounded in some form of relational egalitarianism? Historically speaking, relational egalitarians have long objected to snobbery, viewing it as an enemy of a society of equals. One early relational egalitarian thinker, Jean-Jacques Rousseau (1973 [1754]: 73; cp. 90, 96, 166; cp. Anderson, 2012a: 47–8), observed: '*Amour-propre* is a purely relative and factitious feeling, which arises in the state of society, leads each individual to make more of himself than of any other, causes all the mutual damage men inflict one on another'. He thought luxury goods showed that 'rich and powerful men . . . prize what they enjoy only so far as others are destitute of it' and not because of any real need for luxury goods (Rousseau, 1973 [1754]: 112). Desires for luxury goods are both corrupt – they serve an inflamed form of self-love – and incompatible with Rousseau's ideal of a republic based on relations of equality, where 'no citizen shall ever be wealthy enough to buy another, and none poor enough to be forced to sell himself' (Rousseau, 1973 [1754]: 225).[14] Luxury goods can be used to signal superiority and mark

---

[13] In a sense, this situation involves a form of alienation. The snob prefers a situation in which her circumstances as well as her preferences are different from the present situation. However, this is not the sort of bizarre alienation that Cohen has in mind, i.e. the alienation involved in seeing the expensiveness of satisfying one's preferences as one's bad luck and at the same time thinking that it would involve a loss were one to have non-snobbish preferences despite changes in one's circumstances. By way of contrast, the snob I have in mind has no thought to the effect that, given her circumstances, her personality is not as it should be.

[14] For Rousseau, distribution of wealth does not matter in itself – as Anderson and Scheffler agree – but it matters a great deal nevertheless, because of how it corrupts social relations if it becomes too unequal.

social hierarchies – features which are absent from a society realizing the relational ideal. Indeed, snobbish preferences are one way in which social hierarchies become rigid, because they induce one to distinguish oneself from members of other, less wealthy classes by means of a perspicuous pattern of consumption available to some but not to others.

Admittedly, it is possible to have a snobbish preference for reasons unrelated to those mentioned by Rousseau. You might have snobbish preferences within one subcategory of goods, the satisfaction of which makes you feel refined and special, and at the same time believe that all others are entitled to similar enjoyment of the satisfaction of their snobbish preferences vis-à-vis their own subcategory of goods. In this case the snobbish preferences are motivated by unusual judgements and do not straightforwardly clash with the ideal of a society of equals.[15] Nonetheless, social-relations egalitarians will object to the more usual snobbish preferences for reasons already indicated, and unlike luck egalitarians they can explain why the very fact that people hold them is bad. It is bad because the fact that people are snobs reveals that people do not regard one another as equals, or, at least, that they do not want to regard one another as equals, whether overall or in some particular dimension (cp. Chapters 3.6 and 5.3).[16]

On Anderson's view, acting on standard snobbish preferences – as well as the envy that nourishes them (cp. Chapter 2.3) – is incompatible with expressing equal respect and concern. For one thing, it is in the very nature of snobbish preferences that they are not satisfied if others have similar preferences satisfied. For a similar reason, snobbish preferences are problematic from Scheffler's point of view, in that acting on one's snobbish preferences when the persons to whom one is socially related similarly have snobbish preferences is incompatible with respecting them, as well as incompatible with complying with Scheffler's deliberative constraint. If you and I are both trying to surpass one another, we do not have an egalitarian relationship, where we try to reach a decision about how we should consume which is equally influenced by each other's interests. For

---

[15] I say 'straightforwardly' because a more demanding ideal of a society of equals would presumably require people in each and every sphere to regard one another as equals, and this might rule out the desire to see oneself as special and refined in any particular sphere even if one thinks that others are entitled to something similar in their preferred distributive spheres (cp. Chapter 5.3).

[16] It is, of course, a further question whether they can explain why the bearers of such frustrated preferences should not be compensated for their welfare deficit. However, as noted in the previous section, social-relations egalitarians do not think that people should be equal with regard to welfare, so for them this question arises in a different dialectical context.

one thing, we are not trying to decide how *we* should consume.[17] Moreover, the sort of things people consume because of snobbish preferences are typically reinforcing of and expressing of social hierarchy. Even if social-relations egalitarians cannot condemn all snobbish tastes, they can condemn those whose motivational background is the more usual one. Presumably, it tastes like these that Cohen is concerned with, and presumably his resistance to compensation for frustrated snobbish preferences would be intelligible if he were concerned with how they affect or reflect social relations. From this relational point of view, as with offensive preferences, it is not the case that disadvantages resulting from such frustrated preferences should result in compensation.

This completes this section's argument. In a nutshell, it goes like this: the luck egalitarian impulse to extinguish the influence of brute luck does not oblige us to disregard involuntary snobbish preferences and, thus, Cohen's resistance to compensating for such preferences is not motivated by his luck egalitarianism. However, from a relational egalitarian point of view, snobbish preferences are generally objectionable because of how they prevent people from relating to one another on a basis of equality. Relational egalitarianism implies that offensive or snobbish preferences – both the having of them and their objects – are objectionable and should be disregarded from the point of view of justice. Hence, to the extent that Cohen discounts such preferences, this may reflect that he subscribes to social-relations egalitarianism.[18] This, like the main claim in the previous section regarding frustrated offensive preferences, is significant and ironic, because one of the main targets of social-relations egalitarians' critiques of luck egalitarians is Cohen.

8.5 Dworkinian Bureaucracy

Ronald Dworkin – one of the main luck egalitarian theorists – is very explicit about how his (to use the terminology introduced in Section 8.2:

---

[17] But perhaps two snobs could reach such a decision, e.g. if they decide to take turns surpassing one another. However, as I have argued in Chapter 6.5, relational egalitarians are probably concerned with people relating as equals in each individual interaction.

[18] This argument is far from conclusive. Other ideals might motivate a similarly negative view of the relevant preferences, and Cohen might be reasonably held to ascribe to one of these. Cohen espouses an ideal of community, for example, where people are motivated, non-instrumentally, to serve and be served by others (Cohen, 2009; see Section 8.7 below). Arguably, this ideal of a socialist community clashes with the instrumental attitude to others embodied in typical snobbish preferences. Moreover, assuming that socialist reciprocity involves an equal standing of those among whom relations of reciprocity obtain, it might clash with some offensive preferences, such as sexist, hierarchical preferences regarding how men and women are to serve one another.

first-order) distributive ideal is grounded in a more basic ideal of social relations or, to be more specific, in the relations between a political community, i.e. the state, and its citizens. According to Dworkin, 'equal concern is the sovereign virtue of political community' and it is a necessary condition for a government to be legitimate that it shows 'equal concern for the fate of all those citizens over whom it claims dominion and from whom it claims allegiance' (Dworkin, 2000: 1).[19]

Relational egalitarians have not failed notice this. Scheffler observes that Dworkin presents his luck egalitarianism as 'a spelling out of the idea of equal treatment' (Scheffler, 2003a: 34, 38n78). So apparently Dworkin provides what Scheffler thinks any friend of distributive principles must do in order to show how these principles are attractive: to wit, he grounds them in a normative conception of human relations, or at least, a specific kind of human relations: the social relations between state and citizens. So should not Scheffler be happy about Dworkin's position?

He is not. There are two reasons why. First, he thinks that it is an open question whether showing equal concern for all citizens actually supports luck egalitarian distributive principles. He does not offer any specific arguments in support of this doubt. Instead, Scheffler points out that Cohen finds it unclear that it does and that Anderson thinks it is clear that it does not (Scheffler, 2003a: 34–5).[20] However, even if Cohen's scepticism and Anderson's outright rejection of this claim are both unjustified, there is still a prior question about whether Dworkin's foundational relational ideal is adequate, and Scheffler thinks it is not.

One reason for thinking that the ideal is deficient is that it is statocentric and, thus, significantly restricted in its scope (Cohen, 2000: 164). Accordingly, it does not apply to sub-state-level relations such as the family and private companies, and it does not apply to relations between citizens of different states, or to the relations between different states, implying that no conception of international justice can be based on Dworkin's relational ideal.[21] In fact,

---

[19] There is a difference between being equally concerned with each and every citizen and showing or expressing that one is equally concerned with each and every citizen. At least, on one ordinary understanding of what it is to express or show something, this involves a certain communicative message and surely the state, or its officials, can be equally concerned with all citizens even if they do not communicate it. However, Dworkin's use of the terms 'show' or 'express' is not intended to signal that he thinks that the state is required to do anything other than be equally concerned with all citizens.

[20] One might think that there is simply no way of telling whether or not it does, because there are no clear criteria for when a 'spelling out' of some idea is sound and when it is not.

[21] It is less clear what it implies with regard to justice between citizens of a state who live at different times. If the state has a duty to treat all of its citizens with equal concern at whatever time they live, arguably, Dworkin's relational ideal supports some kind of intrastate, intergenerational justice (cp. Chapter 5.2). One can express equal concern for future people even if one is not socially related to

Dworkin's statocentric ideal is vulnerable to even stronger objections. Dworkin embraces distributive equality because he thinks the state should treat citizens with equal concern and respect. From his perspective it is – as shown in Section 8.3 – clear that the state would fail to do so if it were to compensate some citizens' frustrated offensive preferences for the lesser welfare or freedom of other citizens. As Dworkin sees it, in view of the state's duty, it should simply disregard frustrated offensive preferences. Whether or not this is so, Dworkin's reason for denying compensation for offensive tastes does not apply to the case of, say, racists who live in an all-white country and are frustrated by the fact that blacks prosper in some other state, say, Ethiopia. If the state were to take their frustrated offensive preferences into account, it would not thereby fail to treat any of its own citizens with equal concern and respect. True, it would not treat Ethiopians with equal concern and respect. However, since, *ex hypothesi*, they are not citizens, this is not an issue. But, of course, showing that Dworkin's relational egalitarianism has an implausibly narrow scope is different from showing that Dworkin does not subscribe to some form of relational egalitarianism.

Alternatively, one could deny that Dworkin's normative conception of human relations is an egalitarian one. This is precisely Scheffler's second objection to Dworkin's position. In Dworkin's conception, 'citizens are represented . . . as objects by some kind of centralized object . . . Dworkin's ideal of equality, as applied to questions of distribution, is not itself a model of social or political equality at all; it is perfectly compatible with social hierarchy, inasmuch as it involves one relatively powerful party choosing how to distribute resources among those with relatively less power . . . Dworkin's ideal represents what might be called an *administrative* conception of equality' (Scheffler, 2003a: 35–7). Scheffler contrasts this with the relational ideal, which 'begins from the question of what relationships among equals are like and goes on from there to consider what kinds of social and political institutions are appropriate to a society of equals' (Scheffler, 2003a: 37).[22]

Given that luck and relational egalitarians are often portrayed as being of fundamentally different kinds, it is striking in itself that Dworkin, who after all is seen by most as one of the most prominent representatives of

---

them. However, Dworkin thinks that our '[c]oncern for future generations is not a matter of justice at all' (Dworkin, 1994: 77).

[22] There are considerable affinities between Scheffler's critique of Dworkin and Anderson's emphasis on how an egalitarian theory of justice 'must supply principles for collective willing – that is, for what citizens should will together, not just for what each can will individually' (Anderson, 1999: 310).

luck egalitarianism, is one who explicitly grounds his first-order distributive ideal in a foundational ideal about a particular kind of social relation. Indeed, the fact that he does so coheres well with my overall line of argument in this chapter. Admittedly, Scheffler rejects Dworkin's relational ideal as inadequate. That, however, is also compatible with the main point of the present chapter.

Moreover, one could argue that even if Scheffler's criticisms of Dworkin's ideal (and for that matter, Cohen's critique of its statocentrism) are well-taken, when Dworkin's relational ideal is taken to be a general ideal of relational equality, social relations between persons or human beings take many forms. So even if Dworkin's administrative ideal might not be attractive when imposed on all social relations, it is less clear that it might not be attractive when applied to some forms of social relations. Take the relation between children and the state. Arguably, the state should treat all citizens who are (small) children with equal concern and respect and, arguably, for the purpose of figuring out what distributive implications this has, Dworkin's administrative model might be well suited. As Scheffler notes, many human relationships involve 'differences of rank, power and status' (Scheffler, 2005: 17) and, accordingly, it is unclear on what basis he can deny a circumscribed role for the conception of justice defended by Dworkin.

In sum: Dworkin explicitly grounds his first-order distributive views in a relational ideal. It might not be a plausible relational ideal and, specifically, it might not be plausible as an egalitarian relational ideal, but that does not qualify the claim that some form of relational ideal – even relational egalitarian ideal – plays a crucial role in Dworkin's position, notably when it comes to the way in which he thinks his distributive ideal of equality of resources is grounded.

8.6 Cohen on Justificatory Community

I now turn to the role that community plays in the work of G. A. Cohen. As he notes, 'community' can mean many different things. In this section, I explore his idea of a justificatory community. In the next section, I scrutinize his idea of a community of reciprocal caring. Whatever else a community is, it obtains between people who are socially related in a certain way. Hence, to the extent that Cohen's idea of equality is animated by an ideal of community, he appears to subscribe to some form of relational equality and, thus, is best seen as someone who subscribes to both a distributive and a relational ideal of equality.

As we saw in Chapter 3.5, Cohen introduces the notion of a justificatory community in the course of his critique of the view that the Rawlsian difference principle permits inequalities that are necessary to make the least well off as well off as possible: 'A justificatory community is a set of people among whom there prevails a norm (which need not always be satisfied) of comprehensive justification. If what certain people are disposed to do when a policy is in force is part of the justification of that policy, it is considered appropriate to ask them to justify the relevant behaviour, and it detracts from justificatory community when they cannot do so' (Cohen, 2008: 43–4). Moreover, if the people who are relevantly disposed are asked to justify the relevant behaviour and refuse to provide a justification because they think that they do not need to provide one, 'then they are forswearing community with the rest of us in respect of the policy issue in question' (Cohen, 2008: 44).

There are many ways in which it might be true that people fail to justify a behaviour which is presupposed in a justification offered for a certain policy. In Cohen's critique of incentives, he focuses on failures which consist of failing to meet the so-called interpersonal test (Chapter 4.5). As we have seen, Cohen thinks that Rawlsians must concede that incentive-based justifications for inequality fail to meet the interpersonal test, since talented people cannot justify a policy of providing them with incentives to induce them to be more productive. To do so they would have to justify their being less productive in the absence of incentives and they cannot do so, Cohen contends, since from a Rawlsian perspective they are not worse off than untalented people, and it is simply their good luck that they are talented.[23]

Suppose Cohen is right – whether he is right or wrong is irrelevant for present purposes – that deviations from equality cannot be grounded on the need for incentives. What follows from that? One thing that follows is that the insistence on incentives by talented people in a Rawlsian well-ordered society detracts from community. But this, of course, leaves open that deviations from equality are just and morally permissible, even if incompatible with justificatory community. However, while Cohen might not be clear about it in his initial formulation of his critique of the incentive-based argument for inequality, he wants to say more than just that. Indeed, he believes that another thing that his critique shows is that incentives are unjust and something that, at least from the perspective of perfect justice, ought not to exist.

---

[23] In this way Cohen's use of the interpersonal test connects with an important luck egalitarian theme.

To render this interpretation plausible, it is useful to quote a later piece of his:

> The question, 'Who can say what to whom?' [i.e. the sort of question to which the interpersonal test speaks], goes largely unexplored in contemporary moral philosophy. To be sure, if all that moral philosophy were interested in were which acts are right and which wrong, then this phenomenon [what Cohen refers to as the 'interpersonal dimensions of moral utterances'] might deserve little attention. ('Might': I do not myself believe that the phenomenon carries no lessons as to what is morally right, because I believe that what I call the 'interpersonal test' . . . has non-interpersonal moral implications [i.e. implications for what is right or wrong].) (Cohen, 2013: 119n8)

Admittedly, Cohen uses the phrases 'right' and 'wrong' here and not 'just' and 'unjust'. I suspect, however, that to the extent the use of the former pair of terms, rather than the latter, for him signalled a substantive difference, he would say that the interpersonal test has similar non-interpersonal moral implications with regard to justice (and injustice). And even if this is not so, it would still be the case that his then broader conception of egalitarian rightness has an important interpersonal dimension and involves some notion of egalitarian social relations, egalitarian in the sense that any member of the relevant community can ask any other member of the community to justify his or her behaviour when that behaviour is used as a premise in a justification for a policy within that community. At least, Cohen's justificatory community and its norm of comprehensive justification seems egalitarian in much the same way as Anderson's democratic community: 'By contrast [to luck egalitarianism], democratic equality regards two people as equal when each accepts the obligation to justify their actions by principles acceptable to the other, and in which they take mutual consultation, reciprocation and recognition for granted' (Anderson, 1999: 313). In Cohen's justificatory community, everyone accepts 'the obligation to justify their actions' and everyone accepts that everyone is in a position to ask anyone to justify their actions – something which involves a significant form of 'mutual consultation, reciprocation and recognition'.

In sum: the central role played by the notion of a justificatory community in Cohen's critique of distributive inequality shows that Cohen's vision of egalitarian justice (or, if you like, egalitarian rightness) did include not only a strong emphasis on interpersonal relations but also an ideal about proper egalitarian social relations. Cohen might have been a luck egalitarian, but he was also a relational egalitarian.

8.7 Communal Camping

Cohen's concern for communal social relations was not limited to justificatory communal relations. In some of his latest works, he introduced what
I shall refer to as a community of caring: '"Community" can mean many
different things but the requirement of community that is central here is
that people care about, and where necessary and possible, care for one
another, and too, care that they care about one another' (Cohen, 2009:
34–5).[24] Not only does Cohen think that it is desirable for people to stand
in social relations of caring to one another – indeed, he thinks part of the
attraction of socialism is that, in this respect, it is a bit like a camping trip
on a societal scale – he also embraced the view that 'certain inequalities that
cannot be forbidden in the name of socialist equality of opportunity [e.g.
inequalities resulting from differential outcomes of gambling freely
engaged in] should nevertheless be forbidden, in the name of community'
(Cohen, 2009: 37). One possibility which he suggests is that the ideal of
community 'define[s] the terms within which justice will operate' (Cohen,
2009: 37), i.e. socialism involves both a principle of egalitarian justice and
one of community (cp. Cohen, 2009: 12). If so, Cohen's use of the term
'forbidden' in the preceding quote suggests that he has a broader idea of
egalitarian rightness, of which both luck egalitarianism and community of
care were constitutive parts. Another possibility is to say that what is
forbidden is unjust and, thus, that his notion of egalitarian justice – of
which socialist equality of opportunity is just one part – included his
principle of communal caring.[25]

  Is Cohen's ideal of a community of caring an *egalitarian* relational ideal?[26]
Note first that it does not follow from the fact that his idea of a justificatory
community is an egalitarian one that the idea of a community of care is one
too. This is so because the two forms of community are quite different.
While it might be true that, in some rather thin sense, you care for another if

---

[24] Because this aspect of his thinking of relational egalitarianism appeared in print ten years after
Anderson's critique, it might (though I doubt it), in part, have been a result of her criticisms of his
luck egalitarian position. No such claim, however, can be made about the role of a justificatory
community, whose presence in Cohen's work predates Anderson's and Scheffler's critiques. Cohen
thought that 'communal caring' had 'two modes': community of conditions – or, as Cohen (2009:
38) puts it, 'common life' – and community of reciprocal caring.

[25] Cohen expresses agnosticism at this point: 'But is it an injustice to forbid the transactions that
generate those inequalities? Do the relevant prohibitions merely define the terms within which
justice will operate, or do they sometimes (justifiably) contradict justice? I do not know the answer
to that question' (Cohen, 2009: 37).

[26] Cohen does say in his opening description of the camping trip that there is no hierarchy among us
(Cohen, 2009: 3).

you accept an obligation to justify your actions to that person if your justification of a certain policy is premised on those actions, you can care strongly about someone (and they can care strongly about you), and both parties might care strongly about that relation of caring, even if you do not accept an obligation to justify yourself to each other. For instance, in one important sense of 'acceptance of an obligation to justify one to another', that is true of the relation between parents and children. Parents care greatly about their children and about their caring, but at least when their children are small they might not stand in any justificatory social relations to them, nor think that they ought to.

Patrick Tomlin notes that although 'the focus' in Cohen's later ideal of community of care 'is on "caring" rather than respect, recognition or anti-domination, it nevertheless condemns inequalities that are endorsed by luck egalitarianism in the name of another value – a value that tells us that it is better when we are able to recognize and empathize with one another's struggles; a value that tells us it is better when we live as equals' (Tomlin, 2015: 153). I agree with the first part of Tomlin's observation. However, for the reason indicated in the previous paragraph, I am not sure that Cohen's principle of community of care says that 'it is better when we live as equals'. It certainly tells us more than that because it includes the reflexive requirement that people care that they care about one another. But perhaps it also tells us less than that we should live as equals, because, as already indicated, presumably two persons can care about one another reciprocally – even strongly, lovingly so – and yet not relate as equals. For instance, in most cases parents and children form a Cohenian community of care. Yet their relation is not one of relating as equals – or at least it is not so in the full sense of that term.

This is not to say that Cohen's ideal of community of care has no egalitarian elements (and, in any case, not all relational ideals are egalitarian relational ideals – see Chapter 1.1). For one thing, it seems to involve everyone caring *about* everyone, even though this far from implies that everyone cares *for* everyone (cp. Baker, 2015: 74). (I might care about someone I do not care for, e.g. because that person is a child who has her own parent who cares for her.) Also, Cohen's communal caring involves an important element of reciprocity – we care that we care about each other – which, interestingly, is different from a sort of market-based reciprocity – I scratch your back because you scratch mine, and I don't if you don't – and also a different sort from the conditional compliers' reciprocity involved in

Anderson's idea of a cooperative scheme for mutual benefit.[27] As Cohen puts it: 'I desire to serve [my fellow human beings] while being served by them, and I get satisfaction from each side of that equation' (Cohen, 2009: 41).

In sum: it seems safe to infer from Cohen's embrace of a community of care that his vision of egalitarian rightness (or justice) involves an important relational ideal. It might be that this relational ideal – community of care – is less clearly egalitarian than his ideal of a justificatory community, but at least it is clear that Cohen did not simply focus on distribution having no non-derivative interest in social relations.[28]

8.8 Conclusion

My main claim in this chapter is that there are much greater affinities between luck and relational egalitarian theorists than one might think. In particular, I have argued that G. A. Cohen – one who whole-heartedly embraced the label 'luck egalitarian' as fitting in his own case – in several respects embraced relational egalitarian elements – sometimes implicitly, sometimes explicitly, sometimes clearly egalitarian, sometimes not. However, I have also argued that distributive concerns play an important, unacknowledged role in Anderson's thinking and pointed to the fact that Dworkin's official grounding of his account of distributive equality is in the proper social relations between the state and its citizens. While these points are of independent interest in relation to the interpretation of the relevant political philosophers' views, I am not putting argumentative weight on points made in the present chapter in my attempt to justify the ecumenical account of egalitarian justice that I proposed in Chapter 7. However, the present chapter provides additional motivation for the reconciliatory project pursued there.

---

[27] Presumably, I cooperate with you on the basis of principles of justice not simply because that is best for myself, but at least also because, assuming that you are willing to cooperate with me on those grounds, I care about your benefiting too. See also her previously quoted remark on 'reciprocation' being part of what democratic equality takes to be part of what it is to be an equal.

[28] Perhaps Cohen's remarks about how community constrains socialist equality of opportunity shows that just as Scheffler thinks that relational egalitarianism is not normatively autonomous, then neither is Cohen's distributive egalitarianism.

CHAPTER 9

Conclusion

Some years ago, luck egalitarianism was probably widely perceived to be *the* account of egalitarian justice. This is no longer the case. For a number of years now, many have thought of relational egalitarianism as an important alternative. In much of the literature, these two accounts are seen as radically different and rivalling accounts between which egalitarian theorists must make a choice. In this book I have tried to argue that this view is misleading at best. We do not need to choose between luck egalitarianism or, more generally, distributive egalitarianism on the one hand and relational egalitarianism on the other.

In my view, luck and relational egalitarianism are, even if different, compatible with each other, and many of the concerns that relational egalitarians have accused luck egalitarians of ignoring – sometimes rightly so – can be accommodated within a luck egalitarian framework and indeed are misarticulated as objections to luck egalitarianism per se as opposed to particular variants of luck egalitarianism. In fact, I have proposed an ecumenical account of egalitarian justice which includes luck egalitarian as well as relational egalitarian components and have argued that it might be seen as a theory which is not merely an arbitrary conjunction of two quite different theories, but one that is grounded in the value of fairness. Moreover, many of the dimensions in which different versions of luck egalitarianism differ are dimensions along which different versions of relational egalitarianism differ. This attests to the fact that the two accounts of egalitarian justice are far less different from one another than the discussion so far has assumed. Indeed, I have argued that to the extent that relational egalitarians acknowledge that there is such a thing as intergenerational justice – a topic of extreme importance given present and future predictable climate change – they must supplement their account of justice with a distributive ideal.

Some relational egalitarian readers might reject the ecumenical project of this book – in its specific version or in entirety. However, I hope that even they will find much in this book to be of use. In particular, I have pointed to a number of issues that, independently of how relational egalitarianism relates to luck egalitarianism, are issues that must be addressed in future explorations of relational equality. First, this book offers an analysis of what it is to relate as equals. No doubt, others will find ways to expand, improve or critically revise the analysis offered, but it is significant in that, as far as I am aware, it is the first elaborate analysis of this crucial notion. Second, I have argued that our practice of giving and accepting blame provides a powerful illustration of our commitment to relating as equals. It is important because the practice of giving and accepting blame embodies important insights into the way in which we are committed to relating as equals. Third, I have addressed in a more direct way than is presently done in the literature the issue of what makes relating as equals desirable, defending the view that relational egalitarianism is best construed in deontic terms. Also, I have pointed to a few connections between the analytical details of what relating as equals amounts to and what makes relating as equals desirable – something which, *mutatis mutandis*, is standard procedure in normative theory, but which up until now relational egalitarians have neglected to do at length and systemically. Fourth, I have introduced some novel conceptual tools, e.g. the distinctions between first-order versus foundational relational egalitarianism, and an internalist versus externalist characterization of relating as equals, that I hope have proven their usefulness in this book and will prove useful in others' future work. As should be amply clear by now, while this book is critical of many aspects of relational egalitarian theorizing, it is nevertheless written by someone who is sympathetic to some basic relational egalitarian ideas. Hence, insofar as this book has any impact on the present discussion of its topic in political philosophy, my hope is that it will spark a renewed interest in articulating precise accounts of relational equality and its relations to different versions of the distributive ideal. My hope is not that, given the stated assumption, it will result in a return to the recent past of luck egalitarian hegemony.

The debate regarding luck and relational egalitarianism is not just about the logical and conceptual relations between different normative and axiological principles or about different understandings of the notion of equality. It is also very much a debate between different theorists who hold related, though different, views on a number of different issues in political and moral philosophy as well as on real-life political and moral issues, and who identify themselves and are identified by others as either luck or relational egalitarians. In the preceding chapter, I spent some time explaining why differences between self- and other-identified luck and relational egalitarians are smaller than is often assumed. As we have seen, Anderson seems to slip into the distributive paradigm when it comes to equality of opportunity, and G. A. Cohen and Dworkin rather explicitly endorse relational egalitarianism in some form or other. If I were to allow myself a moment of frivolity – though frivolity with a twist of seriousness: after a long book, which for the most part has been a rather standard piece of academic analytic philosophy – or, at least, that is how I myself would like to think about it – I would paraphrase Marx and Engels and end the book with a slogan: '(Relational and luck) egalitarians of the world, unite!' thereby expressing the hope that future work will focus on how to refine and combine what I believe to be two important strands in egalitarian thinking.

References

Anderson, E. (1999). What Is the Point of Equality? *Ethics* **109**(2), 287–337.

Anderson, E. (2008a). Expanding the Egalitarian Toolbox: Equality and Bureaucracy. *Aristotelian Society, Supplementary Volume* **82**(1), 139–60.

Anderson, E. (2008b). How Should Egalitarians Cope with Market Risks? *Theoretical Inquiries in Law* **9**(1), 239–70.

Anderson, E. (2010a). The Fundamental Disagreement between Luck Egalitarians and Relational Egalitarians. *Canadian Journal of Philosophy, Supplementary Volume* **40**, 1–23.

Anderson, E. (2010b). *The Imperative of Integration*. Princeton, NJ: Princeton University Press.

Anderson, E. (2012a). Equality. In D. Estlund (ed.), *The Oxford Handbook of Political Philosophy*. Oxford: Oxford University Press, 40–57.

Anderson, E. (2012b). Epistemic Justice as a Virtue of Institutions. *Social Epistemology* **26**(2), 163–73.

Anderson, E. (2015). Feminist Epistemology and Philosophy of Science. *Stanford Encyclopedia of Justice*. https://plato.stanford.edu/entries/feminism-epistemology/#auth [last accessed 16 May 2017].

Anderson, E. and Pildes, R. H. (2000). Expressive Theories of Law: A General Restatement. *University of Pennsylvania Law Review* **148**(5), 1503–75.

Arneson, R. (1989). Equality and Equal Opportunity for Welfare. *Philosophical Studies* **56**(1), 77–93.

Arneson, R. (1999a). What, if Anything, Renders All Humans Morally Equal? In D. Jamieson (ed.), *Singer and His Critics*. Oxford: Blackwell Publishers, 103–28.

Arneson, R. (1999b). Egalitarianism and Responsibility. *Journal of Ethics* **3**(3), 225–47.

Arneson, R. (2000). Luck Egalitarianism and Prioritarianism. *Ethics* **111**(2), 339–49.

Arneson, R. (2006). What Is Wrongful Discrimination? *San Diego Journal of Law* **43**(4), 775–807.

Arneson, R. (2010). Democratic Equality and Relating as Equals. *Canadian Journal of Philosophy, Supplementary Volume* **40**, 25–52.

Axelsen, D. and Nielsen, L. (2015). Sufficiency as Freedom from Duress. *Journal of Political Philosophy* **23**(4), 406–26.

Baker, J. (2015). Conceptions and Dimensions of Social Equality. In C. Fourie, F. Schuppert and I. Walliman-Helmer (eds.), *Social Equality*. Oxford: Oxford University Press, 65–86.

Barry, B. (1989). *Theories of Justice*, Vol. I. London: Harvester-Wheatsheaf.

Bell, M. (2013). The Standing to Blame: A Critique. In D. J. Coates and N. A. Tognazzini (eds.), *Blame: Its Nature and Norms*. New York: Oxford University Press, 263–81.

Bidadanure, J. (2016). Making Sense of Age-group Justice. *Politics, Philosophy and Economics* 15(3), 234–60.

Brighouse, H. and Swift, A. (2014). *Family Values: The Ethics of Parent-Child Relationships*. Princeton: Princeton University Press.

Brown, A. (2014). What Should Egalitarians Believe if they Really are Egalitarian? A Reply to Martin O'Neill. *European Journal of Political Theory* 13(4), 453–69.

Burke, E. (1987 [1790]). *Reflections on the Revolution in France*. Harmondsworth: Penguin Classics.

Caney, S. (2005). *Justice Beyond Borders: A Global Political Theory*. Oxford: Oxford University Press.

Carter, I. (2011). Respect and the Basis of Equality. *Ethics* 121(3), 538–71.

Casal, P. (2007). Why Sufficiency Is Not Enough. *Ethics* 117(2), 296–326.

Cohen, G. A. (2000). *If You're an Egalitarian, How Come You're So Rich?* Cambridge, MA: Harvard University Press.

Cohen, G. A. (2008). *Rescuing Justice and Equality*. Cambridge, MA: Harvard University Press.

Cohen, G. A. (2009). *Why Not Socialism?* Princeton, NJ: Princeton University Press.

Cohen, G. A. (2011). *On the Currency of Egalitarian Justice: And Other Essays in Political Philosophy*. Princeton, NJ: Princeton University Press.

Cohen, G. A. (2013). *Finding Oneself in the Other*. Princeton, NJ: Princeton University Press.

Cordelli, C. (2015). Justice as Fairness and Relational Resources. *Journal of Political Philosophy* 23(1), 86–110.

Crisp, R. (2003). Equality, Priority and Compassion. *Ethics* 113(4), 745–63.

Darwall, S. (2006). *The Second-Person Standpoint*. Cambridge, MA: Harvard University Press.

Dworkin, G. (2000). Morally Speaking. In E. Ullmann-Margalit (ed.), *Reasoning Practically*. Oxford: Oxford University Press, 182–8.

Dworkin, R. (1994) *Life's Dominion*. New York: Random Hounce Inc.

Dworkin, R. (2000). *Sovereign Virtue*. Cambridge, MA: Harvard University Press.

Fabre, C. (2007). *Justice in a Changing World*. Cambridge: Polity Press.

Fabre, C. (2018). *Economic Statecraft*. Cambridge, MA: Harvard University Press.

Fourie, C. (2012). What Is Social Equality? An Analysis of Status Equality as a Strongly Egalitarian Ideal. *Res Publica* 18(2), 107–26.

Fourie, C. (2015). To Praise and to Scorn. In C. Fourie, F. Schuppert and I. Walliman-Helmer (eds.), *Social Equality*. Oxford: Oxford University Press, 87–106.

Fourie, C., Schuppert, F. and Walliman-Helmer, I. (eds.) (2015). *Social Equality*. Oxford: Oxford University Press.

Fourie, C. and Rid, A. (eds.) (2017). *What Is Enough?* Oxford: Oxford University Press.

Frankfurt, H. (1988). *The Importance of What We Care About*. Cambridge: Cambridge University Press.

Frankfurt, H. (1999). *Necessity, Volition and Love*. Cambridge: Cambridge University Press.

Fraser, N. and Honneth, A. (2003). *Recognition or Redistribution*. London: Verso.

Frick, J. (2016). What We Owe to Hypocrites: Contractualism and the Speaker-Relativity of Justification. *Philosophy & Public Affairs* 44(4), 223–65.

Fricker, M. (2007). *Epistemic Injustice*. Oxford: Oxford University Press.

Garrau, M. and Laborde, C. (2015). Relational Equality, Non-Domination and Vulnerability. In C. Fourie, F. Schuppert and I. Walliman-Helmer (eds.), *Social Equality*. Oxford: Oxford University Press, 45–64.

Geach, P. T. (1956). Good and Evil. *Analysis* 17(2), 33–42.

Gheaus, A. (2016). Hikers in Flip-Flops: Luck-Egalitarianism, Democratic Equality and the Distribuenda of Justice. *Journal of Applied Philosophy*, online first, 1–16.

Gosseries, A. and Meyer, L. H. (eds.) (2009). *Intergenerational Justice*. Oxford: Oxford University Press.

Griffin, J. (1986). *Well-Being*. Oxford: Clarendon Press.

Hausman, D. M. and Waldren, M. S. (2011). Egalitarianism Reconsidered. *Journal of Moral Philosophy* 8(4), 567–86.

Hellman, D. (2008). *When Is Discrimination Wrong?* Cambridge, MA: Harvard University Press.

Hinton, T. (2001). Must Egalitarians Choose between Fairness and Respect? *Philosophy & Public Affairs* 30(1), 72–87.

Hirose, I. (2015). *Egalitarianism*. New York: Routledge.

Holroyd, J. (2017). *The Social Psychology of Discrimination*. In K. Lippert-Rasmussen (ed.), *Routledge Handbook of the Ethics of Discrimination*. London: Routledge, 381–93.

Holtug, N. (2010). *Persons, Interests and Justice*. Oxford: Oxford University Press.

Honneth, A. (2007). *Disrespect*. Cambridge: Polity Press.

Hooker, B. (2005). Fairness. *Ethical Theory and Moral Practice* 8(4), 329–52.

Hume, D. (2004 [1751]). *An Enquiry Concerning the Principles of Morality*. Oxford: Oxford University Press.

Hurley, S. (2003). *Justice, Luck and Knowledge*. Oxford: Oxford University Press.

Huseby, R. (2010). Sufficiency: Restated and Defended. *Journal of Political Philosophy* 18(2), 178–97.

Kukla, R. and Lance, M. (2009). *'Yo!' and 'Lo!': The Pragmatic Topography of the Space of Reasons*. Cambridge, MA: Harvard University Press.

Kymlicka, W. (2002). *Contemporary Political Philosophy*, 2nd edn. Oxford: Oxford University Press.

Langton, R. (1993). Speech Acts and Unspeakable Acts. *Philosophy and Public Affairs* 22(4), 293–330.

Lippert-Rasmussen, K. (2001). Equality, Option Luck and Responsibility. *Ethics* 111(3), 548–79.

Lippert-Rasmussen, K. (2006). The Badness of Discrimination. *Ethical Theory and Moral Practice* 9(2), 167–85.

Lippert-Rasmussen, K. (2008). Publicity and Egalitarian Justice. *Journal of Moral Philosophy* 5(1), 7–25.

Lippert-Rasmussen, K. (2011). Luck-Egalitarianism: Faults and Collective Choice. *Economics and Philosophy* 27(2), 151–73.

Lippert-Rasmussen, K. (2012). Who Can I Blame? In M. Kühler and N. Jelinek (eds.), *Autonomy and the Self*. Dordrecht: Springer, 295–316.

Lippert-Rasmussen, K. (2013a). *Born Free and Equal?* Oxford: Oxford University Press.

Lippert-Rasmussen, K. (2013b). Offensive Preferences, Snobbish Tastes and Egalitarian Justice. *Journal of Social Philosophy* 44(4), 439–58. Oxford: Wiley.

Lippert-Rasmussen, K. (2014). Justice and Bad Luck. *Stanford Encyclopedia of Philosophy*, http://plato.stanford.edu/entries/justice-bad-luck/ [last accessed 16 May 2017].

Lippert-Rasmussen, K. (2015a). *Luck Egalitarianism*. London: Bloomsbury.

Lippert-Rasmussen, K. (2015b). Luck Egalitarianism versus Relational Egalitarianism. *Canadian Journal of Philosophy* 45(2), 220–41. London: Taylor & Francis.

Lippert-Rasmussen, K. (2017) (Luck and Relational) Egalitarians of the World, Unite! *Oxford Studies in Political Philosophy* 4, 81–109.

Lippert-Rasmussen, K. (2018a). Affirmative Action and Relational Egalitarianism. In H. Collins and T. Khaitan (eds.), *Foundations of Indirect Discrimination Law*. Oxford: Hart Publishing, 173–96.

Lippert-Rasmussen, K. (2018b). Reply to Critics. *Critical Review of International Social and Political Philosophy*, online first.

Lippert-Rasmussen, K. (forthcoming). Discrimination and Disrespect. In H. Hurd (ed.), *Festschrift for Larry Alexander*. Cambridge: Cambridge University Press.

Locke, J. (1960 [1689]). *Two Treatises of Government*. Cambridge: Cambridge University Press.

Mason, A. (2015). Justice, Respect and Treating People as Equals. In C. Fourie, F. Schuppert and I. Wallimann-Helmer (eds.), *Social Equality*. Oxford: Oxford University Press, 129–45.

McKerlie, D. (1996). Equality. *Ethics* 106(2), 274–96.

McKerlie, D. (2012). *Justice between the Young and the Old*. Oxford: Oxford University Press.

McMahan, J. (2002). *The Ethics of Killing*. Oxford: Oxford University Press.

Miklosi, Z. (2017). Varieties of Relational Egalitarianism. *Oxford Studies in Political Philosophy* 4, 110–140.

Mill, J. S. (1972 [1861]). *Utilitarianism, On Liberty, and Considerations on Representative Government*. London: J. M. Dent and Sons Ltd.

Mill, J. S. (1988 [1869]). *The Subjection of Women*. Indianapolis: Hackett Publishing Company.

Miller, D. (1995). Complex Equality. In D. Miller and M. Walzer (eds.), *Pluralism, Justice and Equality*. Oxford: Oxford University Press, 197–225.

Miller, D. (1998). Equality and Justice. In A. Mason (ed.), *Ideals of Equality*. Oxford: Blackwell, 21–36.

Miller D. (2012). *National Responsibility and Global Justice*. Oxford: Oxford University Press.

Miller, D. (2015). Foreword. In C. Fourie, F. Schuppert and I. Wallimann-Helmer (eds.), *Social Equality*. Oxford: Oxford University Press, vii–xi.

Moles, A. and Parr, T. (2018). Distributions and Relations: A Hybrid Account. *Political Studies*, online first.

Moore, G. E. (1989 [1903]). *Principia Ethica*. Cambridge: Cambridge University Press.

Nagel, T. (1979). *Mortal Questions*. Cambridge: Cambridge University Press.

Nagel, T. (1991). *Equality and Partiality*. Oxford: Oxford University Press.

Nagel, T. (2005). The Problem of Global Justice. *Philosophy and Public Affairs* 33 (2), 113–47.

Nath, R. (2011). Equal Standing in the Global Community. *The Monist* 94(4), 593–614.

Nath, R. (2015). On the Scope and Grounds of Social Equality. In C. Fourie, F. Schuppert and I. Wallimann-Helmer (eds.), *Social Equality*. Oxford: Oxford University Press, 186–208.

Navin, M. (2011). Luck and Oppression. *Ethical Theory and Moral Practice* 14(5), 533–47.

Norman, R. (1998). The Social Basis of Equality. In A. Mason (ed.), *Ideals of Equality*. Oxford: Blackwell, 37–51.

Nozick, R. (1974). *Anarchy, State and Utopia*. Oxford: Basil Blackwell.

O'Neill, M. (2008). What Should Egalitarians Believe? *Philosophy & Public Affairs* 36(2), 119–56.

Otsuka, M. (2004). Equality, Ambition and Insurance. *Proceedings of the Aristotelian Society, Supplementary Volume* 78, 151–66.

Parfit, D. (1984). *Reasons and Persons*. Oxford: Clarendon Press.

Parfit, D. (1998). Equality and Priority. In A. Mason (ed.), *Ideals of Equality*. Oxford: Blackwell, 1–20.

Parfit, D. (2000). Equality or Priority? *Lindley Lectures Delivered at the University of Kansas*. Lawrence, Kansas: 1991. In M. Clayton and A. Williams (eds.), *The Ideal of Equality*. Basingstoke: Palgrave Macmillan, 81–125.

Persson, I. (2001). Equality, Priority and Person-Affecting Value. *Ethical Theory and Moral Practice* 4(1), 23–39.

Pettit, P. (1997). *Republicanism*. Oxford: Clarendon Press.

Plato (1983 [377–370 BC]). *The Republic*. Harmondsworth: Penguin Books.

Pogge, T. (2006). Relational Conception of Justice: Responsibility for Health Outcomes. In S. Anand, F. Peter and A. Sen (eds.), *Public Health, Ethics and Equity.* Oxford: Oxford University Press, 135–61.

Pogge, T. (2008). *World Poverty and Human Rights.* Cambridge: Polity Press.

Rawls, J. (1993). *Political Liberalism.* New York: Columbia University Press.

Rawls, J. (1999). *A Theory of Justice, Revised Version.* Cambridge, MA: Belknap Press of Harvard University.

Rawls, J. (2001a). *Law of Peoples.* Cambridge, MA: Harvard University Press.

Rawls, J. (2001b). *Justice as Fairness.* Cambridge, MA: Harvard University Press.

Raz, J. (1986). *The Morality of Freedom.* Oxford: Clarendon Press.

Risse, M. (2015). *On Global Justice.* Princeton: Princeton University Press.

Robeyns, I. (forthcoming). Having Too Much. In J. Knight and M. Schwartzberg (eds.), *NOMOS LVI: Wealth. Yearbook of American Society for Political and Legal Philosophy.* New York: New York University Press.

Rousseau, J. J. (1973 [1754]). *A Discourse on the Origin of Inequality.* London: J. M. Dent & Sons.

Scanlon, T. M. (1998). *What We Owe Each Other.* Cambridge, MA: Harvard University Press.

Scanlon, T. M. (2000). *The Difficulty of Tolerance.* Cambridge: Cambridge University Press.

Scanlon, T. M. (2008). *Moral Dimensions.* Cambridge, MA: Harvard University Press.

Schapiro, T. (1999). What Is a Child? *Ethics* 109(4), 715–38.

Scheffler, S. (1982). *The Rejection of Consequentialism.* Oxford: Clarendon Press.

Scheffler, S. (2003a). What Is Egalitarianism? *Philosophy and Public Affairs* 31 (1), 5–39.

Scheffler, S. (2003b). Equality as the Virtue of Sovereigns: A Reply to Ronald Dworkin. *Philosophy and Public Affairs* 31(2), 199–206.

Scheffler, S. (2005). Choice, Circumstance and the Value of Equality. *Politics, Philosophy and Economics* 4(4), 5–28.

Scheffler, S. (2006). Is the Basic Structure Basic? In C. Sypnowich (ed.), *The Egalitarian Conscience: Essays in Honour of G. A. Cohen.* Oxford: Oxford University Press, 102–29.

Scheffler, S. (2015). The Practice of Equality. In C. Fourie, F. Schuppert and I. Walliman-Helmer (eds.), *Social Equality.* Oxford: Oxford University Press, 21–44.

Schemmel, C. (2011). Why Relational Egalitarians Should Care about Distributions. *Social Theory and Practice* 37(3), 365–90.

Schemmel, C. (2012a). Distributive and Relational Equality. *Politics, Philosophy & Economics* 11(2), 123–48.

Schemmel, C. (2012b). Luck Egalitarianism as Democratic Reciprocity: A Response to Tan. *Journal of Philosophy* 109(7), 435–48.

Schemmel, C. (2015). Social Equality – Or Just Justice? In C. Fourie, F. Schuppert and I. Walliman-Helmer (eds.), *Social Equality.* Oxford: Oxford University Press, 146–66.

Schuppert, F. (2015). Being Equals. In C. Fourie, F. Schuppert and I. Walliman-Helmer (eds.), *Social Equality*. Oxford: Oxford University Press, 107–26.

Segall, S. (2013). *Equality and Opportunity*. Oxford: Oxford University Press.

Segall, S. (2016). Incas and Aliens: The Truth in Telic Egalitarianism. *Economics and Philosophy* **32**(1), 1–19.

Sen, A. (1979). Equality of What? The Tanner Lecture on Human Values. http://tannerlectures.utah.edu/documents/a-to-z/s/sen80.pdf [last accessed 16 May 2017].

Sher, G. (2006). *In Praise of Blame*. Oxford: Oxford University Press.

Shields, L. (2012). The Prospects for Sufficientarianism. *Utilitas* **24**(1), 101–17.

Singer, P. (1990). *Animal Liberation*, 2nd edn. New York: Random House.

Smilansky, S. (2007). *Ten Moral Paradoxes*. Oxford: Blackwell Publishing.

Smith, A. M. (2007). On Being Responsible and Holding Responsible. *Journal of Ethics* **11**(4), 465–84.

Stemplowska, Z. (2011). Reconciling Two Egalitarian Visions. In C. Knight and Z. Stemplowska (eds.), *Responsibility and Distributive Justice*. Oxford: Oxford University Press, 115–35.

Strawson, P. F. (1962). Freedom and Resentment. *Proceedings of the British Academy* **48**, 1–25.

Tan, K.-C. (2008). A Defense of Luck Egalitarianism. *Journal of Philosophy* 105, 665–90.

Tan, K.-C. (2014). *Justice, Institutions and Luck: The Site, Ground and Scope of Equality*. Oxford: Oxford University Press.

Temkin, L. (1993). *Inequality*. Oxford: Oxford University Press.

Todd, P. (2017). A Unified Account of the Moral Standing to Blame. *Noûs*, online first, 1–27.

Tomlin, P. (2015). What Is the Point of Egalitarian Social Relationships? In A. Kaufman (ed.), *Distributive Justice and Access to Advantage: G. A. Cohen's Egalitarianism*. Cambridge: Cambridge University Press, 151–79.

Upadhyaya, K. (forthcoming). No Discrimination in Disapproval: Basic Equality Does Not Explain the Wrongness of Hypocritical Condemnation.

Vallentyne, P. (2015). Justice, Interpersonal Morality and Luck Egalitarianism. In A. Kaufman (ed.), *Distributive Justice and Access to Advantage: G. A. Cohen's Egalitarianism*. Cambridge: Cambridge University Press, 40–9.

Voigt, K. (2017). Kasper Lippert-Rasmussen:Luck Egalitarianism. *Ethics* **127**(4), 939–43.

Voigt, K. (forthcoming). Rational Equality and the Expressive Dimension of State Action.

Wallace, R. J. (1994). *Responsibility and the Moral Sentiments*. Cambridge, MA: Harvard University Press.

Wallace, R. J. (2010). Hypocrisy, Moral Address and the Equal Standing of Persons. *Philosophy & Public Affairs* **38**(4), 307–41.

Wallace, R. J. (2011). Dispassionate Opprobrium: On Blame and the Reactive Emotions. In R. J. Wallace, R. Kumar and S. Freeman (eds.), *Reasons and*

Recognition: Essays on the Philosophy of T. M. Scanlon. Oxford: Oxford University Press, 348–72.

Walzer, M. (1983). *Spheres of Justice*. New York: Basic Books.

Williams, A. (1998). Incentives, Inequality and Publicity. *Philosophy & Public Affairs* 27(3), 225–47.

Williams, B. (1973). *Problems of the Self*. Cambridge: Cambridge University Press.

Wolff, J. (1998). Fairness, Respect and the Egalitarian Ethos. *Philosophy & Public Affairs* 27(2), 97–122.

Wolff, J. (2010). Fairness, Respect and the Egalitarian Ethos Revisited. *Journal of Ethics* 14(3/4), 335–50.

Wolff, J. (2015). Social Equality and Social Inequality. In C. Fourie, F. Schuppert and I. Walliman-Helmer (eds.), *Social Equality*. Oxford: Oxford University Press, 209–25.

Young, I. M. (1990). *Justice and the Politics of Difference*. Princeton, NJ: Princeton University Press.

Index

advantage
  equal access to, 220, 225
agent
  moral, 54
agent-relativity, 81–2
ambition-sensitivity, 44
Anderson, Elizabeth, vii–viii, 3, 8–16, 19, 23–42,
      49–51, 57–73, 78–80, 84, 86, 95, 111–17,
      122, 125, 127–8, 132, 134–5, 137, 140,
      144–54, 161–2, 167, 171, 174–5, 181–200,
      204, 209–33, 235, 238–9
Anderson, Elizabeth and Pildes, Richard, 8,
    200, 239
approach
  individualist, 136, 140, 143–4
Arneson, Richard, xiii, 2–3, 30, 35, 44, 47, 62, 128,
      151, 154, 156–7, 184, 192, 214, 222, 239
attitude
  disrespectful, 37, 58, 139
authority, 42, 44, 53, 55, 65–7, 83, 87, 91, 115–16,
      184–5, 187, 189–90, 195, 200, 208
Axelsen, David & Nielsen, Lasse, 2

Baker, John, 67, 132, 234, 240
Barry, Brian, 124, 240
Bell, Macalester, 97, 240
bias
  gender, 67
  implicit, 86, 142
  racial, 67
Bidadanure, Juliana, xiii, 122, 132, 240
blame, viii, xi, 17, 46, 82–117, 219, 237
  hypercritical, 107–10, 117, 219
Brown, Alexander, 6, 240
Burke, Edmund, 10, 66, 158, 240

Caney, Simon, 17, 146, 240
capabilities, 38, 78, 84, 135, 148, 193, 213–14, 216
care
  reciprocal, 230, 233
Carter, Ian, xiii, 62, 240

Casal, Paula, xiii, 2, 240
caste, 51, 174
challenge
  arbitariness, 207
  reductionist, 192–201, 205–6
choice
  exercise of, 45, 48, 183
civil society, 9, 15, 38–9, 57, 67, 84, 130, 163, 215
coercion, 36
Cohen, G. A., ix, xii, 1–3, 8, 17, 19, 25, 35, 47, 50,
      62, 66, 71–2, 96–7, 111–17, 122, 136, 138,
      142–3, 145, 148, 154, 182, 184, 188, 196–8,
      204–5, 211–12, 214, 218–35, 238, 240,
      244–5
community, ix, 14, 19, 28, 36–7, 54, 116, 118, 127,
      135, 213, 217, 227–35
  democratic, 232
  justificatory, 212, 230–5
  pansexual, 84
compensation, 23, 33–4, 49, 144, 211, 218–29
concern and respect, equal, 3–4, 8, 29, 40–1, 79,
      139–40, 143, 191, 212, 229–30
condescension, 36–7
conservatism, 28
constraint
  deliberative, vii, 46, 51, 54–9, 63–4, 71, 76, 91,
      135, 182, 201–7, 221, 226
  dispositional, 15
  luck-egalitarian deliberative, 205, 207
content, expressive, 7–9, 16, 32, 139
cosmopolitan, 5, 17–18, 122, 146–53, 164
Crisp, Roger, xiii, 2, 240
critique
  theorist-focused, 34–5, 48, 111, 212
  theory-focused, 16, 19, 34–6, 212
Crusoe, Robinson, 25, 28, 128, 203

Darwall, Stephen, 114–16, 182, 187, 190,
    240
deference, 10, 65, 156, 161
democracy, 158, 215

deontology, 199–200
desert, 13, 28
determinism
  hard, 47
dignity, 14
discrimination, 221
distribuendum, 2–6, 20, 185, 196
distribution
  of goods, 1–2, 6, 15, 25–7, 61, 116, 125, 186, 195, 197
  of resources, 1, 213–14
  of well-being, 2
  pattern of, 24, 56, 201
domination, 8, 12, 37, 70, 72–3, 124, 132, 168, 171, 208, 216, 234
Dworkin, Ronald, 1–4, 7–8, 13, 23, 29, 35, 42, 96, 146, 183, 191, 200, 206, 211–12, 218, 222, 224, 227–30, 235, 238, 240, 244

egalitarianism, vii, viii, xi, xii, 2–20, 23–5, 27–37, 40–1, 43–6, 48, 50–8, 61–97, 102, 105, 110–13, 115–18, 121–30, 134–9, 142–8, 151–77, 181–196, 190–238
  deontic, 171
  dispositional, viii, 201, 204
  distributive, 93, 167, 171
  distributive outcome, 2–3
  ecumenical, 191, 206–7, 209, 236
  first-order equality of opportunity
    distributive, 216
  luck, vii, xi, xii, 3, 6–7, 11–20, 23–36, 41–55, 58–9, 69, 78, 89, 97, 111, 114, 116, 121, 136–9, 144, 149, 154–5, 158, 164, 171–5, 181–201, 205–14, 217–37
    deontic, 171
    outcome, 3–4, 23, 26, 48
    outcome relational, 7, 26
    real-life, 29, 84, 155, 174–6
  relational, vii, xi, 4, 7–20, 23–4, 27, 31, 36, 41, 43–4, 51–3, 55, 57, 60–1, 69–70, 80, 88, 92–3, 96–7, 103, 111–12, 114, 121–4, 128–9, 132–5, 143, 146–7, 150–7, 164, 167, 170–7, 181–5, 189–206, 210–12, 216–17, 221–2, 225, 227, 229, 233, 235, 236–8
    complete lives, 135
    cosmopolitan, 150, 164
    deontic, 171–3, 177, 191
    first-order, 216
    foundational, 216
    lifetime, 134
    luck, 7
    outcome, 3–4, 23, 26, 48, 182, 184
    telic, 132, 166–7, 171–2, 181

time-relative, 134
telic, 171
  welfare, 218–19, 222
emotions
  reactive, 97–8
endowment-insensitivity, 44
envy, 33, 36, 226
equalisandum, 19, 69, 192, 200, 207, 213–14
equality, xi
  administrative conception of, 229
  democratic, 13, 15, 23–5, 28, 31, 34, 36–41, 58, 64, 68, 78, 122, 127, 147–50, 212–15, 232, 235
  distributive, viii, xii, 2, 4, 6, 10, 13–15, 17, 20, 24–5, 45, 47, 53, 61, 63, 87–9, 92, 122–3, 129–30, 135, 139, 146, 154–5, 158, 167–8, 171–2, 174–5, 190–3, 200, 210, 213–14, 229, 232, 235
  moral, 81
  moral equality of, 104
  of fortune, 24, 40, 78, 212
  of resources, 13, 176, 230
  of status, 13–14, 193
  of welfare, 176, 193, 218–19, 223
  political, 57, 171, 229
  relational, vii–viii, xi, 5, 12, 16–20, 31, 40, 43–6, 51–63, 68, 79, 87–92, 110, 113, 117, 122–5, 129, 131–7, 142–9, 152–74, 177, 181, 199, 201, 211, 217, 230, 237
  social, 13–14, 71, 83, 88, 144, 157, 217
equals
  aesthetic, 83–4
  communicative notion of treating as, 76–7, 160, 165, 217
  empirically, 84–5
  epistemic, 64, 82–3, 106
  expressive notion of treating as, 77
  externalist conceptions of relating as, 216
  internalist conception of relating as, 216
  moral, 62–7, 70, 73, 75, 81–2, 104, 150–2, 155, 161, 170
  motivational notion of treating as, 71, 75–6, 87, 165
  normative notion of treating as, 74–6, 217
  presuppositional notion of treating as, 79–80, 93
  regarding as, 16, 85–7, 160
  relating as, vii, xii, 6–7, 10, 14–20, 24, 26, 32, 36–41, 44–6, 51–73, 76, 82, 84–93, 97, 103, 107–9, 112–13, 116–18, 121–2, 124–5, 130–5, 139–40, 142, 145, 147, 150, 152, 154–77, 181–4, 192–3, 199, 201, 204, 206–7, 209, 213–17, 227, 234, 237

social, 63, 65–6, 82–4, III, 165
society of, 25, 38, 43, 51, 54, 56, 67, 88, 194,
   225–6, 229
treating as, 16, 74
eugenics, 174
exercise of responsibility, 47
exploitation, 6, 9, 12, 37, 72, 132, 168, 198, 208,
   216, 219

Fabre, Cécile, 95, 146, 240
fairness, 13, 19–20, 45, 47, 155, 164, 172–3, 177, 182,
   206–11, 219, 236
Fourie, Carina, xiii, 2, 15–16, 67, 71, 166, 183,
   240–6
Fourie, Carina & Rid, Annette, 2
Fourie, Carina et al., 16, 183
Frankfurt, Harry, 2, 107, 241
Fraser, Nancy & Honneth, Axel, 11, 70
freedom, 38, 48, 70, 78, 147–8, 156–7, 161, 183, 188,
   216, 221, 229
Fricker, Miranda, 64, 241
functionings, 213

Garrau, Marie & Laborde, Cécile, 70
Geach, Peter, 63, 241
Gheaus, Anca, xiii, 5, 194, 241
goodness
   constitutive, 164
   for persons, 155, 164–5
   impersonal, 155
   non-instrumental, 157, 159, 163–6
   person-affecting view of, 167
goodness, impersonal, 166
goods
   divisible, 29, 213–14
   divisible, privately appropriated, 29
   material, 11–12
   public, 35
Gosseries, Axel & Meyer, Lukas, 124
Griffin, James, 161, 241
groups
   age, 18, 122–3, 131, 134–5, 153

Hellman, Deborah, xiii, 77, 79, 200,
   241
heterosexuals, 29–30, 56, 197
hierarchy, 8, 10, 13–14, 30, 37, 39, 44, 46, 51, 53, 57,
   64, 66–7, 83, 89–90, 101, 121, 127, 132,
   139–40, 147, 156–62, 169, 189, 200, 203–4,
   206, 226–7, 229, 233
Holroyd, Jules, 86, 241
homosexuals, 29–30, 56, 197
Hume, David, 129, 204, 209,
   241
humiliation, 159

Huseby, Robert, 2, 241
hypocrisy, viii, 17, 46, 94–118

ideal
   distributive, vii, 1–11, 14–16, 23–4, 26, 29, 38–9,
      54–5, 88, 117, 123, 132, 145–6, 148, 150, 153,
      158, 170, 172, 174, 177, 192–3, 203, 214, 217,
      228, 230, 236–7
   moral, 51, 125, 144–5, 148–9, 152
   political, 42–3, 45, 51, 145, 148–9
   relational, vii, xi, 4–20, 24–5, 27, 29–30, 39–41,
      52, 54–6, 59–62, 68, 87, 92–3, 116–18, 123,
      125, 129, 134, 136, 142–53, 156, 181, 193,
      211–12, 217–18, 226, 228–30, 233–5
   social, 5, 13, 51, 125, 148
   statocentric, 228
illa quoque, 101, 104
impartiality, 141
imperialism
   cultural, 12, 72
inequality
   age-based, 133–4
   diachronic, 132
   incentive-based justification of, 113, 231
   natural, 187, 190–2
   synchronic, 132
injustice
   hermeneutical, 59, 152
   testimonial, 59, 64, 86
interpersonal justification, 188
intrusiveness, 143

justice
   between young and old, 130
   climate, 125
   distributive, xi, 1–5, 11–14, 29, 34, 61, 122,
      129–30, 136–7, 139, 144–6, 153, 170,
      174, 218
   egalitarian, 173, 175–6, 181
   global, 146–7
   ideal of, 2, 5, 7, 15
   individualist approach to, 137–8, 143, 145
   institutionalist approach to, 136–8, 140, 145
   intergenerational, 17, 121, 123–9, 153, 173,
      228, 236
   locus of, 5–6, 31, 205–7
   metric of, 33
   pluralistic view of, 5
   relational, 6–8, 20, 31, 90, 121, 123, 125, 129,
      137–41, 150, 153, 173
   retributive, 1, 5, 181
   scope of, 5, 12, 146, 153
   site of, 5, 136–8, 141, 144–6, 153
   spheres of, 132–3, 199
   strong distributive ideal of, 26

justification
    comprehensive, 114, 231–2
    context-relative, 187
    interpersonal, 188
    moral, 15, 19, 27, 182, 186, 208, 211
    second-person, 185–6, 189–92
    third-person, 185–91

Langton, Rae, 112, 242
libertarianism, 46–8
Lippert-Rasmussen, Kasper, 7, 13, 23, 28–9, 32, 35,
        39, 56–7, 72, 95, 100–2, 107–8, 128, 142,
        169, 184, 189, 192, 194, 201, 212, 241–2, 245
Locke, John, 67, 242
luck, vii, 3–4, 7, 9, 11, 20, 242
    bad, 219, 224–5
    brute, 23, 28, 32–3, 78, 144, 211–12, 219, 227
    good, 231
    option, 4, 7, 23, 32, 35–6

marginalization, 12, 64, 72, 171
margins
    problem of relational equality at the, 121
marriage, 54, 56, 71, 205
Mason, Andrew, xiii, 156, 242–3
McKerlie, Dennis, 17, 122, 242
McMahan, Jeff, 62, 151, 242
Miklosi, Zoltan, xiii, 184, 204, 242
Miller, David, 11–16, 65, 132, 146, 193,
        199–200, 243
monism, 6, 156
Moore, G. E., 92, 243
moralism, 49–50, 55

Nagel, Thomas, 17, 140, 146, 155, 166, 243
Nath, Rekha, 8, 18, 122, 146–7, 217, 243
Navin, Mark, 12, 243
norm
    deontic, 155
Norman, Richard, 8–9, 12, 15, 146, 198, 206,
        217, 243
Nozick, Robert, 2, 243

O'Neill, Martin, 6, 11, 15, 45, 65, 124, 134, 146, 161,
        166, 168, 240, 243
objection
    counterintuitiveness, 42–3, 51–2, 60
    equal-status monsters, 135
    fetishism, 45–6, 49, 51
    from irresponsibility, 3–4, 23
    harshness, 28, 30–2, 38–9, 42, 53, 58, 78, 134
    levelling-down, 53, 167–8
    metaphysical, 47–8, 50
    moralism, 49
    pity, 32–4

site, 28, 31
opportunity
    equality of, viii, 2, 39, 78, 211–17, 233, 235, 238
oppression, 12, 28, 37–9, 51, 67, 72–3, 112, 214, 216
overdemandingness, 137, 140–1, 150

paradigm
    distributive, xi, 11–12, 118, 123, 196, 210, 238
    relational, xi
Parfit, Derek, 2, 159, 161, 166, 168, 171, 181, 243
paternalism, 18, 36, 52, 130
pattern, distributive, 6, 10–11, 26, 45,
        56, 142
perspective
    time-relative, 18, 58, 135
    whole-lives, 58–9, 134, 153
Pettit, Philip, 70, 243
pity, 28, 32–6, 42, 49, 57, 147
pluralism, 5, 19–20, 43, 48, 50–1, 53, 63, 88, 92–3,
        103, 123, 129, 137, 169, 181–2, 186, 210,
        213, 218
Pogge, Thomas, 8, 15, 18, 89, 126, 139, 244
power, 12, 15, 29–30, 38, 44, 51, 64, 66–8,
        83, 117, 143, 161, 171, 173, 194, 199, 206,
        229–30
    distribution of, 12, 30, 51, 200, 213
    social, 8
powerlessness, 12, 72
preference
    cheap, 221
    expensive, 222
    hypothetical, 160
    offensive, 211, 218–23, 225, 227,
        229
prejudice, 64, 86
principle
    difference, 2, 8–9, 27, 41, 113–14, 122, 137–8,
        142, 188, 215
    transmission, 208–9
Prioritarianism, 2, 129, 208
    relational, 10
problem
    pervasiveness, 52–3, 60, 66,
        83, 101
publicity
    constraint of, 33, 54, 137, 142–3

racism, 17, 65, 72–3, 77, 84, 86, 138, 142, 174–5,
        221, 229
Rakowski, Eric, 30, 35
rank, 15, 44, 66, 196, 230
Rawls, John, 1–2, 5–6, 10–12, 19, 27, 41–2, 55,
        113–14, 122, 124, 129, 137–8, 141–6, 150, 152,
        161, 187, 201, 207, 215, 218, 231, 244
Raz, Joseph, 107, 244

reason
  second-personal, 115
  third-personal, 115
reciprocity, 54, 91, 95, 150, 227, 234
relationendum, 6–7, 16, 70, 123
relations
  social, xi, 4–11, 17, 24–31, 39, 44, 48, 51–3, 57, 61,
    67, 72–3, 87–91, 97, 110–11, 121–8, 131, 134,
    139, 145–50, 152, 162–6, 169–70, 174–5,
    184, 196, 189, 192–207, 212–13, 217, 225,
    227–35
  interpersonal, 25, 46, 145, 232
  non-social, 193, 195–9, 217
requirement
  deontic, 19, 97, 155
  expressive, 31
  no disrespect, 37, 57
  no-ranking, 38, 58, 64
  time-relative sufficiency, 38, 58
respect, 14
  equal, 11, 27, 31, 36, 40, 59, 70, 78–9, 144,
    221, 226
  expression of, 33, 78
responsibility, 2–3, 7, 9, 15, 19–20, 25–6, 29, 36–8,
    41–3, 47, 50, 53, 68, 78, 155, 164, 171, 181–4,
    191–2, 199–200, 205–7, 209, 214, 220
revelations
  shameful, 13
Risse, Mathias, 146, 244
Robeyns, Ingrid, 39, 244
Rousseau, Jean-Jacques, 11, 225–6, 244

Scanlon, Thomas M., 6, 15, 45, 51, 77, 96, 98, 117,
    131, 161, 171, 190, 244, 246
Scheffler, Samuel, vii, 5, 15–16, 19, 23–30, 39,
    41–67, 70–1, 76, 79–80, 91–2, 117, 122,
    125, 134–8, 140, 144–9, 152, 156–7, 166,
    174–5, 181–3, 194–5, 197, 200–205, 210–11,
    213, 217, 221, 225–6, 228–30, 233, 235, 244
Schemmel, Christian, 5, 8, 11, 15–16, 18, 78, 89–91,
    122, 138–40, 143–4, 147, 150–1, 171, 174,
    199–200, 244
Schuppert, Fabian, 5, 52, 64, 87, 217, 240–6
segregation, 15, 117, 215
self-respect, 12–13, 44, 108, 124, 156, 203, 218
Sen, Amartya, 2, 213, 244–5
sexism, 8, 17, 40, 73, 85, 138, 142–3, 174–5,
    208, 227
Sher, George, 97, 245
Shields, Liam, 2, 245
Singer, Peter, 62, 239, 245
slavery, 4–5, 8–9, 11, 72, 113, 161, 166
Smilansky, Saul, 96, 245
socialism, 12–13, 88, 175, 227, 233,
    235

society
  well-ordered, 138, 215,
    231
solidarity, 14, 53, 155–7
standing
  aesthetic, 67
  epistemic, 64
  exploitation, 198
  moral, 64–6, 69, 103, 107, 115–16
  social, 10, 19, 56, 65, 69, 125, 148, 182, 193–5,
    199, 201
status, 13, 15, 30, 33, 37, 40, 42, 44, 51, 62, 66, 70,
    79, 91, 106–7, 125, 134, 142, 145, 148, 155,
    184, 189, 193–4, 197, 200, 230
  moral, 10, 19, 62–4, 70, 85, 103, 151, 174
Stemplowska, Zofia, xiii, 30, 32, 196, 245
stereotype, 86
Strawson, Peter, 98, 245
structure, basic, 2, 8, 122, 138, 142
subordination, 112–13, 117
sufficientarianism, 2, 4, 14, 26, 31, 39, 84,
    208
  luck relational, 9
  relational, 9
sufficients
  relating as, 9, 27
superiority
  sense of, 44, 156–7, 203

Tan, Kok-Chor, 5, 17, 55, 136–8, 140–2, 144, 146,
    150, 244–5
taste
  snobbish, 219, 222–7
Temkin, Larry, 2, 17, 20, 122, 167, 184, 245
test
  interpersonal, 113–14, 148, 212, 231–2
Tomlin, Patrick, xiii, 16, 45, 154, 161, 169–71,
    234, 245
tu quoque, 39, 46, 96, 100, 111

Upadhyaya, Kartik, xiii, 101, 104–5, 245
utilitarianism, 23, 31

value
  distributive, 25
  impersonal, 19
van Parijs, Philippe, 35
view
  complete lives, 131–3
  time-relative, 131
violence, 12, 37, 72
Voigt, Kristin, xiii, 8, 32, 245

Wallace, R. J., viii, 94, 97–105, 110, 116, 245
Walzer, Michael, 14, 65, 132, 246

welfare
    equal access to, 218
well-being, 1–2, 6, 108–9, 161
    mental state-based accounts of, 159–60
    objective list accounts of, 159–62
    opportunities for, 6
    preference-based accounts of, 159
Williams, Andrew, xiii, 141–2, 243, 246
Williams, Bernard, 62

Wolff, Jonathan, 11–13, 15–16, 61, 70, 88, 174, 198,
    207, 246
worth
    equal, 51, 66, 125, 145,
        148
    intrinsic, 37

Young, Iris Marion, 11–12, 16, 29, 72–3, 123, 174,
    194, 242, 246

CPSIA information can be obtained
at www.ICGtesting.com
Printed in the USA
LVHW050640210221
679533LV00032B/2327

9 781316 613672